# UNDERSTANDING
# MILAN KUNDERA

# UNDERSTANDING MODERN EUROPEAN AND LATIN AMERICAN LITERATURE

James Hardin, *Series Editor*

### ADVISORY BOARD

**Understanding Günter Grass**
*by Alan Frank Keele*

**Understanding Max Frisch**
*by Wulf Koepke*

**Understanding Graciliano Ramos**
*by Celso Lemos de Oliveira*

**Understanding Erich Maria Remarque**
*by Hans Wagener*

**Understanding Gabriel García Márquez**
*by Kathleen McNerney*

**Understanding Elias Canetti**
*by Richard H. Lawson*

**Understanding Claude Simon**
*by Ralph Sarkonak*

**Understanding Thomas Bernhard**
*by Stephen D. Dowden*

**Understanding Mario Vargas Llosa**
*by Sara Castro-Klarén*

**Understanding Heinrich Böll**
*by Robert C. Conard*

**Understanding Samuel Beckett**
*by Alan Astro*

**Understanding Céline**
*by Philip H. Solomon*

**Understanding Jean-Paul Sartre**
*by Philip R. Wood*

**Understanding Gerhart Hauptmann**
*by Warren R. Maurer*

**Understanding Albert Camus**
*by David R. Ellison*

**Understanding José Donoso**
*by Sharon Magnarelli*

**Understanding Milan Kundera:**
Public Events, Private Affairs
*by Fred Misurella*

UNDERSTANDING

# MILAN
# KUNDERA

*Public Events, Private Affairs*

FRED MISURELLA

UNIVERSITY OF SOUTH CAROLINA PRESS

Chapter Two, "Human Possibilities," is an adaptation of
the article "Not Silent, But in Exile and with Cunning,"
published in *Partisan Review 2*, 1985


Copyright © 1993 University of South Carolina

Published in Columbia, South Carolina, by the
University of South Carolina Press

Manufactured in the United States of America

**Library of Congress Cataloging-in-Publication Data**

Misurella, Fred, 1940–
   Understanding Milan Kundera : public events, private affairs /
Fred Misurella.
      p.    cm. — (Understanding modern European and Latin American
literature)
   Includes bibliographical references and index.
   ISBN 0–87249–853–0 (alk. paper)
   1. Kundera, Milan—Criticism and interpretation.   I. Title.
II. Series.
PG5039.21.U6Z8   1993
891.8'68509—dc20                                92-27444
                                                         CIP
                                                         r92

*To novel readers
and all their possibilities*

# CONTENTS

# EDITOR'S PREFACE

*U*nderstanding *Modern European and Latin American Literature* has been planned as a series of guides for undergraduate and graduate students and nonacademic readers. Like the volumes in its companion series, *Understanding Contemporary American Literature,* these books provide introductions to the lives and writings of prominent modern authors and explicate their most important works.

Modern literature makes special demands, and this is particularly true of foreign literature, in which the reader must contend not only with unfamiliar, often arcane artistic conventions and philosophical concepts, but also with the handicap of reading the literature in translation. It is a truism that the nuances of one language can be rendered in another only imperfectly (and this problem is especially acute in fiction), and the fact that the works of European and Latin American writers are situated in a historical and cultural setting quite different from our own can be as great a hindrance to the understanding of these works as the linguistic barrier. For this reason, the UMELL series emphasizes the sociological and historical backgrounds of the writers treated. The peculiar philosophical and cultural traditions of a given culture may be particularly important for an understanding of certain authors, and these are taken up in the introductory chapter and also in the discussion of those works to which this information is relevant. Beyond this, the books treat the specifically literary aspects of the author under discussion and attempt to explain the complexities of contemporary literature lucidly. The books are conceived as introductions to the authors covered, not as comprehensive analyses. They do not provide detailed summaries of plot because they are meant to be used in conjunction with the books they discuss, not as a substitute for study of the original works. The purpose of the books is to provide information and judicious literary assessment of the major works in the most compact, readable form. It is our hope that the UMELL series will help to increase knowledge and understanding of European and Latin American cultures and will serve to make the literature of those cultures more accessible.

Professor Misurella's *Understanding Milan Kundera* provides a much needed overview of the literary and critical works of Milan Kundera, one of the seminal writers and theoreticians of our time. Kundera, born in Brno, Czechoslovakia, and now living in France, has been much influenced by German and especially Austrian literature, as well as by western European writers. His multicultural background and his broad knowledge of European fiction have made his work a daunting challenge for American critics drawn to his immensely popular novels. Misurella's own extensive reading has enabled him to meet the challenge, so that the present book casts much light on Kundera's artistic place in European culture. Misurella's discerning analysis of Kundera's debt to the writers who influenced him will be especially helpful to students of comparative literature and will also be welcomed by those interested in German, Austrian, French, and contemporary literature in general. Of special interest also is Professor Misurella's translation of an essay in which Kundera evaluates and discusses his own works. The essay, part of the author's introduction to the new Czech edition of his writings, appears for the first time in English in Misurella's chapter nine.

J. H.

# ACKNOWLEDGMENTS

Many people have helped with this project, but particularly I want to thank the East Stroudsburg University Faculty Development and Research Committee for a grant of time to work on the study and Emil Wagner for a travel grant to meet with Milan Kundera in Europe in May 1991.

As important, if not more so, are others who have helped with interest and effort: Dr. James Gilbert, who wrote several letters on my behalf to make this work possible; librarian Patricia Jersey, who, with her colleague Leslie Berger, became a relentless and dogged detective in finding bibliographic resources throughout the United States; Allan Benn, my department chair, who read parts of the manuscript and contributed key ideas concerning themes; Ralph Vitello, who read the manuscript chapter by chapter, helped with translations from French, and provided important encouragement and advice concerning language; and Carolyn Grossman, who read with insight and understanding. Thanks to all of them.

I also want to thank Vera Kundera for always making my visits to Paris welcome as well as interesting and informative; Milan Kundera, for his ideas and interest as well as his friendship and conversation and for his permission to print, in translation, a portion of the author's note to the Czech edition of *The Joke*. Thanks also to Warren Slesinger and James Hardin, for listening and acting positively from the first mention made of the book; and finally Kim McKay, whose ideas about narrative have been central to my conceptions and whose daily presence has made living and working with this project an exciting, pleasurable experience. She and the Kunderas are the book's real sine qua non.

# CHRONOLOGY

| | |
|---|---|
| 1929 | April 1, Milan Kundera is born to Ludvik Kundera (pianist, professor of music, and collaborator with Leos Janacek) and Milada Janosikova Kundera, in Brno, a medium-size city in the Moravian section of Czechoslovakia. |
| 1933 | Konrad Henlein organizes the Czech Nazi party. In Germany, Hitler is appointed chancellor and granted dictatorial powers. |
| 1937 | Thomas Masaryk, the popular president who led the democratic Czechoslovak Republic from its beginning in 1918 to 1935, dies. In the Soviet Union Stalin conducts show trials against former party loyalists. |
| 1938 | Demanding independence, Sudeten Germans riot in Czechoslovakia; October 10, German troops invade Czechoslovakian territory to occupy the Sudetenland. Czech President Eduard Benes resigns. |
| 1939 | Hitler extends his control over most of Czechoslovakia. September 1, German forces invade Poland. The Second World War begins. |
| 1939–1945 | The Second World War rages throughout Europe and Asia. Meanwhile, Kundera studies musical composition and theory with Paul Haas and Vaclav Kapral. |
| 1947 | Repulsed by Nazism, Kundera joins the Czech Communist Party, as do most of his country's intellectual avant-garde. |
| 1948 | February 25, the Czech Communist Party seizes the central government in Prague. Kundera attends classes in musicol- |

|  | ogy at Charles University. At the same time he takes classes at the Film Faculty of the Prague Academy of Art. |
|---|---|
| 1949 | His first published poem, a tribute to Paul Haas, appears. |
| 1950 | Expelled from the Communist Party, Kundera leaves the university. |
| 1952–1955 | Kundera studies the twelve-tone technique of musical composition and writes his own music, notably, a cycle of songs after the poems of Apollinaire and "Composition for Four Instruments." |
| 1953 | *Clovek Zahrada Sira* (Man: A Broad Garden), Kundera's first book of poems, is published. |
| 1955 | *Posledni Maj* (The Last May), his second book of poems, is published. |
| 1956 | Kundera is automatically reinstated in the Communist Party after most of the Eastern Bloc, led by Soviet leader Nikita Khrushchev, rejects Stalinism and its methods. |
| 1957 | *Monology* (Monologues), his third book of poems (written between 1946 and 1956), is published. |
| 1960 | *Umeni Romanu* (The Art of the Novel), a critical study of the great Czech avant-garde novelist Vladislav Vancura, is published. Written to qualify Kundera for a teaching position at the Film Faculty of the Academy of Art, this book defends the modernity of the art of the novel. Later, Kundera would use the title *L'art du roman* (*The Art of the Novel*) for a book of essays written in France. |
| 1962 | *Majitele Klicu* (The Keepers of the Keys), a play, is produced by the Prague National Theatre in April. |
| 1963 | *Smesne Lasky: Tri melancholicke anekdoty* (Laughable Loves: Three Melancholy Anecdotes, written between 1958 and 1962) is published. Kundera becomes a member of the editorial board for the important literary journal *Literarni noviny*. |
| 1965 | *Druhy Sesit Smesnych Lasek* (The Second Book of Laughable Loves) is published. |

| | |
|---|---|
| 1967 | *Zert* (*The Joke,* written between 1960 and 1965) is published. The Fourth Czech Writers' Congress is held, June 27–29, and is a key political and cultural event, leading directly to the Prague Spring. Kundera makes a polemical speech encouraging intellectuals to help Czech culture extend beyond its provincial borders. The Communist Party attacks the Congress and engages in a process of legal exclusion against its spokesmen. |
| 1968 | In January, Alexander Dubcek, named First Secretary of the Communist Party, begins to lead Czechoslovakia. The Prague Spring commences. Kundera's *Treti Sesit Smesnych Lasek* (The Third Book of Laughable Loves) is published. He wins the Czechoslovak Writers Union prize for *Zert*. In August, Warsaw Pact troops and tanks cross into Czechoslovakia; Alexander Dubcek is arrested. In Paris, *La plaisanterie* (*The Joke*) is published. |
| 1969 | Dubcek is expelled from power. Kundera's *Ptakovina* (A Farce) is produced; an abridged, rearranged translation of *The Joke* is published in England and repudiated by Kundera. He completes *Zivot je Jinde* (*Life Is Elsewhere*), but the manuscript is denied publication by Czech authorities. |
| 1970 | *Smesne Lasky* (*Laughable Loves*), a selection of stories from three previous volumes, is published. Kundera and other Czech writers and intellectuals lose their traveling privileges and their jobs; their books are removed from shelves. Kundera's wife, Vera, gives private English lessons, their sole means of support until 1975. |
| 1971–1973 | He studies intensively the music of Olivier Messiaen, Edgard Varèse, and Iannis Xenakis and works on a long musicological essay. He writes a Czech version of his play published in English as *Jacques and His Master* and completes his novel *The Farewell Party*. |
| 1973 | *La vie est ailleurs* (*Life Is Elsewhere*) is published in Paris and wins the Prix Médicis. |
| 1974 | *Life Is Elsewhere* is published in United States. |

1975  At the personal request of Edgar Faure, president of the French parliament, the Czech government grants an extensive travel visa to Milan and Vera Kundera. They emigrate to France, where he teaches at the University of Rennes.

1976  *The Farewell Party,* completed in 1972, is published in the United States and in France (as *La valse aux adieux*). Kundera visits Martinique for the first time and meets the Caribbean poet Aimé Césaire.

1978  *The Farewell Party* wins the Premio Letterario Mondello in Italy. Kundera loses his Czech citizenship.

1979  *Le livre du rire et de l'oubli (The Book of Laughter and Forgetting,* written between 1975 and 1977) is published in Paris.

1980  *The Book of Laughter and Forgetting* is published in the United States, and Kundera wins the Common Wealth Award in New York. He becomes a professor at the École des hautes études en sciences sociales in Paris.

1981  *Jacques et son maître, hommage à Denis Diderot (Jacques and His Master: An Homage to Diderot in Three Acts),* written in Czech in 1971, is published and performed in Kundera's French translation in Paris. Kundera becomes a French citizen.

1983  Kundera visits the United States and receives an honorary doctorate from the University of Michigan.

1984  *The Unbearable Lightness of Being* is published in France (as *L'insoutenable légèreté de l'être*) and then in the United States.

1985  *Jacques and His Master: An Homage to Diderot in Three Acts* is published and performed in the United States. Kundera wins the Jerusalem Prize for Literature on the Freedom of Man in Society; he journeys to Israel to deliver an address, "The Novel and Europe." For two years he works on revisions of the French translations of all his work, giving them the same authenticity as the Czech versions.

1986  *L'Art du roman (The Art of the Novel),* a book of essays written in French and concerning the novelistic tradition in

|      | Europe, is published in Paris, winning the Académie française prize. Kundera becomes a member of the American Academy of Art. |
|------|------|
| 1987 | Kundera wins the Austrian state prize for literature and, in Germany, the Nelly Sachs Prize. Both are awarded for the body of his work. |
| 1988 | *The Art of the Novel* is published in the United States. Kundera completes the novel *Immortality*. |
| 1989 | The "Velvet Revolution" overthrows the Communist government in Czechoslovakia. Playwright Vaclav Havel becomes the country's president. |
| 1990 | *Immortality* is published in France as *L'Immortalité*. Kundera lives in Martinique and Haiti, studying the life and culture of French-speaking Caribbeans. |
| 1991 | *Immortality* is published in the United States. Kundera begins editing his books for publication in Czechoslovakia, considering valid seven works of fiction, one play (*Jacques and His Master*), and the essays comprising *The Art of the Novel*. Kundera revises the American translation of *The Joke* and publishes an important essay on black culture in the Caribbean. |
| 1992 | The definitive English version of *The Joke*, fully revised by Kundera, is published in the United States. |

# UNDERSTANDING
# MILAN KUNDERA

# CHAPTER ONE

# Introduction: An Approach to the Novels and Their Forms

*Even though the bizarre drama of politics is often present in my books, their characters aren't taking part in any particular politics, but in other realms—those of humor, irony and imagination.*

—Kundera, quoted in *World Authors 1970–1975*

Born on April 1, 1929, in Brno, Czechoslovakia, Milan Kundera has lived a life dedicated to art and artistic principles while living through, and actively taking part in, some of the major events of Czechoslovakia's, and Europe's, twentieth-century history. As a young man he studied musical composition, but he soon turned to literature, following the surrealistic style of the avant-garde poets of his day and publishing poems at an early age. At nineteen, devoted both to culture and art, he enrolled at the Film Faculty of the Prague Academy of Music and Drama to study film making and script writing. But he continued to write poems, published three volumes of verse (which, later, he grew to dislike), and gradually, by way of theater, film, and critical commentary, worked his way into fiction. He published an early edition of *Laughable Loves* in 1963, and then in 1967, after the publication of *The Joke,* his career took final shape. With that book his reputation as a novelist crossed Czech borders into all of Europe. Since then he has published six additional works of fiction, a play, and an insightful commentary on the development of the European novel, all of which are read internationally and have earned Kundera nominations for the Nobel Prize in literature and a reputation for being, along with Günter Grass, Carlos Fuentes, and Gabriel García Márquez, at the very forefront of twentieth-century novelists.

However, politics often mask aesthetics in literary reputations, and despite Milan Kundera's genuine artistic accomplishments, Westerners have tended to read his work through the lenses of their own historical preferences, liking or disliking his books according to what they think he says about life under a Communist dictatorship. Kundera passionately resists that reading, arguing, at times angrily, that he seeks to respond to larger, human issues and that seeing him as a writer of disillusioned political fables misses the point of his work. His argument is made more pertinent by recent European events: the change to democratically elected governments in Poland, Czechoslovakia,

1

and Hungary; the overthrow of Ceausescu in Rumania; the unification of Germany; and the gradual, halting movement toward free speech, a free economy, and free elections in the former Soviet Union. Has Kundera, a former exile along with other Central European writers, lost his subject? Without Soviet expansionism is there no more reason for him to write? It seems clear that any serious novelist interested in the human condition and the forms it can take, as well as fiction and the forms it can take, would reply with a resounding *No!* to both questions. In his two most recent novels, each written before the events of 1989 and 1990 changed Central Europe, Kundera attempted to answer those who read his work politically.

In *The Unbearable Lightness of Being* he gave his definition of the novel as "an investigation of human life in the trap the world has become."[1] Yet if readers understand that trap as laid by Communists, Marxists, or Russian Imperialists alone, they will have misunderstood his intentions completely and, by the way, relegated him to a group of writers who in fifty years, if Central Europe remains free, will be regarded as antique curiosities. In the same way *Hamlet* might be read as a play about life under a Danish dictator and *Othello* and *The Merchant of Venice* as dramas about racial prejudice in Italy.

Rather, the trap Kundera investigates is existential, placing the fate of complex human individuals in the context of larger forces—historical, philosophic, and psychological. In fact, human life is filled with tyranny, oppression, and frustration, whether in the sexual, emotional sphere of love (sometimes portrayed by Kundera as a battlefield) or in the political, ideological sphere of public life. In novel after novel Kundera portrays characters grappling with morals as they attempt to control their lives and destinies. Usually they are frustrated, by doubt or inner weakness, by fate or, sometimes, other people. Any of these may have ideological trappings, but within the context of a story they fulfill larger dramatic purposes—usually the classical workings of fate and character as described by Aristotle in his *Poetics.*

Within the parameters of these rather classical narrative values, Kundera's favorite writer is Franz Kafka, the German-Jewish Czech author who lived in Prague from 1883 to 1924, and anticipated with his absurd, comi-tragic stories the mood and even some of the circumstances governing the politics of our century. Eventually his stories and life spawned a new word in English, "Kafkaesque," to describe certain human conditions, sometimes religious, sometimes political, sometimes philosophic or technological.

Clearly these Kafkaesque conditions, emphasizing the weight and heft of larger systems, accent the frailty of human needs in all life, not just that lived under dictatorships. And so, just as a reader can interpret Kafka in light of

2

*human* rather than simply political conditions, Kundera insists that his own work, if taken seriously, must be judged in exactly the same context. He would be a European novelist speaking to a world made and dominated by European values, "conceived at the dawn of the modern age, based on the individual and his reason, on pluralism of thought and on tolerance."[2] In that system of values doubt, religious or historical, is a fundamental attitude that cuts through dogma and the comfort of received ideas and, like a scalpel invading the body politic, exposes intellectual disease. In such a system art, especially ironic art, has primacy over politics, and the novel has primacy over history, psychology, and philosophy. "The novelist's job is to say things that only the novel can say. If you don't do that," Kundera says, "why write a novel at all?"[3]

In addition to Kafka, other important writers for Kundera are the Austrian novelist Robert Musil, whose depiction of Vienna on the eve of the First World War, *The Man Without Qualities,* is, even as a massive fragment, one of the great novels of our century; the Viennese writer Hermann Broch, who wrote a trilogy of novels, *The Sleepwalkers,* that spans three decades, from 1888 to 1918, and presents a philosophical, psychological investigation of the human spirit as the nineteenth-century European order crumbles and the twentieth-century world begins; and Witold Gombrowicz, a Polish writer, exiled in Argentina during the Second World War, whose novel *Ferdydurke* dramatizes the frailty of human will and character under the pressure of external circumstances. Kundera sees all these writers as forming a European novelistic tradition that he follows and calls post-Proustian. He describes the practice of the tradition as a kind of research whose principal subject is existence. Broch and Musil investigate the human personality under pressure of the forces of history. Broch describes its ineffectiveness, Musil its near irrelevance. Gombrowicz combines the themes of the other two. Although he is perhaps the least known of the three in the United States, he deserves some special comment concerning writing technique. Parts of his novel *Ferdydurke* and most of the diaries, written during Gombrowicz's years of exile, accomplish the kind of reflexive comment and self-criticism Kundera, as narrative voice, practices in his work, particularly in *The Book of Laughter and Forgetting, The Unbearable Lightness of Being,* and *Immortality.* "We, art, *are* reality," Gombrowicz wrote in one of his diary entries, anticipating Kundera's attitudes on the relationship of art and politics. "Art is a fact and not a commentary attached to fact."

Anticipating Kundera, Gombrowicz resists the twentieth-century novelist's temptation to develop characters through psychological means. Instead he

3

emphasizes physical developments, placing the burden of character motivation on external events such as accidents or human choices, giving action the primary focus in the development of his stories. In *Ferdydurke* the narrator, a thirty-year-old man, is brought to a boys' school and treated like a fifteen-year-old. He resists at first, but in a short while he begins to act like an adolescent despite himself. It is a bizarre story, humorous but troubling, demonstrating Gombrowicz's belief, later echoed by Kundera, that our every social act forces unwanted roles (read *personalities*) on ourselves and others. According to this concept, we are like puppets or marionettes: outside hands control our bodies' motions, inhibiting inner development, both spiritual and philosophic.

In one memorable scene from *Ferdydurke,* two boys fight a duel of grimaces, one of them playing the part of an adolescent trying to be a good adult, the other the bad boy who refuses to mature. The point of the passage is that neither is natural by himself, since each has a role thrust upon him by the other. The confrontation raises important issues that must sound poignant to an exile's ears. Away from home, culture, and language, the question of essence overwhelms the palpable facts of character. What does it mean to be human? Are we anything more than form or physical presence? And in a century that has witnessed two world wars, the collapse of the Austro-Hungarian Empire and Czarist Russia, the rise of Nazism and Communism, Auschwitz and the Bomb, another vital question must be asked: What is individuality before the power of historical events, or as Kundera has put it in *The Art of the Novel,* "in a world where the external determinants have become so overpowering that internal impulses no longer carry weight."[4]

Those issues, according to Kundera, made Kafka cry "Enough of psychology!" in his notebook,[5] and he wrote the stories upon which Kundera and other Central European novelists have founded a style. It is a style, as I have noted elsewhere,[6] with the following tendencies: historical determinism coupled with a flair for narrative caprice (in the guise of fatal and fateful accidents that diminish the value of human effort); an ironic, personal narrative voice that combines sentimentality with an aloof, intellectual, darkly philosophic humor; and finally a willingness to mix forms and content: essay with narrative, reality with fiction, fantasy with history, science or philosophy with art, regarding them as equally relevant to the novel and, as Kundera calls it, the novelist's research. "Real novels examine the palpable," he has said. "Their goal: what is the *sensation* of jealousy? What does it (the *sensation*) mean? What is the *feeling* of loss?"[7]

4

As a result of these opinions Kundera, through the example of Kafka and Gombrowicz, narrates almost exclusively along the plane of action, focusing on the inconsistencies and paradoxes of each act's meaning to humans. With narrative commentary he underlines decisions, accidents, the ideas his characters try to follow, and he develops their motivations only as they relate to guilt, terror, and pain, feelings he sees as themes in their existence, not as emotions to be analyzed. "I am not a psychological novelist," he insists.[8] Rather, like the classical dramatists, and like Kafka, Gombrowicz, and Broch, he seeks to investigate the workings of human action and fate in the outer world.

But Kundera has broad aesthetic and intellectual interests, and it is unrealistic to restrict the influences on his thinking and writing to other novelists and dramatists, no matter how great their accomplishments. In fact, he has taken on twentieth-century consciousness as his theme. Whatever has had political, aesthetic, or intellectual importance in our time (by way of influence from the past or dramatic presence now) will likely find a place in his work. Certainly his interest in music, demonstrated by the period in his youth when he studied composition, has influenced his conception of the novel's form, placing emphasis on a thematic structure that has as much in common with the tradition of the fugue as it does with the works of other novelists. Also, his work at the Film Faculty of the Academy of Performing Arts in Prague, followed by the plays he wrote for the Czech theater, influenced his elliptical approach to plot development as well as his dramatic approach to characterization. Though a novelist, he seems to share the concerns of several film directors: Jean Renoir and Alain Resnais from France, for example, both of whom have brought personal, analytic vision to film, as well as the members of the Czech New Wave who at one time were Kundera's pupils. Like them, he sees art as a means of understanding and criticizing human culture, as well as enriching it, by polarizing the relation between the subjective and objective worlds of his characters. Also, like all the French and Czech directors, he sees art as serious about life but playful at the same time, a game in which the artist's personality and intelligence commingle with the accidental in life, sometimes cooperatively, sometimes not. As a result, readers are often made aware of the author in Kundera's work and are entertained by that interesting, though invented, narrative personality at the same time they believe the characters and story the personality controls. Readers also come to trust the opinions this fictional Kundera conveys, thus being entertained and informed by a very human presence, one whose charm accounts for much of the pleasure of reading Kundera's works, even in translation.

*affected*

Finally, the contemporary reader should make note of Kundera's connection, through his father, to the work of the Czech composer Leos Janacek. Janacek's life touched Kundera's in several ways. He lived in Brno, the city of Kundera's birth, from 1887 to 1928, working closely with Kundera's father, a pianist and professor of music. Those familiar with Janacek's work may see his influence in Kundera's use of Moravian folk motifs in *The Joke*. More important, if they pay attention to the powerful, often truncated line of Janacek's melodies, they may understand why Kundera cuts and juxtaposes story lines so abruptly in his novels, saying in *The Art of the Novel* that ellipsis is "crucial" to his writing technique. Also, in hearing Janacek's operas, especially *The House of the Dead* (a retelling of Dostoevsky's novel of imprisonment), readers can see how the composer's dramatization of the human condition, pitting inner desires against the power of outward events, is a conceptual technique that Kundera practices as well. No doubt this technique results from the shared Czech experience, born of a history of suffering in the middle of many European wars, and is a particularly twentieth-century view of human impotence. But as an essayist who has written about Janacek in ways that illuminate his own fiction as well as the composer's music,[9] Kundera has said that a clear affinity exists between the forms of their art as well as the dramas they make of human lives.

In summation then, contemporary readers have two contradictory ways of evaluating Milan Kundera as a writer. On the one hand, some interpret his novels and stories as a response to the political and social developments in his country during the twentieth century. Those readers regard him as an eloquent, persuasive voice of protest against Stalinism, totalitarianism, and Russian imperialism. It is a voice that may now be relegated to the past since the dramatic liberation of Czechoslovakia and much of Central Europe in 1989.

But others look at Kundera's work aesthetically, analyzing its forms, responding to its many-faceted ironic voice—at once compassionate, ribald, humorous, and grave—and enjoy its characters because, as art does, they make the audience laugh at and think about *all* the world (and *all* humanity), not just small corners of it. With this interpretation, Kundera's stories and novels have lives of their own, independent of historical events, in the same way that Shakespeare's plays, frequently based on history, carry the audience onto a stage more imagined than real that has outlasted the events (or human memory of the events) inspiring them. "Every novel, like it or not, offers some answer to the question: What is human existence, and wherein does its poetry lie?" Kundera says in *The Art of the Novel*.[10] That novelist's, and novel reader's, question, with its concepts of joined experience, palpable and aesthetic, permeates this study.

## NOTES

1. *The Unbearable Lightness of Being* (New York: Harper, 1984) 221.

2. *Jacques and His Master* (New York: Harper, 1985) 11.

3. Personal interview, June 1984.

4. *The Art of the Novel* (New York: Grove, 1988) 26.

5. Cited by Kundera in "Encore sur le roman," *Lettre Internationale* 4 (Spring 1985): 3.

6. See my article "Milan Kundera and the Central European Style," *Salmagundi* 73 (Winter 1987): 33–57.

7. Personal interview, June 1984.

8. Personal interview, June 1984.

9. For Kundera's comment on Janacek, see "Prague: A Disappearing Poem," *Granta* 17 (1985): 98–102, and the rather technical "Janacek: He Saw the Coming Night," *Cross Currents* 23 (1983): 371–80, as well as "A la recherche du présent perdu," *L'infini* 36 (1991): 19–42.

10. *Art of Novel* 161.

# Human Possibilities: Kafka, Diderot, and the World of *Jacques and His Master*

*We were the optimists of skepticism: we believed in its subversive force and eventual victory.*

—Kundera, "Paris or Prague" (1984)

In the introduction to his one play published in English, *Jacques and His Master: An Homage to Diderot in Three Acts* ("My best play," he says), Milan Kundera tells this story about the end of his optimism: During the third day of the Russian occupation of Czechoslovakia in 1968, he was in his car somewhere south of Prague. The highways, fields, and forests were filled with Russian foot soldiers. As he approached the town of Budejovice, three Russian soldiers stopped his car and searched it. When they were satisfied that he carried nothing seditious or contraband, the officer in charge asked Kundera in Russian, "How do you feel? What are your feelings?"

The question was not sinister or ironic, Kundera writes; rather, the officer seemed to reach for some rapprochement. He said, "It's all a big misunderstanding, but it will straighten itself out. You must realize we love the Czechs. We love you!"

Kundera says, "Please understand me. He had no desire to condemn the invasion, not in the least. They all spoke more or less as he did, their attitude based not on the sadistic pleasure of the ravisher but on quite a different archetype: unrequited love. Why do these Czechs (whom we love so) refuse to live with us the way we live? What a pity we're forced to use tanks to teach them what it means to love!"[1]

A white-haired man whose bright blue eyes reveal a smiling, somewhat aloof intelligence, Kundera traveled to the West in 1975 and began a new life in France. Intellectual, private, a man who would rather talk of aesthetics than politics, he is the son of a concert pianist, a former musician, playwright, and teacher of film writing. But as a fiction writer he wants to leave his political past behind him so that he can create it anew in his imagination. When asked about the criticism of his political aloofness by other former dissidents from Central Europe, Kundera defends himself philosophically. Political concepts are inadequate to a proper understanding of human life, he says. He passed twenty years in a country (Communist Czechoslovakia) where *any* human problem, large or small, was considered only in the political context, and now he wants to concentrate on other things. But the terrorists and bureaucrats of all political persuasions are undermining human life. "They are telling us," he says, "you are never free. Even in a democracy, when you are a citizen of another country, we can reach you."[2]

In lumping together bureaucrats and terrorists, Kundera speaks as if it were a matter of structural linguistics. The terrorist and bureaucrat share an interlocked vocabulary that "restricts, reduces, limits" the idea of what we make of ourselves as human. "The terrorist endangers private life, and, as Kafka has shown, the bureaucrat invades it. Because of them we are in danger of hearing Newspeak and Doublethink everywhere."[3]

In January 1980 Kundera published an essay on Kafka in *Le debat,* a French intellectual journal. The essay, translated into English and collected in *The Art of the Novel* as "Somewhere Behind," describes the universe as Kafka saw it and relates it to the absurd in twentieth-century art and life. It is Kundera's clearest statement about the relationship between twentieth-century politics and literature. The term "Kafkan," he says, "determined solely by a novelist's images, stands as the only common denominator in situations (literary or real) that no other word," psychological, sociological, or political, can define. He lists four conditions that typify the Kafkan in contemporary life:

1. Its universe is an immense, labyrinthine institution obeying laws that the ordinary individual cannot understand and that have no relation to human needs or interests. This institution is a mechanism, like the computer, that has been programmed, but we no longer know when or by whom.

2. In the bureaucratic universe of Kafkan social life, the institutional dossier, or file, operates as a Platonic ideal: it, rather than physical existence, represents reality. The human being is only a pale shadow of the contents of his file.

3. In the traditions of psychological and religious thought, human error, fault, or guilt seeks its proper punishment; but in the Kafkan system the individual is punished and then must search for the fault.

4. While Kafka's universe contains humor, it does not allow the luxury of objective laughter; rather, it puts humanity inside the joke, into what Kundera calls the *"horror of the comic."*[4] In doing so, the Kafkan denies individuals the heroic grandeur of tragedy.

Modern history tends to produce the Kafkan on a grand social scale, Kundera goes on to say. He points to the increasing tendency of those in power to try to make themselves divine, the growth of a bureaucracy that institutionalizes the labyrinth for all societies, and the increasing depersonalization of individuals. Having been expelled from the university, seen his books destroyed, and witnessed his name erased from the telephone book, Kundera has experienced this depersonalization firsthand, but he is quick to add that he is not speaking politically. For him the Kafkan has no political, economic, or sociological applications, and he points out that depersonalization marks our century, occurring in the capitalist as well as Communist countries. In fact, Kundera sees the whole planet becoming a technological model of the world Kafka described in *The Trial* and *The Castle*. His description of the Kafkan universe as a mechanism programmed like a computer, but whose operator has left the keyboard, may strike some readers as a conception of the absurd, but it is also an analogy very close to the eighteenth-century deist's mechanical model of the universe as a wound clock. Yet while the organizing principle of time imposed an order eighteenth-century man could measure and anticipate (perhaps even understand), an unknown system organizes now. A circuit might break at any moment or the program could last forever. No one knows; no one can anticipate; no one can because we do not understand the limits of this machine or the original programmer's language.

Kundera relates this philosophic vision to Kafka's experience in his family and at the office. In a totalitarian society, Kundera says, the Kafkan manifests itself by erasing the line between public and private lives. Kafka's writing anticipated twentieth-century political and social developments because those developments corresponded to his private experience. The totalitarian regime attempts to make society one big family: in doing so it denies private life. While many critics have read Kafka's work as an expression of a desire for community and human contact, Kundera sees *The Trial* and *The Castle* as really about the loss of privacy. *The Castle's* Surveyor wants to be accepted not by a community of friends or family but by an institution. He must accept his private life as public, and that, says Kundera, becomes his hell. Two aides sent by the Castle follow him incessantly, observing when he first makes love with Frieda, and after that incident they never quit his life or his bed.

Violation of solitude is also the opening theme of *The Trial*. Two unknown men come to arrest Joseph K. in his bed, and from that moment he has no private life. The organization dominates him, controlling his time, forcing him to live in public while it accompanies him through his trial. The organization, legal yet totalitarian, acts very much like a family. Its members surprise each other in their bedrooms, entering to say good-night as parents might. In the Kafkan universe, the "public is the mirror of the private, the private reflects the public."[5]

In one part of that reflection Kundera sees the office world, a "world of obedience," as similar to the world of the bedroom and, at the same moment, like the Kafkan universe of the programmed computer. The office clerk, like a child, is a small cog in a grand administrative machine. His world is abstract, and Kafka's art is that he found epic poetry in it. "The office is not a stupid institution," Kundera quotes Kafka as writing to Milena. "It belongs more to the realm of the fantastic than of the stupid."

If, because of this vision, Kafka's accomplishment is immense, his work is significant, not because he was politically engaged but precisely because he was *not* engaged. The poet and novelist do not invent; they unveil, like history, what man is, what he has inside, or, in Kundera's phrase, "what his possibilities are." In "Somewhere Behind" Kundera praises Kafka because he set an example for what Kundera calls "the *radical autonomy* of the novel."[6] Examining what he observed of the small, intimate moments of ordinary life, Kafka set in motion a universe, unique as well as private, that the developments of history, according to Kundera, would later reveal on a larger stage.

This is an interesting insight into Kafka that illuminates Milan Kundera's attitudes toward the social obligations of the writer. Yet some Central Europeans have wondered at the conscience of a man who, having been blacklisted himself, could remain aloof and silent in the West. One explanation lies in a skeptical attitude concerning any ideology and a philosophic pessimism that goes beyond Kundera's conception of the Kafkan, perhaps owing more to the thinking of the Prague structuralists, or the French anthropologist Claude Lévi-Strauss.[7] In a passage from *The Book of Laughter and Forgetting,* Kundera writes: "World domination, as everyone knows, is divided between demons and angels. But the good of the world does not require the latter to gain precedence over the former (as I thought when I was young); all it needs is a certain equilibrium of power."[8]

In the context of Kundera's work, this passage bears close scrutiny. His sense of private and public evil, his novelistic essays on the loss of personal and cultural memory, and the absolute futility of his characters' attempts to regain their pasts or to change their present lives bespeak a fatalistic determinism best exemplified (at least in Kundera's experience) by despotism and the presence of Russian tanks. Yet at the same time he has dedicated his life to art, the world of order and meaning, "the reign of the angels," as he might say, and in that context the writer must create, remaining aloof from political events even in troubled times, at the same time he may include those events, as metaphor, in his compositions.

In "Litost," one of the stories in *The Book of Laughter and Forgetting*, a Czech student attends a meeting of his country's major living poets. Kundera imagines the meeting as a symposium of the great European writers, giving the participants names such as Goethe, Voltaire, Boccaccio, Petrarch, and Lermontov. But his description of the meeting is skewed by the perspective of time, distance, and height—the Olympian height of art. After a capsule comment on his and his country's history since 1968, he talks about settling in the town of Rennes, at the top of an apartment building. Speaking of fellow writers still behind the Iron Curtain in the 1970s, he says: "Now I watch them from my tower, but the distance is too great. Fortunately the tear in my eye magnifies like the lens of a telescope and brings their faces closer."[9]

The mixture of aloofness and feeling in this passage, the combination of poignant art and artful composition, are typical of Kundera's writing. They occur again in his sometimes cruel eroticism, in the mockery he makes of his characters' attempts to be significant, and in the cynicism with which he overlays almost all portraits of human suffering. He has been accused of not caring for his characters and of being morally irresponsible. But he uses irony as a primary technique to control the expression of his own feelings. "The more I think of it," he said in the summer of 1982, "the more I think of myself as a man of the eighteenth century."[10] The comment may surprise today's readers, but Kundera, describing the eighteenth century as a time of political dislocation and revolution—as is ours—also speaks approvingly of its art. He admires the sense of play in its musical variations, its improvisation in fictional narrative, its humane emphasis on reason. Most of all he likes what he has referred to as the eighteenth-century habit of doubt and clarity, perhaps best exemplified by Denis Diderot, a major influence on Kundera's work.

Published in the United States in 1985, *Jacques and His Master* furnishes a clear entry into the humor, narrative techniques, and motivations behind much of Kundera's fiction. It may also provide further clues about his political and artistic thinking in general. It was Laurence Sterne's *Tristram Shandy* that inspired Diderot to write *Jacques le fataliste*. Imitating Sterne's pattern of digression, with interruptions, false premises, and asides (rather than plot development) providing the real motivation for adventure in reading, Diderot added further technical complications to his narrative by giving it five distinct voices. Adapting to fiction the polyphonic structure of a fugue,

Diderot interwove three tales of thwarted love as told by four different speakers and made all of them depend upon the whims, caprices, and false premises of a fifth speaker, the book's narrator who, like Tristram, continually reminds the reader of the arbitrary nature of the novel's events. With each speaker's voice working in counterpoint to the other four, Diderot placed his basic theme (and joke) in Jacques's mouth: "Everything that happens to us down here, for good or ill, is written above."

Diderot situates himself "above" as well as at the reader's elbow, and the comedy of the novel plays on the ambiguity of the reference in that phrase. Philosophically it is a statement of determinism, but aesthetically Jacques's comment also says something about the nature of storytelling. For Kundera, who believes in the arbitrariness of history, Diderot's narrative must have seemed a perfect vehicle for his own writing. In his introduction to *Jacques and His Master* Kundera recounts how the idea for the play occurred. As in much of his work, history provided the catalyst. Shortly after the Russian invasion of 1968, when Kundera had lost his university professorship and could no longer publish in Czechoslovakia, a theater director tried to help him earn money. He asked Kundera to write a dramatic version of Dostoevsky's *The Idiot,* but to his own surprise Kundera had problems with the idea. Rereading *The Idiot,* he says, he knew he could not do the work, even if he were starving. The universe, so different from Kafka's, of excessive gesture, obscure profundity, and "aggressive sentimentality" disgusted him, and he felt immediate, inexplicable nostalgia for *Jacques le fataliste.* Soon he began to imagine Jacques and his master as characters in his own play.

But, Kundera asks, "Why the sudden aversion to Dostoevsky?" He wonders if it was an anti-Russian reflex caused by the invasion of Soviet tanks. No, he answers, because he never stopped liking Chekhov. Was it doubt about the value of Dostoevsky's work? No again, because that would have taken thought, objectivity, and his aversion was more visceral than intellectual. "What irritated me about Dostoevsky," Kundera says, "was the *climate* of his novels; a universe where everything turns into feeling"; in other words where feelings and sentiment take on the weight of truth and value (1–2).

Sensibility, in its sympathetic, emotional sense, is indispensable to humanity, according to Kundera. But from the moment feeling becomes a criterion of truth, a justification for behavior, replacing rational thought, it leads to close-mindedness and intolerance, or, as Jung said (according to Kundera), "the superstructure of brutality" (3).

For Kundera the elevation of emotion to the level of value finds its roots in Western history, perhaps beginning when Christianity separated itself from the intellectual foundation of Judaism. Quoting St. Augustine's famous dictum, "Love God and do as you will" (see chapter eight of this book for more comment on this quotation), Kundera analyzes the phrase, deeming it significant because it moves the criterion for truth from the external, objective world to the internal one of the heart. From that point, Kundera says, love replaced the clarity of Jewish law, becoming the standard by which to judge behavior. The image of Jesus on the cross taught us how to adulate suffering; chivalric poetry brought us romantic love; bourgeois family values made us homesick for the hearth; and political images sentimentalized power. From the individual figure on the cross to the political symbols of the state, the power of sentiment broadened, but beginning with the Renaissance, a complementary spirit of reason and doubt and an awareness of the relativity of all human things balanced Western sensibility. During this period,often referred to in Europe as the Modern Era, the West "came into its own" (3), and, Kundera says, when the weight of what he calls "rational irrationality" invaded Czechoslovakia in the form of loving soldiers riding in Russian tanks, he felt an immediate and instinctive need for that era again. Its spirit seemed to be concentrated nowhere more densely for Kundera than in that "feast of intelligence, humor, and fantasy" that makes up *Jacques le fataliste* (4).

The philosophy of *Jacques le fataliste* certainly complements Kundera's perceptions about history, but the feast of intelligence and fantasy that he sees in it also complements his sense of aesthetics. Kundera changed Diderot's original title to *Jacques and His Master* and thereby humanized the original theme at the same time he emphasized the forms of social and spiritual control in Jacques's life. More significant, in adapting the novel's polyphonic structure to the stage, Kundera eliminated its most imposing voice, the narrator's, and his new title is a means of emphasizing that difference. Jacques's theme, "Everything that happens to us down here, for good or ill, is written above," takes on a more contemporary note because of the very absence of the narrative speaker—in this case the author—who must be there if the play exists but who, paradoxically and unlike Diderot, does not address his audience. Thus the play reverberates with twentieth-century intimations of the absurd and the death of God, and Kundera conforms to the traditions of those ideas by describing the set as "abstract" and "completely bare." He also says that while the action takes place in the eighteenth century, it is an eighteenth century that we dream of today, and he advises that the historicity of his characters be "slightly muted" (16).

In the introduction Kundera provides an outline of the history of literary characters that is the reverse of his outline of the history of Christian sentiment. Relating the development of Western literature through five famous pairs of masters and servants, he provides a key to his own attitudes: (1) Don Quixote leaves home accompanied by an "illiterate peasant" to fight his foes; (2) one hundred and fifty years later Tristram Shandy's Uncle Toby re-lives his youth as a soldier while accompanied by his servant, Trim, who limps, Kundera says, exactly like Jacques le Fataliste; (3) ten years after Trim, Jacques joked and philosophized on the road with his master; (4) one hundred and fifty years after that, Josef Svejk, soldier in the Austro-Hungarian army, shocked and amused his master, Lieutenant Lukac; and (5) thirty years later, while awaiting Godot, Vladimir and his servant find them-selves on an empty stage. "The journey is over," Kundera says, summing up the procession (12).

A history of famous picaros, the passage can be read as a history of the reign of sentiment also, moving from Cervantes's broad social commentary to the individual, philosophic one of Beckett. Don Quixote went out to fight the sixteenth century in order to impose on it his romantic visions of chivalry; Toby Shandy relived the glory of his days on the battlefield of Namur; and the good soldier Svejk stumbled his straight-faced way through the collapse of the Austro-Hungarian Empire during World War I. With that empire fallen, bringing down with it the reign of sentiment, the age of modernism began, and Vladimir could strut and fret an hour upon the stage, reasoning his way through the difficult questions of existence. The scene, as Beckett describes it in *Waiting for Godot*—"A country road. A tree"—is as empty as the scene in *Jacques and His Master,* and the Godot whom he awaits is as absent as Diderot's narrator, whose voice Kundera has excised from his adaptation, or "variation," as he calls it.

Kundera opens the play by placing into Jacques's mouth several questions about destiny that Diderot had given to himself as narrator. As Jacques and his master walk onto the stage, Jacques glances at the audience, wonders who they are, and then addresses them. He asks if they cannot look elsewhere. Then he asks what they want. "Where we've come from? . . . Back there. Where we're going? (*Philosophically.*) Which of us knows where we're go-ing?" A few lines afterward he recites his famous fatalistic formula to his apprehensive master: No one knows the future, or the road ahead, "But as my captain used to say, it's all written on high" (17).

From that point the play moves forward, through the characters' travels, the recitation of Jacques's first love, his master's frustrated passion for Agathe, and the famous affair of Madame de La Pommeraye, whose story is told by an unnamed lady innkeeper. The characters move on two levels of scenery. The front of the stage occupies the present, presenting the travels of Jacques and his master, their conversation, and the people they encounter on their journey. The rear of the stage is a raised platform, connected by a stairway to the main stage, that is the setting for the stories Jacques and his master tell about themselves and that the lady innkeeper tells of Madame de La Pommeraye. The characters move freely between the two levels and frequently act within the stories that they narrate, addressing their interlocutors as they do. By that means the raised platform occupies the present as well as the past, and much of the play becomes a dialogue between the real and the imaginary, and the world of experience versus the world that exists in memory. As in Diderot's original, imagination and memory are more interesting than their counterparts; but in Kundera's play the crucial absence of the narrator's voice flattens the action of the present, imparting greater depth and fragility to the events of the past, at the rear of the stage. In dramatizing the importance of the human mind and its ability to conceptualize experience, Kundera has borrowed from structuralism, which he calls one of the greatest impulses of modern culture, as well as from Beckett and Diderot.

But in this play, as often in Beckett's world, the minds of Kundera's characters, comic and energetic though they may be, have little to work with. After Jacques, by a quirk of fate, has been saved from hanging and he and his master have been reunited ("even the worst of poets couldn't have come up with a more cheerful ending for his bad poem!" exclaims Jacques [87]), Kundera presents a resolution not as rich as Diderot's but still in keeping with the streamlined, minimalist proportions he has given the rest of the play. Jacques asks his master to lead him forward, and their final dialogue becomes a comment on the relativity of human thinking:

> MASTER:    Very well, but where is forward?
> JACQUES:    . . . Forward is everywhere. (89)

Having written the play in 1971, while he still lived in Prague, Kundera expressed in it the humor and intelligence that he found in Diderot's original, but his modest variation, as he calls it, contributes a twentieth-century sense of despair. At the time he thought the Soviet Union would allow the Central European states to keep their languages and folklore, but their arts and philosophies would suffer a slow, persistent impoverishment as their populations were reduced to the Russian, or Soviet, image. Now, twenty years later, the former Soviet Union finds itself in disarray and Central European countries struggle anew for identity. Meanwhile, Western culture, in the form of television, popular music, and film, overwhelms their young people like a gigantic Atlantic wave. "It is what is called progress," Kundera says ironically,[11] historical progress that, like Jacques and his master, always moves forward no matter what direction it takes and is supported by idealism, economic ideology, and cultural power, much of which has nothing to do with reason.

Trapped by a distrust of feeling that he strongly argues is the cause of history's human-made disasters, Kundera portrays the world as drably lit and with little potential for human comfort. It is a theme he has returned to continually in his career, and in "Edward and God," the last story in *Laughable Loves,* which he wrote shortly before and, as he says, in the same spirit as *Jacques and His Master,* Kundera treats the problem clearly. Edward, like many of Kundera's characters, feels disillusioned with his world. However, his brother has found peace by leaving the Czech Communist Party, retiring to the country and, like Voltaire's Candide, tending his garden. Edward's brother also prides himself on his directness, and he disapproves when Edward tells him how he has recently won a woman's affections by pretending to be religious. They discuss the need for honesty in life, and Edward's brother says that no matter what else might be said of him, he always says what he thinks. Edward argues against this frankness with an analogy: Suppose you meet an irrational person on the street and he starts a conversation: "If you told him the whole truth and nothing but the truth, . . . you would enter into a serious conversation with a madman and you yourself would become mad. And it is the same way with the world that surrounds us. . . . I *must* lie, if I don't want to take madmen seriously and become one of them myself."[12]

Then, at the end of the story an older, even more disillusioned Edward begins, like a character from Dostoevsky, to long for God. But Kundera's narrator says, "God is essence itself," while Edward has never found "anything essential" in his experience, his work, or his thoughts: "Ah, ladies and gentlemen, a man lives a sad life when he cannot take anything or anyone seriously."

In his cynicism, in his defense of the need for fiction in a godless world inhabited by madmen, Edward states Milan Kundera's quintessential theme: Reason, intelligence, and the clarity of the humanistic European mind are out of place in a chaotic world. "In the month of August 1968," Kundera has written, "the Czechs, naive rationalists, experienced the shock of the irrational."[13] In the fall of 1989, with the empire holding them beginning to crumble, the Czechs experienced that shock again, their life changing for the better this time, but with just as sudden, mysterious, and irrational a cause:

The computer's program had changed. In such a universe human reason functions as a literary trope and history remains unreliable because the Kafkan reigns supreme. For a writer like Kundera, the only truth still lies in fiction, the only politics in the absurd reality of art.

## NOTES

1. *Jacques and His Master* (New York: Harper, 1985) 2; further references to this work will be noted parenthetically.
2. Personal interview, July 1982.
3. Personal interview, July 1982.
4. *The Art of the Novel* (New York: Grove, 1988) 100–104. The term is *kafkaien* in French, normally translated to Kafkaesque in English. Linda Asher, Kundera's translator for this essay, uses *Kafkan* instead, a better, more euphonious word. I have chosen to follow her example in this study.
5. *Art of the Novel* 112.
6. *Art of the Novel* 116, 117.
7. Kundera has mentioned structuralism in passing, acknowledging it to me as an "influence on everyone who reads." For comments on the Prague structuralists, see his essay "Prague: A Disappearing Poem," *Granta* 17 (1985): 96–97, and "A Kidnapped West or Culture Bows Out," *Granta* 11 (1984): 105 n 9.
8. *The Book of Laughter and Forgetting* (New York: Penguin, 1981) 61.
9. *Laughter and Forgetting* 128.
10. Personal interview, July 1982.
11. Personal interview, July 1982.
12. *Laughable Loves* (New York: Penguin, 1987) 237.
13. "Le choc de l'irrationnel," Kundera's preface to "Prague 68" by Petr Kral, *Le Matin de Paris* 17 Aug. 1981: 17 (my translation).

# CHAPTER THREE

# A Different World: *The Book of Laughter and Forgetting*

*The characters in my novels are my own unrealized possibilities.*
—*The Unbearable Lightness of Being*

With *The Book of Laughter and Forgetting* (published in France in 1979, in the United States in 1980) Kundera moved onto a new, perhaps larger, literary stage, becoming a novelist for the world, not Czechoslovakia or Europe alone. He had left his native country for good and, like many expatriate writers in the twentieth century, he had to think clearly and carefully about the future—and his next creative move. His native language, vivid and suggestive, "at the expense of firm order, logical sequence, and exactitude," as he has said,[1] was not spoken or read very widely, and so he had to face the prospect of writing in obscurity for a very small, special audience of Czech readers who were also exiles or find a way to appeal to the larger world through translation. He had the advantage of having three previous books published to great acclaim in the West: *The Joke*, published in France in 1968, had been called by the French writer Louis Aragon, "one of the greatest novels of the century"[2]; *Life is Elsewhere*, published in France in 1973, won the Prix Médicis for the best foreign novel published in France that year; and *The Farewell Party*, published in France and other countries in 1976, won the Premio Letterario Mondello for the best novel published in Italy. With those credentials, as well as the academic and literary acquaintances he had already made in the West, Kundera decided to appeal to a larger audience, and in so doing he chose for his novel a diverse mix of characters and biblical references, a varied combination of literary forms—essay, autobiography, and fantastic tales—and held the mixture together with the persona of the narrator and the unifying themes of memory and loss. He wrote with his French translator in mind, he says, achieving a "cleansing of language"[3] and at the same time opening up and redefining the novel form as he had practiced it thus far. In the process Kundera tried to change the way people read fiction in general and his work in particular.

If he succeeded (and many believe he did), we can say that with this book Kundera created a historic shift in the way the contemporary audience regards the novel. As I have argued before, Kundera's *The Book of Laughter and Forgetting* and *The Unbearable Lightness of Being* follow the tradition of the Central European style, combining real experience with fiction, attending to the comedy as well as the tragedy inherent in the lost opportunities in life, and, as in *The Sleepwalkers* trilogy by Hermann Broch, transforming the stuff of history into works of the imagination by sifting through all human experiences (lived or merely read about), examining them carefully, infusing them with personality, and rearranging them into coherent aesthetic expressions.[4] In that sense the novel becomes something that is read like a poem, not for story alone (although story is very important to a narrative) but for wholeness of expression, for thematic unity despite varied modes of composition, for the way parts reflect the whole as well as each other, and the way, in the end, they have something to say that may be ineffable in another form. It is from that perspective that readers can understand why Kundera is so wary of his translators' intentions and the accuracy of their work, why he sees the process of translation as a nightmare that has to be endured and that he has fought battles over throughout his career. In Czechoslovakia under Stalinist rule Milan Kundera refused publication rather than submit to the state censor, and in the West he has had to fight editors and translators who have wanted to make his narratives read more smoothly by changing or eliminating sections that he considered key to the impact of his work. Because of such battles he is especially sensitive to the integrity of the work as he conceived it, no matter what the language of publication. So, in the present critical age that favors a reader's interpretation over the author's intention, Kundera has had to struggle to maintain authorial control over themes as well as sentences and forms. With *The Book of Laughter and Forgetting* he resorted to an old tale teller's stratagem, stepping from behind the fictional narrator's mask and personally addressing his readers, allowing by turns his sober thinking, his playful accounts of history, and his autobiographical commentary to win us over as he explains the events in his characters' lives.

The technique of speaking directly to the audience is as old as *Oedipus Rex* and as recent as the 1980s television show "Moonlighting." The term for such a scene in drama is *parabasis,* usually thought of as an ode that is addressed to the audience by the chorus in a classical Greek play. Traditionally the parabasis existed independent of the action, commented upon it, and was most frequently performed in Greek comedies, although tragedians, including Sophocles, made use of the technique too. Later, Shakespeare resorted to parabasis in his soliloquies and at the beginning and ending of some of his plays, most notably when Puck speaks to the audience in *A Midsummer Night's Dream* and Prospero bids farewell to his art in *The Tempest*. Among American dramatists Tennessee Williams has his alter ego Tom Wingfield stand before a veil to comment on the story of his mother and sister in *The Glass Menagerie*. And on television Ozzie Nelson, of the 1950s "The Adventure of Ozzie and Harriet," frequently stepped away from the action of the set, turned to the camera, and made amusing comments to the audience about the action in his household.[5]

Parabasis descends from a narrative as well as dramatic tradition, especially among oral storytellers who use the technique to regain an audience's attention during lapses in action, to underline parts of the plot, or to make moral and philosophic statements about their characters' fates. From the beginning of the novel's history writers too have resorted to parabasis. Henry Fielding addressed the reader about the proper composition of novels in *Tom Jones*. The first-person narrator of Laurence Sterne's *Tristram Shandy* comments about a multitude of topics ranging from techniques of book printing to philosophic questions of time and methods of human conception. And Nathaniel Hawthorne wrote directly to the reader to discuss the form of the romance in *The House of the Seven Gables* and to provide a genial, perhaps fictionalized account of the genesis of *The Scarlet Letter* while he worked at the Salem custom house. Present-day novelists such as Kurt Vonnegut use parabasis, but none with greater effect than Kundera in *The Book of Laughter and Forgetting*. In the novel he uses parabasis to interpret his characters' lives, to present essays on history, to reveal his own attitudes toward the fictional events he describes, and to narrate his own experiences. Thus, Milan Kundera, a real Czech expatriate living in France, narrates his fiction, interprets it, and becomes a character in his stories at the same time, using the dramatic device of parabasis to blend the levels of reality and discourse together.

## "Lost Letters"

The first section of *The Book of Laughter and Forgetting* opens with a passage of direct address in which Kundera, the narrator, recounts an incident of recent Czech history that will resonate through every section of the novel. On a cold day in February 1948, party leader Klement Gottwald stepped out on a balcony in Prague to announce that a Communist government had been formed to lead the country. It was a "crucial" historical moment, Kundera says, and yet it is filled with a little human drama as well. On this snowy

February day Vladimir Clementis, Gottwald's advisor and fellow Communist, removed his hat and placed it on Gottwald's head. Communist propaganda put out thousands of photographs of the scene showing Gottwald and Clementis together on the balcony, with Gottwald wearing Clementis's hat. But four years later, when Clementis was charged with treason and hanged, propagandists immediately airbrushed Clementis out of the photograph and erased him from any account of Czechoslovak history. Kundera concludes the brief section with pathos and a touch of rueful comedy: "Where Clementis once stood, there is only bare palace wall. All that remains of Clementis is the cap on Gottwald's head."[6]

Having announced the book's two intertwined themes, laughter at forgetting, forgetting through laughter, Kundera the historian becomes Kundera the narrator who moves on to tell the story of Mirek, a former television crewman, who wants to retrieve some love letters he wrote to a former mistress, Zdena, some twenty-five years before. But prior to laying out Mirek's story, Kundera tells us something significant about his character: Mirek believes that the struggle against power is the struggle to preserve memory, and as a result he keeps a daily diary, saves all his correspondence, and keeps notes on meetings, even those where political opinions that might provoke party leaders are aired. Mirek has come to see, Kundera tells us, that he should hide such potentially dangerous papers, but first he decides to take advantage of the free time gained while convalescing from an accident that broke his arm to retrieve his letters to Zdena.

At this point in the story Mirek's motives concerning the letters are unclear. Zdena, a committed, unquestioning Communist, has not threatened Mirek with them, and we have no sense that they contain incriminating information, as his more recent diaries and notes presumably do. But Mirek is in fact more concerned with them than with the politically dangerous notes, and he makes a long, difficult trip to retrieve them. On the way to Zdena's, Kundera the narrator takes the opportunity to comment on Mirek's motives. Mirek is in love with his fate, feels responsible for it, like a novelist for his book or an artist for his painting, and wants to rework it to bring it closer to perfection. Zdena's presence, and especially her possession of the letters, is a part of his fate that he wants to erase because, Kundera informs us after some psychological musing, she was ugly and her important position in his past made people, including Mirek himself, look at Mirek in a negative light: "A weak will and utter poverty—those were the secrets he had hoped to hide" (13).

So far Kundera has united three ideas concerning the theme of forgetting in Mirek's story. We have the official airbrushing of Vladimir Clementis out of Czech history; we have Mirek's political idea that the struggle of man is the struggle to preserve memory; and third, we learn of Mirek's egotistical, vain attempt to rewrite his own history by erasing part of it. In each of these ideas graphic representation, through writing or photographs, is key to the maintenance of memory (in his comments on Kafka, Kundera said the institutional dossier replaces physical existence as reality) and is critical in shaping our attitudes toward our pasts and, ultimately, ourselves. We have reached a critical juncture, therefore, very early in the book, and it leads us to ask the questions that Kundera the historian, the essayist, and the narrator will meditate upon throughout the seven sections of the novel: What is the self? What importance can it have, being so fragile as to be erased not only from physical life but memory as well, even as we struggle to preserve it? And, finally, though possibly less important, are graphic expressions, such as writing and painting, sufficient for the human wish, individually and racially, to survive?

At this point Kundera the narrator gives over to Kundera the essayist, who presents a capsule history of Czechoslovakia in the 1960s. History, he says, "staged" (we must note that verb) an experiment in revolution never seen before (13). Instead of one group of people rising up to revolt against another group it regarded as oppressors, a whole generation of Czechs in the 1960s revolted against their own youth. Most, Kundera included, had welcomed Communist Party leadership in 1948, but Stalinist party hacks had disillusioned them quickly through repressive measures such as those that erased Vladimir Clementis from history, imposed party propaganda as a standard for measuring the arts, and gradually extended Communist influence into the realm of private live. Through the 1960s this disillusioned generation came into maturity and prominence and gained social and intellectual influence until in 1968 they virtually, with the help of Communist Party leader Alexander Dubcek, ruled the country in what we have come to call the Prague Spring. "Borders were opened," Kundera tells us, and microphones were removed from private dwellings: "The spirit was unbelievable. A real carnival!" (14).

But then in August Soviet tanks led half a million Warsaw Pact troops into Czechoslovakia and brought an end to the celebration. Many Czechs left their country (about one hundred and twenty thousand, Kundera says), and those with records of rebellion who stayed had to change their jobs, performing manual labor whatever their intellectual qualifications, experiencing in less drastic forms the erasure from Czechoslovakian history that Vladimir Clementis knew. By way of ending this page-long essay, Kundera leads us back to the story. "Mirek's was one of the names thus erased," he tells us, and conveys his character's physical existence in terms of a painter's conception: he is "only a white stain, a fragment of barely delineated void" going to Zdena's apartment (14).

Kundera's brief parabatic passage serves to remind us of the many types of fiction that concern him: one is the fiction of the novel we are reading; another is the fiction of historical truth, so easily and arbitrarily changed; and a third, the least comfortable, is the fiction of the self that we constantly work to define. In Mirek's conversation with Zdena we see all three of these fictions at work. We learn that Zdena was not really a Communist zealot but instead remained faithful to the Party to show love and fidelity to him—or to that part of him that had used the Party as a means to success and self-definition. Kundera tells us that in his youth Mirek had worn the mask of a rebel, telling "legends and lies" about leaving his rich family, scorning land and property, and becoming a man of the working classes. Zdena had adored him for all that, and now, scorned despite her loyalty through all these years, she refuses to give up the one palpable proof of their affair.

Leaving Zdena's apartment without his letters, Mirek manages to shake the secret police who have been following him, but upon arriving home, he finds their car parked before his house and inside the apartment three men sorting though his papers, books, and notes. One of the men hands him a list of materials to be confiscated, and the story of "Lost Letters" abruptly ends with Kundera addressing us to compare Mirek and Vladimir Clementis's hat: the generation of rebels that he represents have been effectively erased from Czech history, but Mirek remains, like a patch of blurred and ill-formed color on the official, airbrushed photo (read *fiction*) of the past. Mirek went on trial, received a sentence of six years, while his son and several friends incriminated in his papers received sentences of one to six years.

"Lost Letters" demonstrates five central motifs in Milan Kundera's fiction: Accident precipitates important action in the story (Mirek's fall from the roof provides free time to get his letters from Zdena); private life and public life are juxtaposed, with private life destroyed or, frequently, diminished by changes in public affairs; characters use, or abuse, party membership to define themselves and further personal ambitions; regret for the past, both public and private, infuses the stories; and, finally, love and sex are treated purely as manifestations of self-interest, with very little homage given to finer, gentler feelings.

## "Mother"

In Part Two Kundera turns to the purely personal world of family, but by way of a married couple, Karel and Marketa, who, although normally well-organized in their daily lives, indulge in a three-way orgy with their friend Eva while Karel's mother visits them. Narrating the events of the weekend they spend with Mother and Eva, Kundera uncovers the secret wells of emotion that the couple hide from each other (at least concerning their relations with Eva, who turns out to be as secretive as they are). Also, through an accumulation of narrative detail, he makes seemingly small moments of private perception reverberate throughout his characters' mental lives and ultimately into the larger social world beyond their apartment. He does so by opposing a "giant-pear world," representing the private perspective of Karel's mother, with history and public affairs, or what we might call the "world of tanks." When Soviet forces invaded the country in August 1968, cutting short the Prague Spring, Kundera tells us, Karel's mother hardly noticed, expressing more concern that the ripe pears in the family garden would spoil because they had not been picked. At the time, Karel and Marketa regarded his mother's attitude as irrelevant; but as years pass he comes to see the eternal, recurring pattern of life in the garden, an idyll of fruit ripening on trees, as more important than the public, transitory world of tanks. Kundera writes, "Mother was right after all: tanks are mortal, pears eternal" (29).

In the story Karel, who despite his intelligence must be described as emotionally adolescent in relation to women, especially his wife, his mother, and his lover, becomes transformed by a moment of beauty into maturity. At the end he has changed into a man capable of treating his mother lovingly instead of as an old pest who presents him with obligations. The irony is, and it is a nice, Kunderan twist in this story with a rare happy ending, that his wife who has always played the role of the faithful, "better" member of their marriage (it was part of their contract, Kundera tells us), has been transformed as well, ironically having fallen in love with Eva and secretly agreed to an assignation with her and, possibly, her husband, without Karel taking part.

Kundera treats the motifs of memory and history comically in this section, primarily poking fun at the vague, conflicting details Karel's mother brings to her stories of his youth and her own girlhood. And yet it is her faulty memory that triggers Karel's transformation, the moment of beauty during which he experiences a "rebellion against time" that unites a naive childhood memory with his adult erotic experience. In that way the key words of the book's title, *laughter* and *forgetting,* join together, and, with that juncture as bridge from the motif of forgetting in "Lost Letters," Kundera moves on to treat the subject of laughter directly in the next section.

## "The Angels"

He begins this part very playfully, poking fun at literature teachers and critics, especially their tendency to chase after symbols in whatever they read. Two American girls attending a private school in France are assigned an oral report on *Rhinoceros,* a satirical play by Eugène Ionesco that Kundera describes as about characters "obsessed by a desire to be identical to one another" (55) who turn into rhinoceroses. The two girls, Gabrielle and Michelle, are pets of their teacher, Madame Raphael—all three women with angelic names, by the way—and as they work together on their report, they search for the symbolic meaning of the rhinoceros until Michelle suggests that Ionesco intended a comic effect. The girls stop in the middle of the street, look at each other, and "let out short, shrill, breathy sounds very difficult to describe in words" (56). That is, they laugh (or perhaps giggle).

In the next section Kundera the essayist replaces Kundera the narrator once again and, without precisely describing the sound of laughter, develops its social and metaphysical import in a two-page meditation that begins with his quotation of the feminist Annie Leclerc's discussion of sisterly delight. He ends with her sentence, "Laughing deeply is living deeply," and calls her essay a "mystical manifesto of joy" that has, along with other feminist works, marked our era. Kundera compares Leclerc's book, which he says links death with joy, claiming it to be an experience only men fear because of their egos, with the kind of second-rate movie scene that shows a couple running hand in hand through a summer landscape and laughing. Silly though this scene is, it has a serious theme, "laughter beyond joking," and is shared, Kundera says, by all churches, underwear manufacturers, generals, and political parties—that is, by all those who want the individual to follow them, buy their product, or, in other words, march to the sound of their music. It is the laughter of conformity, and Michelle and Gabrielle experience it as they prepare their report (58).

He then undercuts that pleasant, thought-provoking essay by introducing the next section with a sober sentence about the 1968 Soviet invasion. At this point a third type of writing, indeed a third persona for the narrator, enters the book: Kundera the autobiographer, who speaks to the reader with the full weight of his life experience. After August 1968, Kundera says, he "lost the privilege of working" (58), and, with the help of a woman friend who edited a magazine, wrote a regular astrological column under a pseudonym. An interesting confluence of motif, content, and style: Kundera stands before the audience as himself, telling an anecdote about his former life in Prague, and in doing so once again raises the issue of the self as fiction. Kundera, airbrushed from Czech literature, could publish nothing, so this pseudonymous astrologer wrote for him. Kundera says he developed a fictional character to be the "true" astrologer, telling the editor to describe him as a nuclear physicist who used a false name for fear his fellow scientists would laugh at him. With that note Kundera makes laughter a sign of conformity once again, and moves on to the concluding part of this episode. The editor-in-chief of the magazine, a high party official who owed his position to the Russians, asks the astrologer, without knowing he is Kundera, to do a personal horoscope for him. Kundera's friend, who had been his contact with the magazine, tells him the editor-in-chief loves the astrology columns but feels ashamed because they go against Marxist philosophy. Compounding this joke about identity, the party official wants his name kept secret from the astrologer. Enjoying the ironic twists in the situation, Kundera spends a week on the official's horoscope, accomplishing a change in the man's character by implying that suffering lies in his future and counseling him to act kindly to others.

From that humorous anecdote Kundera moves on to one of the most famous passages in all of his fiction, his essay on the two kinds of laughter, that of the devil and that of the angels. It is a discussion that flows thematically from the previous section on astrology and relates to the story, two sections back, of the two angelic American girls, Gabrielle and Michelle. At the same time this essay on laughter raises metaphysical questions of the most serious kind and treats them with a lightness of touch that no writer since Kafka has managed.

"Angels are partisans not of Good," Kundera tells us, "but of divine creation," and the Devil "denies all rational meaning to God's world" (61). The wording of these statements deserves close attention because they illuminate the book and reverberate throughout Kundera's work. First, note that "Good" is capitalized, signaling that the concept is a fiction, while "divine" and "creation," without capitals but also in dispute as absolutes, are not. Note as well that, while the angels are described as partisans of religious or biblical principles, devils are described in relation to a philosophical principle ("rational meaning") as it may be applied to a biblical construct ("God's world"). The reader can infer from these statements that for Kundera (Kundera the essayist, that is) "Good" and "God's world" are fictions, while "divine creation" and "rational meaning" are not. The reader can

27

further infer that just as the religious idea of "divine creation" and the scientific idea of "rational meaning" may be opposed, "Good" and "God's world" also may be opposed.

With those ideas clear, the paragraph about the laughter of angels and demons who dominate the world takes on deeper meaning. The good of the world (note the lower case *g*—the same thought could not be expressed if the letter were upper case) does not require that angels dominate devils. All the good of the world needs is balance between them, a balance of power that will prevent too much or too little meaning, both of which would crush humanity with the responsibility of either living up to some great meaning or creating it.

Originally, Kundera continues, laughter was the Devil's response, because intelligent beings (humans as well as devils) laugh when important things suddenly seem meaningless, and that relieves them from the burden of seriousness, allowing them a measure of freedom they did not know they had. But the angels in this philosophic drama, less intelligent than the Devil, were horrified by laughter upon first hearing it, and in order to defend God's creation they turned their enemy's weapon around. While the Devil's laugh expressed appreciation of meaninglessness, the angels' imitation expressed happiness at organization and good sense. Put in other terms, the Devil's laugh cynically poked holes in agreed-upon fictions, such as received ideas or general truths, and the angels' laughter innocently reconfirmed them. Whether readers agree or not with this concept, they should also note that while Kundera portrays the Devil laughing alone, he renders the angels laughing in company. So the Devil's laughter represents individuality, cynicism, doubt; the angels' laughter represents belief, innocence, and conformity. These are important moral distinctions about laughter that lead the narrative into the next two sections, an interesting mix of fiction (about Michelle and Gabrielle), essay (about individualism and conformity), autobiography (concerning Kundera's life in Prague, before and after the 1968 invasion), and literary history (concerning the Stalinist execution in 1950 of the Czech writer Zavis Kalandra).

Kundera begins by focusing on a news photograph of armed men in uniform staring at young people in jeans and T-shirts dancing in a circle to what Kundera imagines is a folk melody. He identifies with them, he tells us, understanding their sense of innocence before the soldiers. They do not march, they dance; they do not support imposed order, they play. But he gives their innocence an aggressive edge by saying that they cannot wait "to spit their innocence" at the uniformed men who stare at them (63). Then he describes the schoolteacher Madame Raphael's lifelong search for a circle to dance in. She went from the Methodists to the Communists, from Trotskyites to both sides of the abortion dispute, to the Buddhists and the followers of Mao Zedong, and then to writers like Brecht and Alain Robbe-Grillet, finally settling, as a teacher, on the hope of forming a circular dance with her students by forcing them to think and speak as she did. Her innocence is not completely harmless. The eager-to-please Michelle and Gabrielle fit perfectly into her scheme, and their plan to give a strictly humorous reading of *Rhinoceros* reflects their acceptance of her influence even as they miss the warning about conformity in the play.

Kundera then turns the edge of these less than admirable interpretations of dance and laughter on himself, and he does so by means of confession, admitting that he too danced in a circle, just after Klement Gottwald's ascent to power in 1948. He tells us that "old wrongs were righted, new wrongs perpetrated" (65), and he danced with fellow students (innocently, the reader assumes) to celebrate the changes until one day he too was expelled from the party and had to leave the dance. It was at that point that Kundera discovered the magic quality of circles, how, once they are broken, the individual can never join them again. And since that original separation (Kundera uses the word "fall," as in Satan's fall from grace or innocence) he has had what he calls a "muted nostalgia" for the circular dance.

He then narrates a very powerful historical sequence, made all the stronger for the autobiographical point of view and fantasy injected into it. Kundera tells of walking around Prague in June 1950, looking for a circle to dance in on the day after Zavis Kalandra and a Socialist Party deputy were hanged for plotting against the Communist government. Kalandra had been a friend of two French writers, André Breton and Paul Éluard, but while Breton tried to save Kalandra, Éluard did nothing, "too busy," Kundera says, "dancing in the gigantic ring" of Communist believers circling the major cities of Europe, and "reciting his beautiful poems about joy and brotherhood." He quotes Éluard, some lines about filling innocence with strength so that "We shall never again be alone," and then says he understood, while walking through Prague that June day, that he belonged with Kalandra, not the circle of dancers, even though he felt envious and nostalgic as he watched them. At that moment, in a vision, he sees Éluard before him, dancing with the Czechs and reciting his poems until they begin to rise from the ground, float above the square; he runs after them, hoping to catch "that wonderful wreath" above the city until he realizes that they have wings while he, like Satan (and Kalandra), falls away from them.

This part of *The Book of Laughter and Forgetting* now moves toward completion, and in the next three short sections Kundera gathers the strand of autobiography around the fictional strand of his three angels: Michelle, Gabrielle, and Madame Raphael. First he informs the reader that a year after he began composing astrology articles, he was discovered to be the writer, with the result that his friend who had helped him get the job was fired from the magazine and could not find another position. Also, she had been subjected to interrogation by the police and now, in a secret meeting with Kundera, shows unmistakable signs of shame and fear, her uneasy stomach betraying her emotions. He realized, he tells us, that he had been chosen by the party as courier of warnings and punishments.

In the next section Kundera the narrator completes his story of the angels. Michelle and Gabrielle decide to wear false noses while giving their report, but the class responds with embarrassment rather than humor, presumably because they look foolish and because the point they are making is obvious. Then an Israeli student named Sarah goes to the front of the room, stands behind them, and kicks them, one by one, before returning, dignified, to her seat. After a moment the class laughs, and Madame Raphael, thinking the incident was planned, joins in the laughter. She takes the hands of Gabrielle and Michelle and, as the class watches, horrified, they begin to dance, rising above the floor and ascending through the ceiling until the students in the classroom hear nothing but laughter from above, from the "three archangels" (74).

Closing Part Three, Kundera reviews the account of his secret meeting with the editor of his astrology column. Autobiographical historian once more, he says that the meeting was a turning point for him because, once he realized his presence bore bad news and warnings for his friends, he knew he had to leave Czechoslovakia. But he also considers the meeting important because of something else. He confesses that in the middle of his friend's fear and her constant trips to the toilet, he felt a violent desire to rape her, to possess her body and spirit, "her shit and her ineffable soul" (75), the two sides of her nature that in balance comprise her character (and all human character). The desire has remained with him through the years, he informs us, and he interprets it as an attempt to grab something during his fall from the circular dance. He develops that metaphor in a final peregrination: Falling through the void of the world, a world of meaninglessness in other words, Kundera hears what he calls the "terrifying" laughter of angels, laughter representing an imposition of arbitrary meaning. Ending the chapter with a reference to Sarah, the student who kicked Michelle and Gabrielle, he joins autobiography and fiction, invoking Old Testament parallels by calling her his "Jewish sister Sarah," and plaintively wondering where he can find her. The ending, along with the novel's biblical mixture of form and content, bears some further comment, primarily because of its important reference to the story of Abraham and his wife, Sarah.

In the book of Genesis, God names Abraham the titular father of the Jews, a tribe of political exiles much like those who left Czechoslovakia after 1968. When, during a famine, Abraham travels with Sarah into Egypt, he tells the pharaoh that she is his sister because he fears the Egyptians will kill him on account of her great beauty. The pharaoh makes her a member of his harem until God intervenes to free her and once again promises that the children of Abraham and Sarah shall be numerous. Finally, after years of barrenness, when Abraham is a hundred years old and Sarah is ninety, God promises that she will give birth within a year. In a wonderful moment of Old Testament levity Sarah and Abraham laugh (need I say devilishly?) at this patent absurdity, and for a moment God appears on the defensive, saying, "Is anything too hard for the Lord?" But, as promised, he delivers. Sarah conceives, bears a male child, and Abraham names him Isaac, Hebrew for "he laughs," or "laughter," key words in this book and Kundera's thinking about man, the novel, and fate.

## "Lost Letters"

With "The Angels," the architecture of the novel has been solidly founded, and Kundera moves into the next three parts with an exuberance that belies his subject matter. In this second "Lost Letters," a reprise of the title and theme of the first part of the book, Kundera the essayist opens with a parabatic address to the reader about fictional characters, his uncertainty in naming them when there are two or three new ones "baptized" every second, and then introduces the principal character of this episode, providing her with a completely new name, Tamina, and saying he cares for her more than any other being, presumably fictional or nonfictional.

A native of Prague, Tamina moved to a provincial West European town (seemingly in France) after the tanks invaded in 1968 and now, with her husband dead, she passes her days as a waitress in a small café, listening to customers talk about themselves. Tamina is popular with her customers because, in a world that Kundera describes as combat for attention, she never talks about herself. A good listener who has her own unhappy past, she and her story sum up the motifs of the first three sections: the idea of writing and privacy that Kundera introduced in the first "Lost Letters," the link between memory and desire in "Mother," and the joining of conformity and laughter in "The Angels." Also, in a novel that discusses book writing and story-telling as a means of holding on to life, Tamina represents an audience with a heart, one that pays attention and seeks to retain.

She also is one of the many characters in Kundera's work who seek to re-trieve the irretrievable: their pasts. But unlike Mirek in the first "Lost Letters" chapter, Tamina does not seek it to change it. Rather she seeks to preserve her past because she finds that as the years go by since she left Czechoslovakia (and since her husband died), she recalls things less and less clearly. She had kept a notebook for each of the eleven years spent with her husband, but having left the notebooks behind when they escaped, she finds it impossible to preserve the events of those years in her memory. She cannot bring back all their vacations; she misses Christmases and New Year's Eves; and, most disturbing because they are parts of herself, or selves that she has lost, she cannot recall the long list of twenty or thirty endearing pet names her husband called her, inventing them frequently as their lives changed through-out the years. The pet names, the vacations, the holidays are reference points in what Kundera calls "the rhythm of time," and he emphasizes that Tamina seeks the past to give her present form, to make it meaningful. Without the past the present is "nothing moving slowly toward death" (86).

Two interlocking motifs dominate this second "Lost Letters." First is the plot: Tamina's efforts to retrieve her notebooks from her mother-in-law's apartment in Prague. Second, perhaps more important, is a parabatic discus-sion of a contemporary desire by people in the West to reveal everything about themselves and their personal lives, even when not forced to by a snooping government. In several highly comic passages women talk about their orgasms while watching TV, men write about their sexual adventures and then discuss them on television, and characters express the intention to write books that will bear witness to the world as they see it. In a short essay addressed to this topic, Kundera describes graphomania, defining it as a de-sire not simply to write letters, diaries, and chronicles but to write them with an eye toward publication. In that way Tamina is a foil to the world around her because not only does she listen to her friends instead of talk, she is in-tensely private and wishes no one to read her notebooks but herself.

Kundera presents three social conditions for the development of grapho-mania: general economic well-being providing time for what he calls "use-less activities"; civil atomization leading to a feeling of isolation among the people; and an absence of significant social change. Indicating that France (or almost any Western society) meets those three conditions, Kundera constructs a story about the graphomaniacs in Tamina's café and how they and their self-centeredness influence her fate.

Her friend Bibi, who never reads and leads an absolutely banal personal life with her husband and child, wants to write a book about the world and what she thinks of it. Banaka, described as a "tenth-rate" novelist, says he doesn't exist after he reads a review ridiculing his latest novel. And Hugo, vaguely described as an intellectual who comes into the café to read and ogle Tamina every day, publishes an article of political analysis in a small, unimportant journal and sees himself as boldly taking on all of the repressive governments of Central Europe. Tamina uses these people to attempt to retrieve her notebooks, to keep them out of the hands of the Czech secret police, her mother-in-law, and her father, but in the end her friends, despite promises, refuse to help her. She sleeps with Hugo because he has vowed to go to Czechoslovakia for the notebooks but, disappointed with her lack of passion, he creates a ridiculous story about the danger the country would pose for him because of the article he wrote. Disillusioned, learning that her notebooks indeed have been read by her mother-in-law and probably her father too, Tamina retreats to the toilet of the restaurant where she and Hugo have been dining and, in a scene reminiscent of the one between Kundera and the editor of his astrology column, vomits her dinner, her body physically expressing the inner revulsion of her soul.

### "Litost"

Tamina returns in the puzzling, beautiful sixth part of *The Book of Laughter and Forgetting,* but first Kundera the essayist builds a bridge to it with a complexly formed tale about writers and love that he calls "Litost" (pronounced *lee-toasht*), a Czech word he describes as untranslatable. He defines "litost" as a synthesis of several feelings: grief, sympathy, remorse, and longing. But he also says there are times when its meaning is precise, when, in fact, it relates to the English word "resentment" and is especially associated with youth. In that context Kundera defines the word as "a state of torment caused by a sudden insight into one's own miserable self" (122) and then tells the comic story of a young man's tryst with a married provincial woman on the night he meets some of the leading poets in Prague. The situation is ripe for the emotion of *litost;* and Kundera, who has described Czech literature, especially its poetry, as lyrical and narcissistic,[7] takes the opportunity to poke fun at several romantic traditions in and out of Czechoslovakia: the drunken, squabbling sense of competition among writers, their idolization of love and beauty, the macho nature of their behavior with women, their bumbling egotism in the guise of genius, and the emotional variety with which they respond to a simple lack of sex.

Dividing "Litost" into passages with evocative titles, Kundera begins the story with a description of Kristyna, a butcher's wife of the provinces who loves literature from afar and seeks some romantic escape from the banality of her life. Unlike Tamina's friend Bibi, however, Kristyna does not seek to tell her story to the world. Instead, she wants to take part in life, to see a larger society, and she agrees to visit a young student in Prague. Unfortunately, the student's literature professor invites him to attend a meeting of the best poets in Czechoslovakia, who are gathering at the Writers' Club the very night of Kristyna's visit. Caught between two urgent desires, the student, whose name Kundera never provides, arranges to satisfy both. What follows is an account of a night-long series of disappointments, events that fall far short of expectations for everyone. Kristyna's country clothes and behavior make the student ashamed to be seen with her in Prague, and the inexpensive restaurant where he meets her reminds Kristyna of the places she frequents with her butcher husband. They resolve these difficulties when he tells her of his coming meeting with the poets at the Writers' Club, and she promises to wait for him if he will return with an autographed copy of a book by the country's greatest poet, whose verse Kristyna memorized in school.

By means of yet another parabatic aside to the reader Kundera introduces us to the scene at the Writers' Club. In a short passage entitled "The Poets," he mixes fiction and autobiographical memory by telling of his escape to Rennes, a university town in northwestern France, and saying that from the windows of his high-rise "tower" he looks back toward Prague and sees the poets meeting. But Prague is now his past, and he describes the poets as they might have been in 1962, when Czech writers and intellectuals led the country toward greater freedom. In moving sentences that parallel the opening of Tamina's story, Kundera reveals how he intends to name them now that they have been eclipsed and erased, their books "locked away in the cellars of the state" (128). If he has to hide them behind masks, he says, he might as well make them a gift of their names, honor them, decorate them with the fiction. The most famous Czech poet, old and revered, he gives the name of Goethe, after the most famous poet in the German language, and the others he calls Lermontov, Yesenin, Petrarch, and Verlaine, romantic poets of Russia, Italy, and France respectively. Countering their romanticism he names the student's professor after Voltaire, the eighteenth-century French philosopher of reason; and to one of the others, a fiction writer who doesn't like poetry, he gives the name Boccaccio, a contemporary of Dante in fourteenth-century Florence, whose *Decameron,* a collection of bawdy tales within the frame of a larger story concerning Florentines who want to escape the plague, is one of the first works of prose fiction in the West, one that Kundera refers to as having a novel's form in his book of criticism *The Art of the Novel.*

With the form of this section functioning as a mirror in miniature of Boccaccio's *Decameron* (and *The Book of Laughter and Forgetting* as well), Kundera reports the meeting of the poets as a series of tales within other tales. Read in the context of his comments on graphomania in Part Four, these tales and the poets' conversation about them turn into critical, and comic, discussions on the value and purpose of literature. The poet called Petrarch tells of a night when one of his students, a young woman poet who loves him, visits his apartment just as he and his wife retire for the night. Petrarch tries to make her leave, but the young woman, eager to talk, refuses and ultimately breaks into his apartment to confront him and his wife with a crowbar in her hands. Petrarch describes her at that moment as Joan of Arc with a sword, and the other poets make fun of him for the romantic image. Lermontov doesn't believe the story at all. Boccaccio claims Petrarch idolizes Woman but dislikes individual women; then he adds that all poets cling to their mothers' skirts. Yesenin mumbles in his beer, wondering what Boccaccio has said about his mother. As the poets shout and interrupt each other, Petrarch attempts to complete his story, and when Lermontov again expresses doubt, calling his account worse than Boccaccio's fiction because it is simply bad poetry, the whole group turns on him in ridicule. Goethe sums up by whispering that although Lermontov, a proud poet of the working classes, writes great verse, he is bad-humored because he is starved for sex. The student, feeling empathy with Lermontov's celibacy, defends him, calling on their sense of pride as poets. He impresses the others, especially Goethe.

What follows is a series of comic scenes about drunken poets and particularly their romanticism, which Kundera portrays as fuzzy muddleheadedness, lacking in reason, individuality, and common sense. Boccaccio, whose earthy humor makes him a clear surrogate for Kundera himself, becomes the foil for all that poetic thinking, and we note that despite the powerful impression the student made with his comments on poetic pride, the narrator refers to him as stupid and imbecilic several times, primarily because his "poetic" attitudes ultimately prevent a physical union with Kristyna. Armed with the pride of Lermontov, the words of Goethe (he has signed the book of poems with a paean of praise to Kristyna as a rural queen), and the ideas of Petrarch ("Love is poetry, poetry is love"), the student returns to his attic room for the night. There Kristyna embraces and kisses him passionately but refuses intercourse because, she says, it would kill her. He interprets this as meaning that the emotions would be too strong for her. He responds emotionally himself. Thinking of Petrarch's comment on poets, that they "burn" in the women they love, he accepts her refusal. But excited by an experience he naïvely thinks is unique, he learns next morning that Kristyna feared pregnancy, not her emotions. As she takes the train back to her country town, he feels like screaming with laughter, "hysterical" laughter, a feeling akin to *litost* in that it represents a sudden insight into his miserable self.

If the emotion of *litost* alienates, as it does when mixed with the laughter of the student and the laughter of the Devil that Kundera described in his section about Gabrielle and Michelle, then poetry, romantic poetry at any rate, is like the laughter of the angels in that it speaks of grand harmony, order, and unity without regard to the facts of daily physical life. Poetry often speaks in generalities, while prose fiction, at least the prose fiction of the realist Boccaccio (or Kundera), cuts through order and speaks of discord, individuality, and palpable things: the body as opposed to the soul, sex as opposed to love, sensations as opposed to grand ideas. Put in another, political way, devilish laughter and ironic fiction tend to promote tolerant attitudes, while poetry, romanticism, and angelic laughter lean toward conformity and intolerance. The emotion of *litost* presents an opportunity for all of them to surface, but poetry remains the response of the frustrated and impotent. In the last part of the story the student returns to the Writers' Club and meets Lermontov and Petrarch together. Mistaking Kristyna's hastily scribbled note as a love lyric by the student, Petrarch pronounces him a poet. In his celibacy Lermontov scowls, and Kundera closes Part Five by recalling for the reader that he perceives them all from his high-rise in Rennes, a position above the crowd, much like the balcony on which stood Gottwald and Clementis and toward which—we learn this at the beginning of the following part—Kafka ascended when he was a boy. As Petrarch and the student say good-bye to Lermontov, Kundera refers to him as the genius of *litost*, whose sound in the pronouncing evokes "the plaint of an abandoned dog."

## "The Angels"

A second part entitled "The Angels" follows Kundera's meditation on *litost*, and he opens it by returning to a fundamental scene, the balcony on the old baroque castle in Prague where Gottwald announced the formation of a Communist state and instituted a culture of forgetting—as shown by the photographs with the hat of the "erased" Vladimir Clementis on his head. He also returns to Tamina, the character who, in the second "Lost Letters," "means more to me than anyone ever has" (79), presumably because she sought to preserve memory against overwhelming odds. Essentially Kundera develops the theme of *litost* again, but without mentioning it, expanding the context of the feeling to include the frustration of the Czech people as they seek nationhood and instead experience a series of cultural invasions. He then narrows his consideration more specifically to include the personal: an autobiographical story of his father's loss of memory in his declining years and then the drowning of the fictional character Tamina.

After the opening passage about the balcony in Prague, Kundera discusses national memory. Gustav Husak, the man whom the Russians installed as Czech leader after their 1968 invasion, has become known as *"the president of forgetting"* in Czechoslovakia (158). The Russians used Husak to massacre Czech culture and make the country over in Russia's image. Kundera finds it significant that nearly one hundred and fifty historians lost their positions in Czechoslovakian universities and research institutes and reports with typical cynicism the Czech rumor that for each historian fired a "new monument to Lenin sprang up" (159). Relating the destruction of books, culture, and history (all forms of social memory) to the planned liquidation of a people, Kundera says that from 1968 to the present time of the book, about 1978, the Czech nation could see its death, not as inevitable perhaps, but as a real event, a possibility close at hand. Such a realization, Kundera has said, is what the New World Indians must have felt as white men and women gradually took over the North American continent and crushed their way of life.[8] The emotion tied to that realization must be akin to *litost,* an insight into self on a grander, national scale that makes the individual pale into insignificance and makes memory of the past, embodied by history and personal recollection, all the more precious.

Using Husak's dismissal of Czech historians as transition, Kundera moves to a pair of parallel narratives, one autobiographical, the other fictional, concerning the memories of his father and Tamina. As the historians are being fired, jailed, or sent into exile, Kundera tells us, his father, Ludvik, slowly loses his ability to speak words even as he is acute enough to take up a study of Beethoven's intricate piano sonatas.[9] One day, looking at the score of the Opus 111 sonata with its many variations, Ludvik Kundera points to the music and tries to tell his son that he has finally figured them out. But words won't come, and he barely utters "Now I know." After several more attempts at explanation, he says in amazement, "That's strange," and leaves Kundera (and the reader) with the mystery of his knowing.

We can read that touching anecdote in light of the book's action: Without language, either spoken or written, memory is sealed, and both his father's knowledge and his country's past (as written literature or history) are as irretrievable for Kundera as they are for Tamina. With that established, he begins the final episodes in her life. These episodes contain more fantasy than reality, yet the fantasy is founded on the realism of the first story Kundera told about Tamina and the factual history and autobiography he uses to introduce this second one. The mixture is biblical or, more broadly speaking, mythical in tone, and, appropriately, Kundera infuses the tale of Tamina's final days with moral, philosophic considerations concerning the book's principal themes: body and spirit, understanding and innocence, laughter and forgetting.

After some years, Tamina does not come to work at the café one morning, and when the police fail to find any trace of her, they place her in the file of the "Permanently Missing" (162), a bureaucratic category easily applied to the dead or exiled. We never find out what has happened to her, whether she completed the suicide attempt described in "Lost Letters" or whether she simply decided to move to another country, possibly Czechoslovakia, to escape her present or relive her past. Instead, Kundera explores a possibility, one speculation about what *could* have happened to a woman like her, a speculation made possible because he states clearly to the reader that she is an imagined character, not real. A young man visits her in the café, asks her questions about herself (as no one else in the small town ever has), and then offers to take her to a place where things are light and there is no remorse. "As in a fairy tale," Kundera says, she leaves the counter she has stood behind for several years and drives off with the young man, named Raphael, in a red sports car (164).

After a parabatic aside comparing Tamina's loss of her husband and Kundera's loss of his father with Beethoven's interest in variations during his mature years (like the world of pears discussed in "Mother," all are described as examples of the human interest in the infinitely small as opposed to the "infinity of the stars"), Kundera delivers a short essay about the form of *The Book of Laughter and Forgetting*, "a novel in the form of variations" (165), pointedly telling the reader that he chose the name Raphael on purpose, and then continuing the narration of Tamina's final journey. Taking up that idea of variations and thinking further on the idea of this novel as a mixture of biblical styles and content, the reader may reflect that Raphael is a principal character in the book of Tobit, one of the most delightful stories in all of biblical literature.

Found in the Apocrypha, the book of Tobit has several parallels, in addition to the form of the title, with *The Book of Laughter and Forgetting* and the individual stories within it. First, the story concerns exiles and a journey by one of them (Tobit's son, Tobias, accompanied by the angel Raphael) to regain something from the past. Of course, that is the essence of Tamina's story, as well as Mirek's from the first "Lost Letters." Second, there is a character named Sarah in the story (compare Kundera's "sister Sarah" in "The Angels"), and while she is not the same biblical woman who in old age gave birth to Isaac ("laughter"), this Sarah has a demon lover, Asmodeus, who makes it impossible for her to enjoy sex or bear children. He kills seven of her husbands; then Tobias, with the help of Raphael, frightens him off and spends the night with her, finally achieving a consummated marriage and, ultimately, children. Third, the narrative of the book of Tobit has several points of technical interest that parallel *The Book of Laughter and Forgetting*. It is told from the point of view of a first-person narrator, Tobit, who tells two stories that he could not have witnessed firsthand, underlining the idea that the stories are imagined rather than fact (as Kundera does in his discussion of Tamina). In addition, Tobit relates the stories in a modern way, simultaneously, cutting back and forth, as if he were a movie camera, between Tobias's journey and Sarah's problems with her demon lover, until the two characters meet. Kundera's switches of point of view, content, and character as he moves from chapter to chapter of this novel are similar. And finally, the author of Tobit exercises a very modern-seeming self-consciousness about writing when Raphael, before returning to heaven, tells Tobit to write down his story so that it may function as an eternal hymn of praise to God and his works. In answer, presumably, Tobit has written the very book we are reading, and with a nice bit of Kunderan irony we realize that as part of the Apocrypha (from the Greek word for "set aside" or "concealed") its truth and validity as part of the Old Testament canon have been in dispute from the very beginning of its history. Similarly, *The Book of Laughter and Forgetting* is about the importance of writing, yet it too is a book that was "set aside" and "concealed" in Czechoslovakia until very recently.

With these parallels in mind, the rest of Tamina's story takes on transcendent overtones. Raphael drives into the countryside, past an area that reminds Tamina vividly of Czechoslovakia, and then to a river, where a young boy with a boat awaits them. It is hard not to see this water as mythical—as the Lethe, for instance, the river of forgetfulness in Greek mythology, or the

Acheron, the river Dante has dividing the borderland of Hell from Limbo. Whatever the reference, Tamina clearly embarks on a mythic journey here, and with Raphael and the boy laughing pleasantly but without real humor (reminding us of the laughter of the angels in the first "Angels" story), Tamina steps into the boat and leaves Raphael behind. The boy and she take turns rowing, and we see something ominous about the trip when the boy plays loud music from a tape recorder and moves his body sexually to its rhythm as Tamina rows.

They reach land that seems pleasant enough. Tamina finds green grass, trees, pleasant walkways scattered about, and a white building at the end of one path. A young girl leads Tamina to a dormitory room where, presumably, she will sleep with others. When Tamina, as an adult, demands some privacy, the girl tells her that they are all children here and that Tamina has been assigned to the group of children known as squirrels. Not liking this, Tamina attempts to leave but finds that the is trapped on an island. Cut off from her past, without memory, she is, physically mature or not, like a child, and the reader must now be prepared to understand her trip on other than adult, or "realistic," grounds. Returning to the dormitory, she sees a group of children standing in a circle. In a brief passage like the one in which the French poet Éluard dances as a fellow poet hangs, the children open their circle and invite Tamina in to play. Terrified, she remembers Raphael's smile and runs into the building to be alone.

In two following parabatic chapters about dying, memory, and fear of the human corpse, Kundera brings together the autobiographical, historical, and fictional strands of his story. He tells how Tamina went to the hospital one day to find her husband's bed empty. The man who shared the room with him tells her that after her husband died, the attendants dragged his corpse by the legs, letting his head bump on the floor. Kundera says that her fear of death had to do with the sudden loss of privacy that the body suffers upon becoming a corpse, and that she attempted to drown herself a few months after her husband's death because only fish would witness the shame of her dead body. By association, he moves to tell of his own loss. During his father's final hours President Husak, the President of Forgetting, received an Honorary Pioneer award from the children of Prague. "Children! You are the future!" he shouts. Kundera then joins the political and philosophic meanings of the story's three different strands by having Husak declare, "Children! Never look back!" (174).

In effect, Husak's words become the motif of Tamina's life entrapped on the island. Reluctantly she becomes one of the children, playing their games, sleeping and bathing with them in a loss of privacy, relinquishing all the weight of her past. She becomes a curious figure among them, favored, leaned on, caressed, as if she were important; but at the same time we understand that she has become an object, and when we read about her performing bathroom functions among them in the nude, we perceive her as diminished. Like Karel in "Mother," who in adult orgies has to work through an infantile vision of his mother's friend whom he saw naked, these children are abusers. But they are angelic, innocent abusers because they have no past and no values except for play. In that light the story of Tamina's experience on the island can be seen as a comment on modern life and culture—in Communist Czechoslovakia and the West. If she finds political repression behind the wall of Soviet tanks, she finds mental and spiritual repression in the youthful culture of the West, particularly its music and its emphasis on sport. In another short section Kundera discusses what he calls "the idiocy of music," that is, music stripped of thought, music that is elemental in that it appeals strictly to the senses, a concept that calls to mind the young boy jerking rhythmically to popular music while ferrying Tamina to the island. Such thoughtless music, innocent yet brutal, reflects human life at its most idiotic, Kundera says, an idiocy he has portrayed throughout the book: in orgies, mindless dancing, poetic drunks, political censorship, and in children's games that are simple, sexual, and cruel, even as they are innocent, or "angelic." Like people who see existence through one set of truths or principles, the children simply want to glorify the world as they know it. And they are cruel to Tamina, as well as innocent, because she so obviously exists outside their narrow vision.

In a moving ending that is the dramatic climax of the novel, Tamina throws herself into the water and begins to swim. Despair aside, she does not intend to commit suicide. Rather she wants to escape the island with all that she has left of herself: her body and her desire for life. But the children follow her, and after a night of swimming, when, exhausted, she sees their boat floating nearby, she gives up, letting herself go under as the children, interested in her death but not caring, observe her. Without memory they have little capacity for sympathy and none for love. Like the people who danced in Prague, their interest in games and play gives them innocence, but their ignorance of the everyday world (the world of consequence, the world of pears) makes them unsympathetic, cruel. Unlike Karel in "Mother," they will not find maturity; they will not grow beyond their angelic cruelty, though Tamina has been sacrificed to their pleasures. Weightless, they live in an intolerant world completely cut off from the past.

## "The Border"

A coda to the themes of *The Book of Laughter and Forgetting*, the final part advances Kundera's critique of culture, but in a more direct, realistic mode. In making that critique, Kundera ties together his various narrative motifs: the use of hats, games playing (among adults in this particular story), the closing down of culture, and the sterility of modern life because of its increasing sense of isolation and lack of contact. If Tamina's death among the children is an example of her terminal exile, her final forgetting, then in "The Border" Kundera dramatizes that exile in life, importantly, the life among exiles in the West.

The story opens with a description of the major character, Jan, having intercourse with his lover, Edwige. Kundera makes clear immediately that, even in this most intimate of human situations, Jan is isolated, exiled. First he describes Jan's conception of a woman's face during intercourse as a television screen upon which a film has been projected, and then he increases that sense of isolation by saying that with Edwige, Jan perceives nothing but a blank screen. In addition, they are absolutely silent during their lovemaking, so that we have an image of this perfectly modern couple as spiritually isolated, out of communication with one another, playing out their lives on separate stages. They get along well, but they exist separately, perhaps because their liberal sexual mores lead them to perform sex as automatically as a "man standing at attention" upon hearing his country's national anthem (196). It is an apt, ironic simile, bringing together the private sexual act of love with the public patriotic one and repeating one of Kundera's most perceptive themes: the invasion of private life by ideology on both sides of the Iron Curtain.

As background for that theme Kundera addresses the reader playfully once again and discusses the invasion by blackbirds of the major European cities during the eighteenth and nineteenth centuries. On a global level, he says, that invasion was probably more important than the many human invasions in modern history because the blackbirds' movement signalled a major change in the planetary order, that is the relations between two species. Yet no sane person—historian, biologist, or philosopher—would ever interpret earth's last two hundred years in light of the blackbirds' invasion. We are prisoners, he says, of rigid conceptions concerning what is important in human life, and, like the angelic children in Tamina's story, we are unable to comprehend a broader, more complex vision.

Applying the irony of that concept to private life, Kundera says that a biographer would summarize Jan's life with Edwige positively: It would be a turning point, when his life took shape and he made several advantageous career decisions, especially the one to go to America. But that description would be just as wrong as the historical interpretation that overlooks the blackbirds, because Jan's favorite story while he lives with Edwige is the ancient romance, written by Longus in the fourth or fifth century after Christ, about Daphnis and Chloe, two children who fall passionately in love at a young age but are too innocent (and "angelic") to fulfill their love in any practical way.

With that psychological insight into Jan established, Kundera moves to another major character, Jan's friend Passer, who after an operation for cancer can no longer function sexually, although he still maintains an active social life. To put it bluntly, both Passer and Jan represent sterility in modern thinking, although Passer (whose name means "to pass" in French) takes on larger significance, especially at his funeral, where his death seems to represent the passing of humanism, an aesthetic and philosophic attitude that emphasizes appreciation for life, sympathy for humanity, and respect for the past, qualities that Passer's friends revere in him. Kundera plays off that symbolism comically when he introduces the Clevises, a fashionably avant-garde family whom he describes as a "spiritual air bubble" on a carpenter's level that provides impeccable testimony concerning an idea's fashionable progressivity (201). Jan visits them, and in a discussion like the one Tamina hears from Joujou and Bibi concerning orgasms in "Lost Letters," the Clevises fall into an argument concerning topless sunbathing for women. They begin with ethical and aesthetic concerns, but when the teen-age daughter explodes in anger, saying men are incapable of seeing women as anything but sex objects, the falseness of their rational context is made clear. Naïve style has replaced experience; the Clevises applaud their daughter's words, and in the following section Kundera tells of another fashionable woman Jan knows, a clerk in a sporting goods store who is an orgasm fanatic. Without emotion, without foreplay, she simply seeks to achieve orgasms in sex, like a child collecting marbles, or like a sport enthusiast keeping records.

Against that charged background Kundera builds the story of "The Border" around two scenes, Passer's funeral and an orgy that Jan attends shortly before flying to America. He draws the scenes as two halves of a circle representing the dance of the human spirit in our times. In both scenes laughter interrupts solemnity. At Passer's funeral Papa Clevis's hat blows off his head and falls into the grave, causing the mourners to laugh uncontrollably as they go through the ceremony. At the orgy, Jan meets a bald man, and they are led to separate parts of the room by two different women. In the middle of the sex act they glance at each other, perceive how silly everything looks, and begin to laugh uncontrollably—at themselves, the women, and the others surrounding them. Their laughter is "as much a sacrilege as laughter in church," Kundera says (224), and Barbara, the priestess of the orgy, asks Jan to leave.

The alert reader perceives much in the details of these two scenes, the most obvious of which is the repetition of the hatless head motif from the opening passage (or the headless hat since in both scenes, by a nice sense of ironic inversion, Kundera gives the hat more dramatic presence than the head under it), along with Kundera's variation on that motif by providing a bald mirror image for Jan at the orgy. It is almost as if Vladimir Clementis's hat is a fictional character with a mind of its own and, aware it sits on the wrong head in the famous touched-up photograph, now seeks its proper owner. Leaving Papa Clevis's head (he is too naïve, too fashionably avant-garde politically), it flies to the dead humanist in his grave and provokes chaotic laughter (the laughter of the Devil) in solemn circumstances. At the orgy, on the other hand, the hat is portrayed in its exaggerated absence, the bald man calling to mind Clementis, who was airbrushed out of Czech history after 1948. The hat represents character, intelligence, and presence in the human world. By a nice ironic turn it also represents a form of human hope, a reminder that even in the bleakest circumstances something, no matter how small and ridiculous, remains of the human spirit.

The title of this final part unites the many strands of the story and does so through the multiple meanings Kundera gives to the word "border." He begins with Jan's decision to fly to America as one instance of crossing a border—the boundary line between countries—and then expands to other applications. "Border" also refers to the line between meaning and chaos in existence (the line dividing laughter of the angels from the laughter of the Devil). Human life takes place along that border, touching it from time to time, so that one false step can lead a person into meaninglessness and, consequently, a lack of will to live. We think of Tamina's attempt at suicide after her husband's death and her final moments with the children, and we realize that she died not only from exhaustion, but probably because the children's inhuman curiosity destroyed her hope. They had touched her, sexually penetrated her, but they had never crossed the border of her being, primarily because they lived in another world with different laws. Kundera expands on this last interpretation of "border" by telling how Jan meets a woman on the train and, although they both seem willing, they cannot talk. The simple reason Kundera gives is that they live on opposite sides of the border, occupying different worlds.

The final vision of the book becomes a pessimistic one and, as a summation, leads us to a philosophic dead end: Just before Jan leaves for America, he and Edwige spend a weekend at an island that has a nudist beach, and in the process of telling the story Kundera turns nudism into another kind of border. Thinking of the Jews who were forced to strip before entering the gas chambers, Jan perceives nudity as a uniform, a sign that they lived "on the other side of the border," that is, in another world (226). When Kundera pronounces the uniform a shroud, nudity takes on several meanings: lost individuality because, when naked, everyone looks the same; lost civilization, because, at the concentration camps, barbarism reigned and its regime required nakedness; finally, it means human surrendering to chaos because nakedness obliterates any signs of individual distinction.

In the last scene of the book Jan and Edwige walk to the beach and sit on the sand, listening to some fashionably avant-garde conversation about the decline of Western civilization and the inhibitions of Judeo-Christian thought. Jan has heard these ideas hundreds of times before, and at the moment he can think only of *Daphnis and Chloe*, the romance about innocence at the beginning of civilization. Filled with longing for the world of Longus's story, Jan and his friends are described in terms of biological and psychological futility. Looking at them as they reflect nostalgically on an older, simpler (nevertheless untrue) world, Kundera describes the group in a phrase charged with biblical sterility: Their naked genitals (all that remains of character in this vision of a naked, hatless world) stare "dully, sadly, listlessly at the yellow sand."

## NOTES

1. Quoted in *Contemporary Authors*, ed. Frances Carol Locher, vols. 85–88 (Detroit: Gale Research Co., 1980) 323.

2. Louis Aragon, preface to *La plaisanterie* [*The Joke*] (my translation).

3. *Contemporary Authors* 323.

4. See my "Milan Kundera and the Central European Style," *Salmagundi:* 73 (Winter 1987) 33–57.

5. I am indebted to Holmes's interesting article, "The Wizardry of Ozzie," *Journal of Popular Culture* 23 (Fall 1989) 93–101, for its commentary on the use of parabasis in contemporary popular works.

6. *The Book of Laughter and Forgetting* (New York: Penguin, 1981) 3. Further references will be noted parenthetically.

7. Antonin J. Liehm, *The Politics of Culture* (New York: Grove, 1973) 142.

8. Personal interview, July 1982.

9. Kundera said that his father suffered from aphasia, brought on by a stroke (personal interview, May 1991).

# CHAPTER FOUR

# An Old World in the New:
## *The Joke*

*Spare me your Stalinism, please!* The Joke *is a love story!*

—Preface to *The Joke*

In late June 1967, Milan Kundera addressed the Fourth Congress of the Czechoslovak Writers' Union about the role of literature and culture in the nation's history. Essentially, he told the assembly of writers that at this critical moment, as the Czechs were throwing off the bonds of Stalinism and making ready for the hugely successful flowering known as the Prague Spring, the survival of the Czech nation was in its writers' hands: they must work as a group and as individuals to elevate the country's spirit to assure its survival during this critical time. As a small country, he said, Czechoslovakia has had to struggle for its cultural life because it has always been surrounded by larger, more powerful neighbors: the Austro-Hungarian Empire during one epoch, Germany in another, and Russia for a third. In such a situation, exacerbated by the development of telephone, television, and other communications technology that tend to homogenize culture, the Czech community of readers and speakers is so small that its language is always in danger of being relegated to the level of a European dialect and its culture to that of folklore. In such a situation writers and artists must seek to tie their work to a larger structure, the humanistic tradition of Europe made up of Greco-Roman antiquity and Judeo-Christian thought.

The speech, a comment on cultural history and an impassioned plea for tolerance and the free exchange of ideas and work, contains two passages of note to the reader of *The Joke* and *The Book of Laughter and Forgetting:*

The world of Greco-Roman antiquity and the world of Christianity, those two mainsprings of the European spirit which give it its strength and tension, have almost disappeared from the consciousness of the educated young Czech—an irremediable loss. For there is an iron continuity in European thought that outlasts each intellectual revolution and has created its own vocabulary, its own fund of metaphor, its own myths and themes, without knowledge of which cultured Europeans cannot communicate.

And:

> The vandal [whom, in this speech, Kundera equates with the censor] is a man proud of his mediocrity, very much at ease with himself and ready to insist on his democratic rights. In his pride and his mediocrity he imagines that one of his own inalienable privileges is to transform the world after his own image, and since the most important things in this world are the innumerable things that transcend his vision, he adjusts the world to his own image by destroying it.[1]

We can see the first passage illuminated in the sad ending to *The Book of Laughter and Forgetting*, with the group of friends Jan has gathered about him in exile listening to a speaker who, in the name of liberalism, condemns the very tradition that has engendered him. In that light, the final image of "naked genitals staring" at the sand possesses philosophical as well as biological meaning, the characters' sterility applied to modern thought as much as their bodies. The second passage illuminates *The Joke* by allowing us to see Kundera's portrait of a censor as a vandal of the intellect and the imagination, and in a clear statement preceding this one Kundera tells his audience that he feels institutional evaluation of literature is fundamentally unsound. *The Joke*, which appeared to great acclaim in Czechoslovakia that year, studies the human loss resulting from institutional evaluation, especially as it affects the lives of five major characters: Ludvik Jahn, intellectual, a student Communist who is expelled from the Party for a remark on a postcard and sent to work in the mines of Ostrava; Kostka, a physician whose thinking combines Christianity and Communism in an interesting, if self-centered, kind of charity; Lucie Sebetka, a peasant woman whom Ludvik loves; mistreated in her youth, she is mistreated again by Ludvik in Ostrava; Pavel Zemanek, a Communist youth leader who condemns Ludvik at a Party hearing and later becomes a professor of history, developing his career by following intellectual fashions that reflect changing ideas about the past; and Jaroslav, a friend of Ludvik's boyhood who, as a Moravian folk musician, represents, along with Lucie, the best traditions of the ordinary Czech people, their history and culture.

Structurally the novel presents a group of four narrators, all telling parts of the story from their own perspectives and presenting dramatically different intellectual, social, and cultural views. Ludvik presents the biases of a disillusioned intellectual whose cynicism hides disappointment in love and guilt for having brought on that disappointment himself. Kostka's narration works as a foil to Ludvik's, his voice of compassion representing an optimistic view that can overlook Stalinist obsession with power and combine Christian ethics with the more sober rationalism of Marxist thinking. The third narration, Jaroslav's, is short and, at first glance, peripheral to the story. It fooled Kundera's original English publishers too, who cut and rearranged parts of it, causing him to write a series of furious letters to the *Times Literary Supplement* in London, saying, in essence, that institutional censorship by an editor who follows commercial values is as violent and destructive as censorship according to party dogma.[2] In fact, Jaroslav's brief narration may be seen as central to the novel, its attention to folk customs containing some of the most interesting and trenchant cultural commentary that Kundera has written. Jaroslav speaks of music and the past, his autobiographical past (as a student with Ludvik) and the nation's, or people's, past, which he single-mindedly identifies with folk traditions.

Unlike the other narrators, the fourth, Helena Zemanek, is not important in Ludvik's life. Rather she functions as his means of revenge, after nearly twenty years, against Pavel Zemanek, for Ludvik intends to cuckold him by sleeping with her. More important, Helena's character, in a pointed contrast with Jaroslav and Lucie, epitomizes post-Stalinist Czech culture (and contemporary European culture in general), with its emphasis on the future as opposed to the past, fashion as opposed to tradition, and the urban value of achieving social status through political association. Seemingly a perfect mate for the intellectual weather vane her husband is, Helena works as a radio reporter, her job promoting the cultural homogeneity Kundera said endangered Czech culture in his speech to the Writers' Congress.

### "Ludvik"

The novel opens with a portion of Ludvik's narration. He tells of returning to his hometown near the city of Brno after fifteen years away and admits that although his purpose in being there is cynical and base (he calls the mission a "beautiful demolition job"), he has been drawn homeward because of deep-seated feelings. The opening paragraph, describing the town square with a mixture of affection and disdain, immediately reveals the contradictions inside Ludvik's character. Capable of great sentiment, hinted at here by his reflection that he crossed the town square countless times before, he analyzes his feelings with an intellectual's suspicion of emotion and an urban aesthete's condescension concerning the rough amenities of small-town life.

His hotel room is small, uncomfortable, and noisy, not at all conducive to the mission he has in mind. Unwilling to seek help from anyone who might require him to fill in the gap of fifteen years' absence, he goes to the local hospital to look up Dr. Kostka, a new arrival to the town who gained his position with Ludvik's intervention. Strange, scrupulously moral, unstable, Kostka would be only too glad, Ludvik thinks, to repay one favor with another. They meet, discuss Kostka's past (he has been divorced and is now engaged to a schoolteacher in another town), and joust over philosophic issues as they did in former years. Ludvik refers to Kostka as a "workman on God's eternal construction site,"[3] and they begin a discussion of values that illuminates their characters as well as some of the issues shaking Czech intellectual circles during the postwar years. Ludvik sees reality as made up of backgrounds and sets, underlining his view that life is inherently false, a drama played before an artificial scene. But he recognizes that Kostka's more traditional humanistic view (with God constructing reality, not sets) makes an adequate complement to his own beliefs. He says that he uses arguments as "a touchstone of who *I* was and what *I* thought" (6).

Agreeing to let Ludvik have his apartment next afternoon so that he can achieve his mission in a pleasant atmosphere, Kostka then brings Ludvik to the local barbershop for a shave. The barber, a woman Ludvik sees only in the mirror at first, provides the means by which he fills in the intervening fifteen years of his life. Could she be Lucie Sebetka? he asks afterward. Kostka says she is, although she has a different name now, and Ludvik, moved, wanders through town (his past) without thoughts of dinner, his mission, or anything else in the present.

## "Helena"

But before filling in that past Kundera continues with present matters, using a second narration, Helena's, to provide background on Ludvik's mission and to foreshadow events that occur at the climax of the novel. We perceive her as a bewildered, somewhat shallow woman who has clung to the Communist Party (and her husband, Pavel) out of sheer emptiness rather than conviction. As a radio reporter she fits into Ludvik's philosophic schema because she lives a life that is all public image with very little private substance. Although she says she wants her life to be whole, "to be one from beginning to end" (11), Kundera makes it very clear that her life contains more fragments than Ludvik's, partially because of circumstances but also because she lacks sufficient character to see and think for herself. She depends on the Party, experiencing significant events within its embrace and always with its interpretation. Indeed, the Communist Party functions like a church for her, providing moral support as well as meaning to the important events of her life. She meets her future husband at a speech in Prague given by Italian Communist Party leader Palmiro Togliatti; they court while participating in the

Fucik Song and Dance Ensemble, named after a Communist martyr hanged
by the Nazis; and she receives Pavel's hand in marriage after having him
called up before the Party Committee to discuss his philandering ways.
Though Pavel later protests that pressure, saying they married out of party
discipline rather than love, clearly he and Helena, at least in terms of the
novel's themes, are made for each other. Pavel declares that, in the new world
of Czechoslovakian Communism, society abolished the difference between
public and private events, and by extension Helena's profession further
clouds over the difference, making public events instantly available in the
home and, through gossip, talk shows, and intrusive journalistic interviews,
turning private thoughts and experience into subjects for immediate public
judgment.

With Helena and Pavel we set upon a theme that Kundera later developed
more explicitly in *The Book of Laughter and Forgetting,* especially in Part
Four, where he defines graphomania and pokes fun at public discussions of
orgasm that Tamina and her friends watch on television. In that book Kundera speaks openly of his respect for Tamina and her desire for privacy. In this
Tamina stands at the opposite end of the social spectrum from Helena and
Pavel Zemanek, and she exists as a character whose desires and experiences
in many ways parallel those of Lucie Sebetka in *The Joke.* Both are country
women who represent the best impulses of the Czech people, yet both suffer
because of the Party, sexual ill treatment, and the loss of important loves.
Both also suffer in silence, isolated among strangers, giving comfort to others, especially men, by ministering to basic needs, drinking or barbering, and
listening to them talk. Though lacking social status, the two women represent
Czech (and human) nature at its most generous, their nobility being a matter
of inner strength and kindness rather than position or title. While Helena provides details of a comfortable past, fashionable clothes, party influence, and
a socially prominent husband, none of which makes her particularly admirable or happy, Lucie and Tamina gain our respect because, in trying circumstances, they seem to know who they are and remain true to the privacy of
their inner selves. In that sense they belong to the vision of the world expressed by Kostka, while Helena belongs to the world of props and scenery
described by Ludvik. In a sense, then, the story of *The Joke* becomes a philosophic dialogue between those two views: traditional humanism with its emphasis on religion and individuality, and contemporary modernism with its
emphasis on social politics and doubts about the viability of the self.

Helena continues her narrative, and we learn of her unhappy marriage, the
turning in of a colleague to party moralists, and a little about her extramarital

affairs. We can sympathize with her because we sense in her breathless narration, made up of sentences that run into one another without proper punctuation, a personality seeking to be whole, needing and not finding love, trying to use Party ideas and power to fill the void inside her soul. "Man is one and indivisible . . . only petty bourgeois" thinking fragments him, she says (17), yet we know that her job, her clothes, her values are bourgeois enough to cause her own inner divisions and that while the Party fails to make her whole, she uses it as a means of advancement. In the United States of the 1980s we would have probably called her a yuppie, and it is precisely that self-serving, mindless side of her and Pavel that Ludvik is on a mission to destroy.

She meets Ludvik while doing an interview for a story on the institute he serves. He flatters her, overlooks her incompetence as a journalist, and tells her she must seek more joy in her life. When he learns she is going to his hometown in Moravia to do a story on the Ride of the Kings, an annual folk rite, he tells her he will meet her there. Traveling toward Moravia as she narrates, Helena reflects that he will be waiting for her at the bus stop, closing this portion of her narration and leading the reader back to the beginning of the story.

## "Ludvik"

In Part Three Ludvik speaks again, occupying the most extended piece of narration in the novel, filling in the details of the past fifteen years, especially relating to Pavel, Jaroslav, and Lucie, and giving as fine and unideological a portrait of life under Stalinism in the 1950s as we are likely to find in literature. A talented university student in Prague, Ludvik has an important post in the Party's League of University Students, but he finds himself cited for individualism in committee critiques, and his smile, which, he hears, reveals "you were thinking for yourself" (24), becomes the primary evidence against him. In the spirit of the times he accepts Party judgment and, echoing the theme of fragmentation in Helena's narrative, confesses that he felt a crack open between the person he was and the person he tried to be. "I was a man of many faces," he says (24). Those faces multiply when he begins courting Marketa, a young, sincere student "unable to look behind anything" (25), who, like Helena, believes unreservedly in Party ideology, so much so that she lacks a sense of humor concerning it. Trying to seduce her, Ludvik assumes a mature, cynical tone and jokes, with little effect, in order to demonstrate to her his worldly detachment. Alone, he is unsure and excited; at party meetings, earnest. Yet despite the many contradictory faces, he

52

disclaims hypocrisy, saying that as a young man he did not know his real self. Since the reader already knows that fifteen years later Ludvik will describe reality as false, made up of theatrical sets, it remains to be seen whether he will change his self-evaluation, assuming personal wholeness as opposed to fragmentation, or whether he will, like the character in Witold Gombrowicz's *Ferdydurke* (treated more fully in chapter one of this study), still regard himself as a man of many masks acting in a theatrical scene.

The Party sends Marketa away to summer camp to balance her enthusiasm with revolutionary strategy and tactics. Disappointed at her leaving and upset that she writes to him with admiration for what she is learning, Ludvik responds jealously, sending her a postcard that ridicules her enthusiasm and makes fun of party slogans: "Optimism is the opium of the people!" he writes. "A healthy atmosphere stinks of stupidity!" (26). He ends by lauding Leon Trotsky, the former revolutionary comrade Stalin had murdered in exile. Once again his humor proves useless. It passes over Marketa's head, rebounding to be a fateful joke on him.

Marketa shows the postcard to Party leaders, who call Ludvik before them. He admits his fault, partly because he feels guilty, partly in hopes of avoiding expulsion from the Party. He counts on his friendship with Pavel Zemanek to save him, but at a plenary session of the university's Division of Natural Sciences, Pavel, who knew Marketa and had appreciated Ludvik's sense of humor with her, makes a successful plea for Ludvik's expulsion. Party members go one step further and expel him from the university too, and so Ludvik leaves Prague, ruined because of a joke and the betrayal of a friend and the Party. Returning to his Moravian hometown, he meets Jaroslav again, attends his wedding, a showcase of Moravian traditions, but cannot bring himself to play in Jaroslav's folk band because he remembers dancing with the "Prague-born, Moravian-clad" Pavel during May Day parades in Prague (39).

The following autumn, with no university deferment, Ludvik is called to work for the Czech army in Ostrava, a mining town in northern Moravia. Assigned to the penal battalion, he endures the degradation of person and loss of privacy so frequently revealed in military stories, but here the horror is sharper because national service has become Ludvik's punishment. He works in the mines, enduring truly hellish conditions, is regarded by regular soldiers and civilians alike as undesirable, and, despite all his explanations and pleas for understanding of a crime that is, after all, minor, he learns that the Party apparatus has him labeled as a Trotskyite and imperialist, an enemy of its revolution. The labels, he says, were "more real than my actual self" (42).

The one gleam of hope in all this despair is Ludvik's love for Lucie, whom he meets during a leave. He finds her at a movie theater showing a piece of romanticized Soviet propaganda, but he pays little attention to the film. Lucie's simplicity and air of the commonplace move Ludvik immediately, while their shared sense of melancholy, indicative of past sorrow and lost hope for the future, overcomes differences of intellect, education, and outlook. He feels himself responding to her with genuine feeling instead of one of his social masks, and as their friendship develops, Ludvik responds to a whole new side of life. Lucie exists outside of politics, and while he had always seen the Communist Party as the center of history and life, he learns from Lucie the value of the trivial, the ahistorical ordinary events of daily life. Once again, as in "Mother," in *The Book of Laughter and Forgetting*, we find a character responding to the world of pears as opposed to the world of tanks. Through Lucie, Ludvik learns that the trivial is eternal, while the great historical events of a person's epoch (the world of tanks) are transitory, made falsely great out of human self-interest.

He reads poems to her, moved to see the verses make her cry. We begin to understand that the aloof Ludvik is in fact vulnerable and that Lucie embodies the precise formula of innocence, sensitivity, and naturalness to break through his intellectual arrogance. We know him finally not as artificial, but as a young man whose intelligence has allowed him to hide his innocence behind a mask of cynicism. He has distrusted people, he will distrust people in the future, but for the few brief months that he knows Lucie his guard drops, allowing him to feel affectionate toward a woman for the first (and only, he tells us) time. That affection blossoms into sexual love when Ludvik takes Lucie to buy her a new dress. The sight of her wearing something beside her drab, gray, nunlike uniform bowls him over. He experiences the *"revelation of her body"* (70), presses her to allow him to meet her in her room alone, and with that change removes their affections from the chaste realm of grace.

Kundera's thematic intentions become clearer at this point in the novel. While he says in his preface that *The Joke* is a love story, the overlay of national, social, and political history in the actual narrative has served to obscure the emotional events. In addition, Ludvik's loss of Party attachments, along with his attempt fifteen years later to avenge that loss through Helena, may distract us from Kundera's very real commitment to explore the sensations of love in a world where faith in the past is fragile, where national and international events in the present threaten the very notion of individuality, and where the idea of self has absolutely no clarity. When in *The Divine*

*Comedy* Dante explored love in a complex world with the sins of the body and Satan on one side and God and the ideal love of Beatrice on the other, his divisions were certain, and his understanding of human nature founded itself on distinct ideas of heart, soul, intellect, and body. But in our twentieth-century universe, where Freud, Marx, Darwin, and Einstein have altered our very concept of ourselves, all such clear ideas are suspect, and so a writer like Kundera, employing an imagined Prague and Czechoslovakia as his laboratory (as Dante employed Florence, Rome, and the hereafter), presents us with more ambiguous visions.

Ludvik's love of Lucie and his relations with Marketa and Helena represent a philosophic exploration of body and soul, a dialogue about their relative importance in determining what is essentially human, what is essentially self. The novel asks, What are these feelings we call love and desire? What do they say about us and our possibilities, especially in a world where historical events have eclipsed the notion of a solid foundation to human character? So when Ludvik's chaste affection for Lucie slips over into bodily lust, we see a change in his experience of her. Until he sees her in her new dress, she is an idea, a figure, something eternal (like Beatrice). Made aware of the warmth and shape of her body, Ludvik transforms Lucie into an adventure, ordinary and physical though it may be, something that we might call today an object. But because of his youth and innocence, because of her shame about the awful sexual circumstances in her own past, she becomes an object he can never possess, a possibility he can never explore.

After a failed attempt to make love to Lucie in her dorm room, Ludvik decides he must have her and makes arrangements to meet her in a room he rents for the night. There he sees her wearing the dress that awakened his sexual longing, but Lucie clearly harbors ambivalent thoughts: he feels her shake when they embrace. In addition, the ceiling lamp is bare, and the room lacks personal charm. Dressed in baggy, ill-fitting clothes (Ludvik imitates Charlie Chaplin on first wearing them), he tears them off and lies naked with Lucie while she remains fully clothed. A painful scene follows. Lucie tries to remain affectionate and tender, but Ludvik's patience wears thin when she refuses to undress. Frustrated, he grows angry, forcing himself on her until she fights free of him. Thinking of his failure with Marketa and his sordid sexual encounters while carousing with his fellow soldiers, Ludvik becomes enraged, wondering why he must be punished as an adult, suffer political loss as an adult, and yet fail like an immature boy when it comes to love. He tries to force her again; she breaks free. While she backs against the cupboard, he shouts that she must make love with him or never see him again.

Still she refuses, and Ludvik, feeling a "supernatural force . . . constantly tearing out of my hands everything I wanted to live for" (99), says he hates her and sends her away. Exhausted, regretful, he returns to the barracks where, next morning, he and his fellow soldiers learn that one of them, the most committed Communist, has killed himself in despair because of the heckling of his fellow soldiers and his expulsion from the Party. With the dead soldier as a surrogate for his own failures, Ludvik dates his loss of faith in life and his fellow men—his true cynicism, in other words, not the mask—from that night and day. His mother dies. He spends three more years working in the mines, plus another ten months in jail for leaving camp without permission. Now, fifteen years afterward, he finds himself at home again (and readers find themselves at the beginning of the narrative one more time), with Lucie as his barber and an assignation with another woman in a different borrowed room.

## "Jaroslav"

Part Four is a narration by Jaroslav, Ludvik's boyhood friend who leads a traditional Moravian folk band. The section is a marvelous piece of writing, prefiguring *The Book of Laughter and Forgetting* in the way it dovetails with the brief references Ludvik has made to Jaroslav already and gathers together various intellectual and narrative strands, including Moravian legend, fantasy, musicology, personal reminiscence, and history, along with a discussion of the cultural relationship between Communist ideology and Czech folk values. With a fuguelike narrative of thoughts and feelings that embodies Jaroslav's provincial, folksinging character, we learn about the Ride of Kings in village traditions, get a personal account of Jaroslav's first ride as king and the subsequent meeting of his wife; we hear about Ludvik's past, particularly his father's imprisonment and death by the Nazis and his widowed mother's poor treatment by his father's well-attached sister, married into a prominent family named Koutecky. We see how Ludvik's bitterness developed out of that treatment and learn that it pushed him against "bourgeois" values and into the Communist Party as well as enrollment in a Prague university instead of the one in Brno that the more traditional Jaroslav attends. We read a technical discussion by Ludvik and Jaroslav of traditional folk music and its relation to "new" folk music written to fit Party ideas. Surprisingly, Jaroslav writes the new music, while Ludvik finds it unauthentic. And finally, despite his writing of Party lyrics, we learn of Jaroslav's hope of passing on Moravian traditions, especially the role of the king in the village ride, to his son.

The section combines the mysticism and practical wisdom of folk customs, marrying the eternal with the ordinary, like the "world of pears" concept mentioned earlier, and it functions as a contrast with the modern historical material in the narrations by Ludvik and Helena. Jaroslav's narration provides a more sympathetic view of Ludvik, and it prepares us for an understanding of the complex series of events that occur during the story's climax. If *The Joke* is a love story, then the reader must understand that it is about love in the complex sense: love of country and of self, love of traditions, future and past, as well as the varieties of love between men and women. Jaroslav's narration encompasses all those loves and prepares us for the intricate series of events that close the novel on the day of the Ride of Kings. In that sense it functions as the novel's bridge and keystone, occupying the very center of the book, the fourth of its seven parts, as well as the middle 35 of its 267 pages in English. We can be quite sure that Kundera did not count pages to achieve this structure, but the combination of counting and feeling, a very musiclike blending of intellect and heart, probably led him to allow Part Four to function in such an important technical and thematic way.[4] Without Jaroslav's narration the novel fails, losing meaning and architecture. Thus Kundera's anger when his British publishers cut and rearranged the section upon the novel's first English printing.

### "Ludvik"

In Part Five Ludvik speaks again, providing the reader with details about Zemanek, the Party, and his mission of vengeance with Helena. But first he tells a little about his feelings for Lucie—that she had become an abstraction for him after she left Ostrava and that he believed he could not love her independently of the situation in which he had known her. Without the seedy surroundings, the mines, the days when she brought him flowers and passed them through the camp fence, his love for her would not be the same, might not exist. He compares his love to Hamlet's love for Ophelia, again raising the motif of life as a play and, by extension, human character as action dictated by someone else. Without concrete situations or lines, Hamlet's character would be nothing but essence, a voiceless illusion without shape.

Ludvik goes on to discuss love and the meaning it has in human lives. Does it have something to say? he wonders. And, if it does, what does the reappearance of Lucie in the present say about his own life, especially after a space of fifteen years? Ludvik confesses that despite his cynicism, despite his skeptical attitude toward given beliefs, he cannot rid himself of the need to interpret his life, to *"decipher"* it (141), especially as it relates to his love for Lucie.

With those thoughts in mind he strays into the town hall, where he witnesses a Communist Party service that is equivalent to a civil christening, or a *"welcoming of new citizens to life"* (148), as the presiding official calls it. Combining poetry, art, ceremony, and civic principles, the service is a neat transition, as Ludvik describes it, from the concerns expressed by Jaroslav in the preceding section. Where Jaroslav and Ludvik argue over a joining of folk and Party ideas in Part Four, this scene brings together the sacred and the ideological at a Communist Party function. In both cases Kundera makes the point that although Marxism has sought to banish religious and mythic beliefs as atavistic, the human pursuit of them persists. The result in a socialist society, at least as we experience it through Ludvik's eyes, is empty ceremony, drama without content, spectacle without real cause, a situation that seems particularly modern and evident in the West as well as the East. In that context we begin the story of Ludvik's afternoon with Helena, seeing it as an expression of Kundera's exploration of human character searching for meaning and power in the area of the profane as opposed to sacred.

Ludvik's seduction scene is intricate, difficult to understand, and more difficult to like, particularly in light of current understanding of sexual relations and power. The idea that one man would use a woman to gain revenge on another man repulses us, and it is very hard not to condemn Ludvik's actions or thoughts here and, by extension, not to condemn Kundera for voicing them through his principal character. Ludvik shows himself to be manipulative, callous, and arrogant, using Helena's body in rage rather than affection and debasing her in action and words through his description of her body and behavior. Kundera writes this section so well, so believably, that contemporary readers may find it difficult to divorce the author from his character's words. But in all fairness we must, and to do so we need to place the events and descriptions of the afternoon within the context of the whole chapter, where loving thoughts of Lucie serve as bookends to the rest of the material. We also must try to see it within the context of Ludvik's life as a whole.

After the "christening" scene in town hall, Ludvik tells more about Helena, reviewing their first meeting from his perspective, attacking journalists as shallow invaders of privacy and saying how her response to his flattery led him to conceive of his revenge. Unaware that she and Pavel no longer live as man and wife, Ludvik thinks the ultimate insult will be invading their privacy by taking Pavel's place in bed with Helena. They drink, go to Kostka's room and drink some more, their conversation revealing more and more of the gap between them. In general, she is a believer; he is a skeptic. She has had privileged attachments; he has lost whatever attachments he had. In one sense, therefore, Helena and Pavel (at least, Ludvik's idea of them) represent everything he might have had or might have been—an alternative fate, in other words, had the "joke" of his postcard never occurred.

He recalls the hearing he went through fifteen years before and remembers Pavel reading to him and other members of the committee the words of Julius Fucik as he faced death at the hands of the Nazis. Fucik's words are noble, brave, and optimistic, immediately placing the words on Ludvik's postcard in a bad light and, Ludvik says, dooming him to the committee's censure. He tries to explain himself in humble, confessional terms. He is intellectual and individualistic; he is isolated from the people; he is a skeptic and a cynic. These are masks, of course; we know that much if we followed Ludvik's evaluation of himself when he described his attempts to seduce Marketa. But they are also standard formulae of Party self-criticism, and for the moment Ludvik stands on the verge of winning sympathy. However, when one of the committee asks what he thinks Communists tortured to death by Nazis would say about his postcard, he thinks of his own father's death in a Nazi concentration camp and, furious, says they might have laughed. Pavel Zemanek replies that Ludvik's answer shows he has not learned anything, and he proposes, successfully, that Ludvik be expelled from the Party and the university. Ludvik's reminiscence ends as he gives up his Party card and Pavel refuses to look at him. In a nice transition to the present, Kundera has Ludvik touch Helena's legs and feel that he has Pavel's life in his hands. The thought sounds murderous, perhaps, although we should see also that Ludvik attempts to be Pavel as well. If his life has been a failure, and his rupture with Lucie is the primary experience of his failure, then in seducing Helena he can, for a brief moment at least, achieve success, like Pavel.

Kundera continues, letting Ludvik speak of seeing Helena's body through the eyes of a "third, absent party" (171), obviously Pavel. He says that her naked body and their lovemaking achieve meaning only when his spirit merges with that "absent third party," becoming one with him in thought and flesh to rob his "sacred chamber; to ransack it" (171), and in effect spoil his privacy the way Zemanek, through the Party, spoiled Ludvik's. At this point in Ludvik's narrative life and privacy have become one, wrapped up in some important way with Kundera's concept of being. Note that after they finish making love, Ludvik goes to the other room to enjoy his "sudden privacy" (172), and upon his return Helena compares him to Pavel, saying Ludvik looks like him and possesses his energy. However, she spoils his satisfaction and revenge by telling him that she and Pavel no longer sleep together. His plans thwarted once more, Ludvik induces Helena to leave the apartment before Kostka returns, and, sinking into a chair, frustrated again, he contemplates Lucie, seeing her as incorporeal and abstract compared to Helena. Likening her to a star flashing across his life with a message for him, he at last finds meaning in the story of his love for her, saying Lucie was there "to demolish my vengeance," and calling her a "goddess of vain pursuit," summing up in that phrase a vision of all human life as well as his own (178).

## "Kostka"

Ludvik's mission now completed, Kundera turns the narrative over to Kostka and his more traditional Christian view, a contrast that, dramatically, helps us measure Ludvik at this very dark moment of his life and continues the philosophic debate between him and Kostka. First, we learn that although they have known each other for years, they have met just a few times. Kostka underlines their personal and intellectual differences, referring to an "internal discord" that underlies their good feelings (179), saying that Ludvik has attached greater importance to their external harmonies, particularly the fact that they both occupied important university positions and lost them because of independent thinking. While Ludvik's independence lies along cynical, pessimistic lines of reason and doubt (like the laughter of the Devil in *The book of Laughter and Forgetting*), Kostka's is founded on religious, optimistic ones of faith. The Czech Communist Party liked neither, and, as closed a system of belief as a church, banished both of them—Ludvik from the university to the mines of Ostrava, Kostka to the farmlands of Bohemia.

Both meet Lucie in their banishments and fall in love, but with dramatically different results. Where Ludvik fails, Kostka succeeds, helping her win back self-confidence and trust after her experience with Ludvik has driven her into retreat from other people. She and Kostka become confidants. He learns that her father beat her and that, in rebellion, Lucie took up with a gang of boys who abused her sexually until one day the police burst in and arrested them (and her). Ironically, the police charge theft. After a year in a reformatory, Lucie leaves her hometown for Ostrava and, of course, her encounter with Ludvik. Her experience with him in the miner's room echoes so powerfully the cruelty in her past that she wants never to see him again.

Both Kostka and Ludvik perceive Lucie as innocent, but in different ways. Ludvik, the doubtful rationalist, see her as physically innocent, attributing her sexual reluctance to a wish to preserve her virginity. Kostka sees her as spiritually innocent, astounded by the fact that she seems never to have had religious instruction, that she has only vague notions of Christ, associating him loosely with Christmas, and that she does not recognize a picture of the Virgin Mary when she sees it. He begins to educate her about Christianity, teaching her the values of forgiveness and redemption, and in the process, although Kostka is still married, they fall in love. Torn morally, a spiritual man confused by his physical weaknesses, Kostka looks for a way out of the uncomfortable situation. When Party authorities seek to punish his boss through Kostka, he accepts banishment once more, seeing it as God's way of helping him to leave Lucie. But some years later, after Ludvik helps him gain his present position at the hospital, Lucie follows Kostka to Moravia. Married now, but badly, she remains in the small town to be near him. Clearly Kostka is the one hope in her life, and he responds to her presence with fatherly feelings. "My little lamb, my little dove," he says, "the little child I'd healed and nurtured with my soul had come home to me" (205). He claims Lucie as the one accomplishment in his life and in an aside to Ludvik asks if that is enough. He concludes that it suffices for him.

Until this point Kostka never doubts, never changes, always seeing God's hand in the accidents of his life. He differs from Ludvik in that, although both have suffered at the hands of fate and the Party, he has seen the events as positive, in effect seizing them as opportunities. But in the short last chapter of this section, a mere page and a half, Kundera changes that perception, pulling the rug out from under our conception of Kostka by inverting everything that we have read into his character. After Kostka somewhat lamely repeats three times in his aside to Ludvik that he is happy, he begins his last section with another view: "Oh, how I delude myself!" (205), going on to place a completely different interpretation on everything he has said and done. Lucie is miserable; her husband, not only cruel, is unfaithful too; and Kostka's own vaunted ear for the voice of God turns out to be a mask for his weaknesses, his inability to act responsibly, his unwillingness to take control of his life. As a result we can see that his wife and daughter live in unhappy abandonment; his fiancée, a schoolteacher in another town, waits with little hope for him to gain enough courage to live with her, let alone marry; and, of course, Lucie, suffering in silence, simply watches and waits for precious, momentary meetings that must provide little satisfaction. Summing up the despair of all the characters in the book, Kostka cries out to God, asking for solace in his state of wretchedness and self-ridicule. But his pursuit of satisfaction is just as vain as Ludvik's. The believer's cry ends with a confession that he hears nothing in reply.

## "Ludvik, Jaroslav, Helena"

Part Seven, the fugue, or canon, of Ludvik's, Jaroslav's, and Helena's voices, brings the book to its darkly humorous and, to my mind, tragic close. By now the idea of the joke in Ludvik's life has taken on a metaphysical significance, and we begin to see it as well as a metaphor for Kundera's technique. Many events happen in the story as if occurring in a joke, but Kundera has chosen to provide no context for laughter, as he does in his later books. His narrators' voices are absolutely deadpan, his characters suffer spiritually and physically as a result of ironic twists of fate, and at the end of each episode there is little, if any, psychic release, humorous or otherwise. Yet very little turns out as expected in *The Joke*. Very little is as it appears. Ludvik's little postcard humor transforms his own life, not Marketa's. Helena seeks love and receives vengeance instead. Ludvik, seeking love from Lucie, sends her away into Kostka's life. And Kostka, teaching the ways of spirit, falls into the morass of flesh. Everything works opposite from the characters' expectations. With this last section, a secular canon that by means of a bathroom joke still has metaphyscial meaning, the mist over physical reality becomes more obvious, calling into question our perceptions about life, ourselves, our purposes, and each other.

Part Seven comprises nineteen sections or chapters, the odd ones narrated by Ludvik, the even ones divided unequally between Jaroslav and Helena. Jaroslav narrates chapters two, six, eight, ten, twelve, and eighteen; Helena, chapters four, fourteen, and sixteen, as they tell about the Ride of Kings and the aftermath of Ludvik's vengeance. By means of this canon Kundera renders simultaneous action from several points of view and examines the passions of two parts of Ludvik's life, one before the postcard, the other afterward, hinting at a resolution for the future that in itself raises doubts, at least for Czechoslovakia.

The first chapter begins with irony and a complaint, Ludvik's observation that in his hometown he can find no breakfast for the second day in a row. Leaving the hotel in search of something to eat, he finds himself witnessing the beginnings of the Ride of Kings, the public, communal event against which the private passions of the novel's characters will play themselves out. In this public atmosphere little or nothing is as it first appears. The king and his pages are dressed as young girls during the ride, and Kundera adds a twist to that false appearance by gradually revealing that the person playing the part of the king is not Jaroslav's son, Vladimir, as Jaroslav thinks. Vladimir is in fact at the motorcycle races with Koutecky's grandson, a sign that he and the other young Czechs in the story have lost contact with their traditions and lack all memory of (or lack the wish to have a memory of) the past.

That theme is echoed in Ludvik's experience when he meets Zemanek and his new girlfriend, a student named Miss Broz. She expounds the new, liberal ideas of her generation, simplifying her understanding of human nature by dividing people into those who will pick up hitchhikers and those who won't. Zemanek, as usual, adjusting his opinions to the times, praises the new generation as freer than his and Ludvik's, particularly because they are less fearful of their bodies. Ludvik agrees, but counters that they won't remember the past. Although he finally expresses grudging admiration for Miss Broz, he cannot really like her because he realizes that to her Zemanek and he, despite their vastly different fates and characters, are the same, with the usual political and social biases of their post–World War II generation. Much as he wants to be different from his enemy, much as he needs Zemanek to hate in order to maintain equilibrium, he is trapped by Miss Broz's limited understanding and, we must add, the forces of history that push him, irrevocably, into the past.

Kundera moves from that important, signature perception to the events that form the climax of Part Seven. As Jaroslav walks home to seek the truth about his son, Ludvik speaks to Helena, who has come upon him during his conversation with Zemanek and Miss Broz. After Zemanek leaves, believing the affair between his wife and Ludvik absolves him from guilt and obligation to either of them, Ludvik tells Helena that he does not love her and won't see her any more. His words wound her deeply. She returns to the District Council building and, in despair, decides to commit suicide. She goes through her technical assistant's pockets, finds a vial of pills labeled analgesics, and decides to take enough to kill herself. First she writes a note to Ludvik telling him she loved him body and soul and that, since he has left her, "body and soul . . . have nothing left to live for" (241). She sends her assistant to deliver the letter to Ludvik, who sits in a café thinking about his fate, conceiving of his whole life as an error, with history playing jokes on him rather than following rational Marxist laws of physical and social necessity.

As Ludvik broods, Helena's assistant, Jindra, delivers her letter. Ironically, the message, about as personal as one can be, comes written on the public letterhead of the District Council's office. When Ludvik reads it, he and Jindra run to the District Council building and find Helena, having swallowed a vial of laxatives instead of analgesics, sitting in an outhouse. What follows is a painful, comic scene that deromanticizes all the important themes of the book: the idea of pure love, the excesses of romantic passion, even the pessimistic philosophy of despair that, after his meeting with Zemanek, has driven Ludvik to say that "everything will be forgotten and nothing will be rectified" (245). At the end of this section Ludvik even questions the seriousness of Helena's suicide; she had not taken very many pills, certainly not enough to kill herself, and she knew he and Jindra would be nearby.

In the meantime, in the complementary story, Jaroslav learns that his son is at the motorcycle races. His wife defends Vladimir, saying he didn't like the use of privilege that got him the role of king, but Jaroslav counters by asking why Vladimir associates with the grandson of the "petty bourgeois" Kouteckys (256). When she points out that the Kouteckys cannot send their son to the university because of their bourgeois status, while Vladimir, son of the peasant Jaroslav, has the privilege of doing whatever he wants, he loses his temper. Methodically, Jaroslav breaks most of the dishes, glasses, and furniture in the house, destroying the home he tells us he loved. Brooding on himself as the last king, Jaroslav picks up his violin and leaves, going to the river's edge. There, he lies down with his head on his violin case and stares at the sky until Ludvik, also brooding after Helena's suicide attempt, arrives. Looking for some kind of stability in his past, Ludvik asks if he can play with Jaroslav in the band that afternoon.

In the very last chapter of the book Ludvik brings the day's events (and his unacknowledged mission) to a close. Feeling at home in the atmosphere created by the folk ensemble, he tells us he thinks of himself while playing as falling through the ground "into the depths of years and centuries past" (265). Realizing that his true home is in that fall, he savors "the sensuous vertigo" of the music until he looks into the crowd of young people in the audience (265). They are busily drinking and socializing instead of listening, and when Jaroslav perceives that, he tells the ensemble that they should leave the stand to play in the field, spontaneously, presumably the way their ancestor folk musicians did. But the group decides to meet their obligation to the town committee who planned the event. As they continue to perform Jaroslav collapses from a heart attack. The novel ends when Ludvik and the others lift Jaroslav from the floor, escorting him through the crowd while members of the indifferent audience break into a fight in a distant corner. Although the pathetic and the comic are joined in this scene, past and present remain forever separate. Hope glimmers, but dimly, and not in love. Rather it exists in the fact that music has provided one last opportunity for Ludvik to find his home.

## NOTES

1. In Dusan Hamsik, *Writers against Rulers* (New York: Random House, 1971) 173, 174.

2. *Times Literary Supplement* Oct. 2, 30; Nov. 13, 20, and 27, 1969. *The Joke* is reviewed October 2; Kundera's letter appears October 30. The other issues have letters from the publisher, translator, and readers of the novel.

3. *The Joke* 5–6. Further references will be noted parenthetically.

4. For further remarks on the mixture of feeling and form in Kundera's narratives, see "Dialogue on the Art of Composition," *The Art of the Novel* (New York: Grove, 1988) esp. 85–95.

# CHAPTER FIVE

# Poet, Traitor, Mama's Boy, Spy: *Life Is Elsewhere*

*My own youth, my own "lyrical age" and poetic activity coincide with the worst pe-
riod of the Stalinist era. And this of course has done much to prejudice me against
youth and lyricism.*
—Kundera, quoted in *The Politics of Culture*, by Antonin J. Liehm

Although Ludvik Jahn finds solace in the traditional art of Moravian folk
music at the end of *The Joke*, we should be careful to say that for Kundera,
while art often provides a means to such comfort, it does not possess unqual-
ified, or intrinsic, value. In fact certain kinds of art, or art techniques, may
delude and disillusion, according to his thinking, placing themselves in blind
service to demagogic political, social, or religious visions. Consequently he
sees certain kinds of art—particularly lyric art, emphasizing youth, sensitivity, and emotions (instead of experience, understanding, and intellect)—as
philosophically naïve and suspect, no matter what their political attachments.
As we saw in the two sections entitled "The Angels" in *The Book of Laughter and Forgetting*, Kundera treats innocents negatively, seeing their reliance
on enthusiasm, their need to please a higher power, and their shallow disregard for the suffering of others as signs of cruel inexperience and selfishness.
In "Litost," another section of that book, poets and their work are just as
much a subject for Kundera's satire as Communist Party loyalists, and in *The
Joke* we come to realize that for all of Ludvik's ironic humor, intelligence,
and skill with music, he needs to face up to defeat and loss by giving up his
vengeful emotions before he can move on to a fuller life.

In *Life Is Elsewhere*, completed two years after *The Joke*, in 1969, but not
published until 1973, Kundera once again combined the two traits of youth
and artistic sensitivity in one character. The two novels are companion pieces
in a certain sense, *The Joke* presenting the devilish, doubtful side of youth
(Ludvik) in a Stalinist society, while *Life Is Elsewhere* presents the enthusiastic, angelic side in the person of a young lyric poet, whose enthusiasm for
verse in the service of revolution leads to tragedy. The novels have other similarities: They demonstrate Kundera's interest in the theatrical aspects of human character, his emphasis on betrayal and accident as a means of
determining human fate, and his laughter at the ambiguities of sexual rela-

tions between men and women as they coalesce by turns into scenes of combat and tenderness.

In an interview with Antonin J. Liehm in February 1967, Kundera discusses poetry, especially lyric poetry, at some length and provides an idea of why he holds it up to doubt: A country's excessive love of poetry may create a social mentality that, while not necessarily irrational, could be described as "rather hysterical, sentimental, and partial to kitsch." Exclusive interest in lyricism creates an attitude turning "everything into perfumed, rosy, clouds." When Liehm challenges him about those opinions, Kundera responds that "in periods of angry bias it seems to me that among the accused standing before the court—somewhere between Enthusiasm and Gullibility—I recognize the face of [Abused] Lyricism."[1]

Unpalatable as those comments may sound to Western ears (our most beloved poets tend to be lyricists, after all), we can place them into greater perspective if we consider Kundera's belief in reason and his comments to the Fourth Czech Writers' Congress in June 1967. In this speech, Kundera made an impassioned plea for aesthetic and intellectual freedom, emphasizing pride in the country's native traditions. "The very principle of authoritative, institutional evaluation" is unsound, he said, "institutional" referring to government or party censors and critics. He went on to discuss the Czech nation and culture, recalling its nineteenth-century national revival, underlining the idea that the Czech nation must elevate its spirit through art and culture in order to survive, simply because, hemmed in by larger, more aggressive neighbors (Germany and Russia), its art and thought provided the most practical historical weapons for defense. From that principle, Kundera criticized the motivations of censors, whom he called cultural vandals attempting to transform the world after their own image, and he equated them with the adolescent thug who knocks the head off a statue because the very act of self-assertion appeals to him. "People," Kundera said, "who live purely in their own immediate present tense, without culture or awareness of historical continuity, are quite capable of turning their country into a wasteland."[2]

Later, in *Life Is Elsewhere* he would call that attitude lyrical, and, opposed to it, we can place three of Kundera's antidotes: his sense of the importance of historical memory (especially of the Judeo-Christian, Greco-Roman traditions of Europe); his emphasis on human responsibility toward culture and works of the intellect; and, last, his feeling for the important role the novel can play in exploring individual human relationships to the past. In *Life Is Elsewhere*, perhaps the most personal novel he has written—at least in terms of the main character's preoccupation with Czech literature, politics, and the Prague literary scene—Kundera portrays the inner and outer life of a young poet named Jaromil. In the process he lays bare what he sees as the intellectual and psychological weaknesses of the lyric attitude, underlining its emphasis on emotion instead of reason, its dependence upon traditional, mothering, women for security, and its tendency to ally itself with political authoritarianism under the guise of creating a better world. In other words, this attitude, often associated with liberal or radical thought in America, has conservative underpinnings in Kundera's vision, and we might say that if Shelley saw poets as "unacknowledged legislators of the world,"[3] Kundera sees them, at least lyric poets, in much less exalted terms: blind innocents who can easily (as Éluard did in *The Book of Laughter and Forgetting*) turn their backs and dance in joy while the dictator's police go about their brutal work.

On the surface the narrative theme of *Life Is Elsewhere* is nearly as old as the history of the novel. Charting the affections, adventures, and attitudes of a sensitive young man with artistic ambitions makes up one of the great themes of literature, with examples in the work of Goethe, Dickens, Proust, and Joyce. Kundera takes the tradition a step further and, by means of satire and irony, dissects the character, and the myth behind such a character, exposing him as a laughable figure whose life, upon examination, reveals blatant egotism and self-centeredness—signs of weakness and inconsistency in the inner and outer life of human existence.

## "The Poet Is Born"

Part realism, part dream and myth, often an ironic mixture of the two, the first section of the novel examines the private and public background of a poet, born in the 1930s, who grows up during World War II, comes to a doubtful maturity and dies suddenly during the 1950s, just before Stalinism succumbed to history and, ultimately, the demands for free expression by Czech writers and intellectuals. Adopting a tone that is at once humorous and inquisitive, Kundera writes the narrative in a third-person voice commencing with a discussion of the main character's probable beginnings. But, comparable to the famous conception scene in Sterne's *Tristram Shandy,* this section of the narration is mock serious in form, its distinct undertone of irony exploring and then exploding the relationship between husband and wife in regard to sex and conception and, later, mother and son in regard to artistic inspiration. The poet's mother, "Maman," as Kundera's narrator calls her, believes the conception of the poet took place during an idyllic afternoon in the country with her lover, while the poet's father, bribed by a large dowry to marry before the child's birth, insists conception was an unlucky accident taking place in a friend's apartment when, unexpectedly, they heard a key turn in the door.

By means of a meditation on Maman's ripening pregnant body, Kundera traces her gradual loss of love for her husband to an intense, smothering obsession with her son, whom she identifies with a cheap statue of Apollo, god of light, poetry, and masculine beauty, until she sees herself and the boy as one, excluding the father and promoting a relationship that is, if anything, beyond Freudian. She hears his first word, "Mama," conceives of herself as filling his developing mind, and, as his utterances increase in complexity, buys a notebook in which to collect those statements, some rhymed, some metaphorical, that she believes demonstrate his prodigious talent. In fact, Jaromil has learned the rhymes from his doggerel-minded grandfather. But he begins to appreciate the magic of language in any case, seeing that certain expressions win admiration or laughter and that others possess the power to prevent a spanking. On his sixth birthday Jaromil's parents give him a room of his own, and Kundera turns the occasion into a media event. Maman decorates the room with a desk and posters of Jaromil's poetic sayings, in a sense becoming his first publisher and editor by picking and choosing appropriate expressions and changing some for propriety.

With a sense of his own importance now (Kundera says Jaromil felt as if he filled a whole house, his words becoming an extension of his self as they hung on the wall), the poet finds himself alienated among his schoolmates, except for the school janitor's son, who will later become his means of earning fame. Meanwhile, Maman remains his closest friend, and in a typically Kunderan situation she causes another important event in Jaromil's aesthetic development. The spring after Hitler's invasion of Czechoslovakia, she travels to a small spa to rest her nerves, takes Jaromil with her, and meets a man who claims to be an artist. She shows him some of her son's sketches. The man admires what he calls their "original inner world"[4] and says that when he moves to Prague to teach, he would like to see more. Two years later, with Prague still staggering under Nazi control, Maman brings Jaromil to the artist's studio, and he volunteers to teach drawing to the boy. Kundera soon makes it clear, however, that the artist's real interest centers on Maman rather than Jaromil's work, and in the incidents that follow, a double story of Jaromil's developing awareness of sex and his mother's reborn interest in it, he explores two distinct notions about imagination and its relation to the real world.

Once again Kundera places the devilish and the angelic side by side, contrasting them here in relation to sexual love and the inspiration an artist derives from it. On one side, the angelic, Jaromil feels love and sexual longing for the family maid, but his inexperience prevents any concrete action. He peeks at her while she bathes, and, without ever touching her body or seeing it whole, his fantasies move him to write love verses that, in a parabatic aside, Kundera calls variations on romantic lyrics that Jaromil has read. At the same time Kundera treats the devilish impulse in the human character. While Jaromil innocently sketches in the studio, the artist breaks down Maman's inhibitions in his private quarters. He makes love to her, and afterward, during their affair, he insists on painting her naked as he breaks down further inhibitions. Ultimately he turns the brush on her, creating her body (and character) anew in a sense as she becomes a fresh work of art. In this scene the artist is a parodist, adult, realistic, a painter who impresses his inner visions on the world, remaking it through the medium of his work and imagination. Jaromil, on the other hand, works as a romantic, an adolescent idealist, who escapes reality through his art (in this case the art of poetry as well as sketching) and renders experience without real engagement or originality. While it may seem unfair to make these statements on the basis of a comparison between adolescent and adult experience, we should remember that as Kundera develops the story, escape and evasion of concrete experience remain Jaromil's basic character traits. The adolescent prank of keyhole peeping becomes a metaphor for Jaromil's tendency to remain apart and, while unobserved, study others. By extension, while the artist is a rake manipulating and entering a woman's body, Jaromil violates a woman's privacy. In that way Kundera has allowed Jaromil his innocence but given him the character traits of a voyeur and spy.

## "Xavier" and "The Poet Masturbates"

Parts Two and Three of the novel present contrasting images of Jaromil's experience, dream and reality respectively, and Kundera asks us to consider them as we see the young lyric poet approach maturity. Xavier is an internal character; that is, he exists in Jaromil's fantasies; he is a man of action and success, leaping boundaries, seducing women, winning fame and affection while destroying authority figures. At the same time, the Jaromil who lives externally is sadly bogged down by doubt and his close relationship with Maman. When we finish the "Xavier" fantasy section and begin "The Poet Masturbates," we learn that the Gestapo has taken Jaromil's father to a concentration camp where, toward the end of the war, he dies. The only man in his grandmother's and mother's life now (Maman long since having ended her affair with the artist), Jaromil gropes his way toward maturity and independence, believing he has been chosen to be a great poet and struggling to find some experience to propel his vision into words. But timidity inhibits him, and, as has been constant in his life, his experience remains limited to language and daydreams, the "land of tenderness, the land of *artificial childhood*" (112) where dreams and fear of reality take the place of experience itself.

Once again the artist assumes an important role in Jaromil's life, reading his poems with admiration, corroborating Jaromil's sense of himself so that he feels himself to be "one of the *elect*" (99) and can take his talent seriously. Furthermore, when Jaromil attends a meeting of young high school Marxists who are debating the idea of progress in art, he finds courage to speak by thinking of the artist and using his words, his gestures, and even his voice to make a point about the value of modernism versus socialist realism. But, importantly, the subject of the argument possesses less significance for Jaromil than his presence in the limelight. Again Kundera portrays Jaromil as an imitation, a "variation" on words and gestures that originate with someone else and yet win attention and approval for him.

At the end of the meeting a young woman, a university student, approaches to commend his speech, and Jaromil begins his first love relationship with a woman other than Maman. In a series of chapters that mix Jaromil's clumsy attempts at seduction with both his mother's reluctance to let him go and his growing facility with progressive slogans of art and politics, Kundera moves Jaromil toward his final development as a lyric poet and Communist Party enthusiast. During one argument Maman recognizes in her son the condescending tone and manner her former lover, the artist, used toward her and shouts that Jaromil is killing her (120). At another point, as he and his uncle argue over Klement Gottwald's efforts to create a Communist government, Jaromil spontaneously erupts into a party slogan about the dustbin of history (127). Soon afterward he defends the firing of non-Communists in his mother's office and tells her that despite their bourgeois background he has decided to join the Party.

Kundera intertwines these political developments with some detailed scenes of Jaromil's failed attempts at sexual experience. Clearly the young woman he met at the students' discussion is eager to have sex with him, but despite several opportunities he lacks the confidence to successfully bring her to bed. His fears about real life, his tendency to withdraw into self-consciousness during critical moments, and his lack of a male model make every sexual situation an insurmountable challenge. Like Ludvik in *The Joke*, he hides his lack of courage behind a façade of cynical, Byronic experience, but different from Ludvik, he uses the façade to escape sex rather than accomplish it. Frustrated, he visits his artist friend's apartment during an informal meeting of intellectuals who debate the relationship between modern art and the Communist Party. Jaromil feels as overwhelmed among these people as he does in bed with his girlfriend, but, coaxed out of his timidity by several of the women present, he defends the Communists' aesthetic of social realism against his mentor's condemnation in the name of modern art. The artist says that modernism had always supported the Party against bourgeois values and that the Party's interest in resurrecting classical realism for didactic purposes betrays the true roots of the revolution. Jaromil, finding himself using the artist's tone of voice and gestures against him, argues the Party's dustbin theory again: Real revolution and change surprise people, and since the ideas of modern art have held sway for years, it can no longer be revolutionary. He even admits that his own poems, much as they give pleasure to him and others, are useless and should be sacrificed to change. His words shock the others, but their reaction merely increases Jaromil's sense of accomplishment. In his own mind at least he has argued successfully against his mentor, and he no longer feels like a child.

Despite his success, Jaromil's new sense of himself as mature and manly crumbles under another challenge in the person of his schoolboy chum, the janitor's son, who is married, with a child and apartment of his own. Working for the police, the janitor's son refers to the leader of the high school Marxists' discussions as a Jew and advises Jaromil to watch out for him. We get a new insight into Jaromil's callous character when we find that the comment, mixed with the racial epithet, does not disturb him in the least. Instead Kundera describes him as excited, even exalted, feeling the conversation at his schoolmate's apartment has been decisive and that, at last, things have become clear. When, in the last chapter of "The Poet Masturbates," Jaromil runs away from the mothering attention of Maman and her friends at the beach, we know that the conflicts between his search for manhood and his need for his mother, having first resulted in the powerful impulses of his lyrical poems, may now ripen into something distinctly less sweet.

## "The Poet on the Run"

The title of Part Four picks up the action in the last scene of the previous section and extends it into a metaphor describing Jaromil's emotional state during the next important stage of his life. The title also hints at a larger

72

theme Kundera has in mind, the biographical similarity among lyric poets of all countries and times wherein they break from their mothers and start running after manhood—some writing revolutionary poetry, as Rimbaud did, some fighting in wars, as Lermontov did, some renouncing poetry in favor of political action. Jaromil takes the path of political action, like Ludvik in *The Joke,* and attends the Faculty of Political Science at the university while becoming active in the Party Youth Council. He hears a poet, a former idol, read some poems that mix modernist elements with revolutionary politics and rises to denounce the poems and their surrealist elements. The scene recalls Jaromil's speech to the group at the artist's apartment and repeats the sense that he rejects an important, imaginative side of his own character. At the same time Kundera very nicely conveys the impression that Jaromil has learned to perform skillfully in public now, underlining the fact that the Party and its revolutionary clichés go well with him, yielding a sense of self-confidence. He no longer writes poetry, but, repeating Maman's use of posters to publicize his sayings as a child, he becomes adept at making up, or remembering, slogans to be painted on placards used for marches.[5]

Growing up, socially active, engaged in public events as well, Jaromil still feels incomplete and alone. Eros beckons him. Longing to meet a cashier in a store where he and his mother shop, he lacks courage to speak to her and, consistent with his earlier behavior toward the family maid, occasionally follows the girl home after work. But he bungles that bit of voyeurism too, and in the kind of foolish accident that Kundera sees as changing lives irrevocably, Jaromil learns that what he thought was the cashier's apartment really belongs to her redheaded friend. The redhead sees him looking in her window and mistakenly thinks Jaromil is interested in her. She invites him inside next time and seduces him before he has time to worry about the intricacies of approaching the topic of sex with her. Thus, erotic experience, like many other important events in the Kunderan world, surprises, and, of course, like those other important events erotic experience also changes Jaromil's life forever. The redhead responds passionately to his lovemaking, making him feel mature and powerful. In a beautifully written final page of the section Kundera brings together parts of the biographies of Rimbaud and Shelley with Jaromil's lyric quest for adulthood. Having used Rimbaud's "Life is elsewhere" as title and leitmotif in the narrative, Kundera now applies it to the idea of the lyric poet's need to be on the move, to escape. Lying next to the redhead after they have made love, Jaromil feels content and at rest, not "after two bouts of love but after a long, long run" (181). Of course, Kundera mitigates Jaromil's satisfaction with the irony that the girl he dreamed of making love to is very different from the one who actually takes him into her bed.

## "The Poet Is Jealous"

This section is perhaps the most important in the novel, taking the reader step by step from Jaromil's first extended affair through poetic fame, political betrayal, and literary inspiration based upon his attempts to unify socialism and sexuality—that is, general, idealistic human love and love for one individual. Here Kundera also touches on the theme of privacy again (especially the invasion of it) and the idea of the face as the self, the public image somehow becoming the definitive image of character. This latter idea, returned to in *Immortality* and other novels, is a favorite theme of Witold Gombrowicz, and in this section Kundera performs an early variation on it, commenting on the role of poets as well as their audience in a culture already dominated by electronic communications.

The chapter begins with the facts of history forcing themselves on the well-ordered lives of Maman and Jaromil. The government jails Jaromil's uncle and expels his aunt and cousin from Prague. Then his grandmother dies, and with the first floor of Maman's villa empty the government assigns the apartment to a working-class family who, while enjoying the luxurious surroundings, resent the fact that one family has owned them for so long. The arrangement works awkwardly for everyone, but Kundera uses this public threat to family privacy to underscore Jaromil's adolescent need to step out from his mother's shadow and rule his own life. Maman has always read his diary in secret, even opening a locked drawer with a spare key to get at it. Once he starts seeing the redhead, she rejoices that she finds poems in the diary again (ones that for the first time she really enjoys, by the way), but she regrets that the source of inspiration is another woman. For a time the new poems reconcile the three characters, despite difficult moments between Maman and Jaromil. Clear, rhymed, with standard rhythms and about conventional subjects rather than modern, fractured ones, the new poems allow Maman to note her son's progress and pronounce him, once again in her mind, a poet.

Ironically, the redhead likes Jaromil's new work too, especially after one of the poems appears in the daily newspaper. He revels in her admiration even though her presence counters his mother's fondest desires. She is a working girl, after all, uneducated, unspoiled by bourgeois values, as he and Maman have been. He speaks to her of his fantasized alter ego, Xavier, who will leap through windows rather than merely look in them, recounting for her a fantasy (he describes it as a poem he wrote) concerning one of Xavier's adventures. Jaromil claims the woman whose window Xavier jumped through had red hair (in fact, her dark eyes are the only detailed feature the dream narrator mentions in Part Two), and the redhead responds to the similarity between the fantasy and their first meeting by nicknaming Jaromil "Xavy."

Voyeurism still works as one of Jaromil's primary motivations, along with his need to run. Enjoying the manipulation of words, the attention it wins him in the press, and the affection of the women in his life, Jaromil, for all his angelic innocence, now begins the journey toward character fulfillment, one that yields not maturity or adulthood, as he had hoped, but treachery and a farcical need to disappear. Jealousy sounds the note of the change, providing a less than admirable insight into his character.

During a moment of lovemaking the redhead playfully alludes to a visit to a gynecologist, and Jaromil can barely control his rage at the thought of another man touching her in an intimate place. Brusquely, he covers the girl's mouth with his hand, and the fear in her eyes "intoxicates" him, Kundera says, echoing a phrase about poetry that he used earlier.[6] We see that the effect of his threat to use physical force excites Jaromil as much as the power he exerts with words. He puts his hand to her throat and finds that the control over her life and death sexually excites him. In a parabatic aside Kundera explains this complex set of emotions by saying that Jaromil feels the girl eluding him, and although she swears her love for him, the security of the moment cannot satisfy him. Rather, he seeks eternity, "or at least the eternity of this girl's life" (202) and begins to rage inwardly about the first man in her life and even the male members of her family. Although he can deny knowing her when a school friend mocks the redhead's appearance (Kundera pointedly compares Jaromil to Peter denying Christ in this incident), we know his obsessive wish for complete control remains powerful. Linking the emotion to his criticism of the lyric attitude, Kundera quotes Keats's letter to his love, Fanny, *"You must be mine to die upon the rack if I want you"* (211). Jaromil's desire for the redhead's martyrdom results from romantic innocence, his angelic, Kundera might say *lyric*, sense of considering God's world and his ego as one. Some writers have criticized Kundera as sexist, but a close reading of *The Joke* and *Life Is Elsewhere* reveals his sympathetic attitude toward women who are victims of men, especially men like Ludvik and Jaromil, who in their naïve self-centeredness try to exercise power through the women they love.

75

The fifth chapter of "The Poet is Jealous" begins with another of Kundera's novelistic essays, this one on the traits of lyric poets and their poetry. He compares lyric poetry to a world where truth is measured by the intensity of emotion and inexperience equated with genius, while the poet of such a world writes to define himself, to sharpen his features in the hope of projecting a loved and even worshiped image to the public. From that disquisition on egotism and image making Kundera moves on to the most important public event so far in Jaromil's career, his first reading as a poet, and the means by which that reading ironically fulfills his wish to be a worshiped figure.

Fittingly, at least for the lyric world as Kundera portrays it, the reading comes at the invitation of the janitor's son and takes place at another center for thought control and power, a school for the Czech National Security Police. Entering the world of action at last, Jaromil impresses everyone with his recitation, other poets as well as the audience. At a discussion afterward his remarks concerning the quality of love under socialism, delivered with the tone and gestures of his former mentor, the artist, carry the argument in his favor even though Kundera undercuts the scene comically by introducing some villagers who begin a debate over the placement of a bus stop.

Despite that laughable conclusion to the meeting, the reading yields significant results for Jaromil. At it he meets a cinematography student, a young, beautiful woman whose dark eyes center on him with a hypnotic power similar to those of the dream woman described in the novel's "Xavier" sequence. Invited with the rest of the poets back to her apartment, Jaromil, by the consensus of the other poets, has an obvious opportunity to spend the night with her, but his timidity, self-consciousness, and innocence prevent him from turning this possibility into reality. History intervenes as well, Kundera tells us, and in explaining the situation he comically extends the evening's topic of discussion: love under socialism. In the proletarian fashion of those Stalinist days, he informs us, men wore ugly underwear that they would exchange for sexier-looking gym shorts whenever they went out with women. Jaromil, thinking only of his poetry, wears his ill-fitting proletarian shorts for the reading and, because he cannot bear to be seen in them, must leave the cinematography student behind. Later he defends his action by nobly and eloquently speaking of the glory of monogamous, socialist love.

But Jaromil has not heard the last of the cinematography student. As the novel progresses, Kundera provides her eyes with a haunting quality that feeds Jaromil's ego and, because of the camera in front of them, complements his lyric wish to become an adored public image. Jaromil learns that the student and Maman know each other and have contrived to make a film about his life. The script, written primarily by Maman, will emphasize her reminiscence of his childhood, a cinematographic equivalent of showing Jaromil in diapers, or ugly underwear, instead of at his work. Flattered at first, he balks at their plans, but the strength of the two women together, along with the power of their egos, wins him over. They shoot the film, concentrating on boyhood pictures, voice-overs of Maman's memories, all culminating in a scene where Jaromil recites a poem before the landscape in which Maman believes he was conceived. Inevitably the scene has problems. On camera Jaromil cannot recite as well as he can before an audience. He stumbles over his own words, and his voice makes little dramatic impression. Finally the cinematography student tells him to mouth the words silently and she will find an actor to read them for the soundtrack. Thus, the lyric portrait becomes reduced to the poet's face framed before an empty landscape, his voice and words inaudible because they are controlled by someone else.[7]

The timid poet speaking grandly because of his underwear; the public poet whose image is more important than his voice: Kundera develops these two opposing ideas of his hero as he moves him simultaneously toward triumph and defeat. But we must witness Jaromil's treachery as well, and Kundera portrays that side of him through his obsession with the control of his girlfriend's life. Waiting for her outside her apartment, Jaromil becomes angry at her lateness, and Kundera portrays the frustrated, dictatorial qualities of his character moving him to punish the girl in a way that is worse than physical, revealing Jaromil's lyrical innocence at its most repugnant. Learning that her brother caused her to be late because, the redhead says, he was about to defect from Czechoslovakia and she wanted to say good-bye, Jaromil becomes enraged. Intoxicated by his feelings, he visits the janitor's son at the office of the National Police and informs on the redhead's brother, also agreeing to keep his eyes open for any similar occurrences among university colleagues. Fully compromised by this collusion, Jaromil feels no remorse later when he learns that the girl has been arrested along with her brother. Instead, in a twist of ideological logic, he feels ennobled, manly, as if he has suddenly broken through to maturity because he has willingly given up his love for the betterment of the socialist fatherland. This is innocence at its most angelic, and Jaromil is appropriately inspired. The end of Part Five shows him writing "the greatest poem of my life" (266), no longer feeling jealous or childish and, he thinks, finally solving the complex problem of love and duty under socialism.

## "The Middle-Aged Man"

Part Six of the novel works in two ways: it advances the plot of the story through oblique means and forms a realistic companion piece for the "Xavier" dream section. At the same time it works as a variation, having a similar relation to the rest of the novel as a guesthouse has to an estate, Kundera tells us. Small and separate, yet obviously a part of the whole, it has a thematic unity that also provides the reader, as "Xavier" does, with a different yet related point of view of the novel's characters.[8]

We enter the "guesthouse" by means of the title character, the middle-aged man who, alone yet at peace with himself, represents an idea of masculine maturity completely opposite from that struggled after by Jaromil in the previous chapters. Here the man lives a dream that is real rather than fantastic, humble rather than exalted, private rather than public. Having stepped off the stage of history, so to speak, he lives in the world of pears instead of the world of tanks, supporting himself with laborer's work but returning home at night to dip into books by Greek and Roman authors. Clearly one of those Czech intellectuals who have fallen into displeasure with the Stalinist regime, he has survived his devilish independence, and in certain ways is wiser and perhaps better off than before. He might be the artist who taught Jaromil to draw or the "Jew" who invited high school students to his apartment to discuss Marxism. He might be, but probably is not, because Kundera gives us no real hints, making his anonymity the point of the section. The character is an Everyman we can contrast with the romantic dream self of Xavier and Jaromil's hopes for his maturity.

Reading in his bath one day, the man answers the doorbell and greets a young woman whom he last saw three years before. We learn that she is Jaromil's girlfriend, the redhead, and that she has just been released from prison. On her way home she has stopped at his apartment because she fears facing her family. She says her brother has never been released, and the man understands that she feels responsible. They discuss Jaromil. He died of an ordinary illness soon after the redhead disappeared, and the reader learns that the story she told him about her brother's defection was a lie. In fact, she had been the middle-aged man's lover then and had spent time with him on the day she arrived late for her meeting with Jaromil. Ironically, she had met the man that afternoon to say she would never see him again because of her love for Jaromil.

In a very tender scene the man's sexual feelings for the redhead surprise him, yet, in a marked contrast to the youthful Jaromil, his sympathy for her pain helps him to forbear making demands. They sleep side by side with the window open, calling to mind the window that, in Part Two's dream narrative, Xavier jumped through—and that Jaromil retreated from when he saw the redhead in her apartment. Kundera ends the passage with a parabatic comment on the purpose of the section. Not a story or adventure, it is "a quiet interlude" in which the middle-aged man "lights a lamp of kindness" (286). Underscoring the theme of this part of the novel, as well as its narrative purpose (which is to give us another, more humane point of view, to balance the doubt and cynicism inherent in Jaromil's story), he asks us to gaze at the light for a while before continuing to Part Seven.

## "The Poet Dies"

The final section furnishes no surprises in terms of plot. Kundera completes his ironic portrait of the poet, providing a final dramatic scene that realizes Jaromil's worst fears about his manhood and allows his foolish pride to lead to sickness and death. At the same time Kundera combines biographical incidents from the lives (and deaths) of several other lyric poets, principally Lermontov, Rimbaud, and Shelley, that add weight to his primary theme and balance with fact the fictional parody of Jaromil's death.

Invited by the cinematography student to a party at her villa, Jaromil attends, romantically believing that the evening will be a dramatic one in his life, one that will allow him finally to unite his Xavier dream self with his passive poetic self. Clearly he intends to seduce the cinematography student at last, and as he rings the bell that night he whispers to himself over and over that he is Xavier. Entering the villa, he finds artistic-looking people like himself, and Kundera describes them as young, fashionable, and attention-seeking. Once again, as with Helena and Zemanek in *The Joke,* Kundera provides an interesting portrait of ambition under communism, observing people with the universal human impulse of using others, selling images, or compromising important ideas for career advancement. Called apparatchiks in the former Soviet Union, yuppies in the United States, they are people who support the system (sometimes cynically, sometimes innocently) for their own purposes and seem, as Kundera portrays them, to care primarily for themselves.

Jaromil talks to the cinematography student, who stares at him "with her large brown eyes" (293) while he complains that he has not had a chance to be with her alone. Promising a chance, she leads him up the stairs to her room. It is a comic moment. His heart pounding, Jaromil believes he will finally live up to his dreams, but when the student opens the door they find her room crowded with people. One man in the crowd recognizes Jaromil and talks to him of his old friend the artist, who has been declared a bourgeois enemy of the people because of his art, lost his teaching job, and now works as an ordinary laborer. He accuses Jaromil of avoiding the artist to further his own career. Jaromil eloquently defends his behavior, saying the revolution has passed his old mentor by. "Real life is elsewhere," he says (297), repeating a theme concerning his own inner motivations. When he goes on to declare the artist and the man both dead, the man reacts angrily. Jaromil, no doubt with the image of Xavier on his mind, swings his fist. The man spins him around, catches him by the seat of his pants and collar, and, as the crowd at the party laugh, deposits Jaromil on the balcony where, once again, he stands outside of life, or at least his dream of it.

The night air is freezing, and, we find out, Jaromil has a cold. What's more, he took off his jacket inside because he felt too warm. With the shame of the party's laughter in his ears, he refuses to reenter the villa, not even for his jacket. Writing a pastiche of death scene parodies from the lives of Shelley, Lermontov, Pushkin, and Rimbaud, Kundera pokes ironic fun at Jaromil's pride, satirizing the lyric attitude that prefers death to dishonor and aggrandizes suicide as a preferable way to die. Kundera portrays Jaromil as "trapped in a farce" because, having been humiliated, he cannot return to the party, cannot climb down from the balcony because it is too high, and yet cannot end it all by jumping because he fears the balcony is not high enough to kill him. So, for the rest of the night he shivers and stares through the cinematography student's window until he sees a lamp lit and two naked bodies on her bedroom couch. The image reminds us of the end of "The Middle-Aged Man" and "Xavier" sections. Freezing, Jaromil imagines that his alter ego, Xavier, has cuckolded him, ending in ignominy the night that he had anticipated with such high hopes. Adding insult to injury, as he lies in his own bed a few days later, dying of pneumonia, Jaromil dreams that Xavier is leaving him. Before parting through the open window, Xavier caresses Jaromil's cheek and announces, "You are very beautiful, but I must betray you" (304), using romantic tenderness against, rather than for, him as Jaromil earlier did so treacherously against the redhead.

In the novel's final pages, with Jaromil's dream self gone, Kundera shows him and Maman drawing closer together and, in doing so, evokes the story of Narcissus, the mythical Greek youth who could not love a woman but who saw his own image in a pool and died of love for it. Maman says Jaromil looks like her. He reciprocates by saying that she is the only woman in his life, the only one he ever really loved. Tying together the Greek myth with a post-Freudian vision of the lyric poet's life, Kundera describes Jaromil and Maman as staring into each other's eyes as the novel ends, their faces so close that "it seemed he was bending over a still pond watching his own likeness" (306). Of course, Maman is bending over, but Kundera's inversion underlines the Narcissus theme. Having wanted to die by fire, Jaromil realizes he will die by water, which will weigh him down rather than liberate him as he has imagined a death by flames would. Kundera closes with the idea that even in death Jaromil cannot escape the trap of self-consciousness or Maman's overly possessive love. Dying yet still innocent, he sees an expression of fear cross his mother's face, and Kundera underlines it as a leitmotif; he describes the look as the last image of himself that Jaromil ever saw.

## Conclusion: *The Joke* and *Life Is Elsewhere*

Known, loved, but somehow unknown and unloved at the same time, especially to himself, the lyric poet dies. The conclusion to *Life Is Elsewhere* is a particularly stringent comment on the human condition, especially since the sensitive reader experiences little more than a sinking feeling, perhaps equivalent to a chuckle of remorse, at the death of this less than admirable young man. We feel a far different experience at the end of *The Joke,* when the more honest, and perhaps more talented, Jaroslav has a heart attack and a saddened but wiser Ludvik plays in his band. The difference is a matter of seasoning, maturity, but, more important, attitude. For while the angelic Jaromil may strike the reader as more appealing at first, principally because Kundera portrays him as victimized by his mother's ambitions, we view him less sympathetically as he ages without change, without genuine maturity. Unchanging innocence is a characteristic of angelic characters as Kundera defines them, but he means this character change to apply to life as well as art, so that Jaromil's weakness has dire political and sociological results. In effect, Jaromil behaves more selfishly as he grows older, while Ludvik behaves less selfishly, especially in relation to Kostka. His behavior toward Helena and Lucie may revolt us, but the misery of his life as devil in his society—first as ironic commentator on Marxist conformity, second as a conscript obliged to perform forced labor—can make us at least accept his anger. We have no such feeling toward Jaromil since his violence comes from angelic self-righteousness. Also, Jaromil never feels remorse, never understands the human errors he has committed in the name of faith; Ludvik, on the other hand, suffers genuinely for them because he is more doubtful, rational, and, ultimately, kind.

In addition, both characters are trapped by roles they cannot escape: Jaromil must play the lyric poet his mother conceived as a role for him before his birth; Ludvik, by birth more than choice, remains an ambitious, if intellectual, provincial. Their attempts to escape lead them to terrible blunders and awful acts of unkindness. Both choose a woman who complements those roles and then betray her because of the pressures of manhood. These suffering women represent something deep and lasting: plain, generous, from the working class, sexually active at an early age, they survive the bad treatment they receive at the hands of their men, going on to find someone kinder (Kostka or the Middle-Aged Man) even though they still feel pain.

A final, and perhaps more important, point, because this one has to do with novelistic form, both characters exist in novels that should be considered variations in the same way Kundera asks us to regard the stories in *The Book of Laughter and Forgetting*. In this case the two novels are variations on the *Bildungsroman*, traditionally a novel that traces the education and development of a young man or, sometimes, woman from youth to spiritual adulthood, or the *Kunstlerroman*, a novel that traces the education and development of a young artist. *Bildungsroman* (and *Kunstlerroman*) stories feature the following themes or events: childhood experience, the conflict of generations, provinciality, entrance into the larger society, self-education, alienation from the world, ordeal by love, the search for a vocation and a working philosophy.[9] If *Life Is Elsewhere* emphasizes the childhood experience of the form and *The Joke* emphasizes provinciality, both novels give equal treatment to the other themes: conflict of generations (Jaroslav and his son, Jaromil and the artist); entrance into the larger society (by means of university attendance in both novels); self-education (through experience and working in party politics); alienation (Ludvik's exile in Ostrava, Jaromil's retreat into his dreams); the ordeal of love (Lucie and the redhead); and the search for a vocation and working philosophy (Ludvik's research and musicianship, Jaromil's poetry of socialist realism).

In treating these themes, both novels work out Kundera's notions of Czechoslovakia's conflicting experience—that is, its angelic and devilish history: its entrapment by larger social and political powers; the people's lyric self-consciousness (in ''The Poet Is Jealous'' section of *Life Is Elsewhere* an editor, without a touch of humor, speaks to Jaromil of the possibility of exporting Czech poetry as a national resource); the country's inability to escape provincial feelings in the face of larger European cultures; and, last, the Czech leaders' historical inability to control the country's fate. While *The Joke* treats these ideas seriously with a heavy dose of irony, *Life Is Elsewhere* parodies them, along with the *Bildungsroman* genre, making fun of the idea that angelic youth and innocence, national or individual, can be taken seriously when the very idea of faith in ideology implies the helplessness of the blind.

In truth, Jaromil has lived according to fragile codes of conduct. The bombast of poetic feeling and his mother's longing pumped him up with grandeur. While he (and his country) may have experienced some important lyric moments, in the light of history (and reader's hindsight) those moments appear smaller and far less significant than he thought. Once again, the world of pears outlives the world of tanks. So we perceive the poet's life through an aura of shabbiness, containing gray, clouded visions and only a very few shining ones, as if he too were surrounded by coal dust, earth, and shadow, another Ludvik forced to labor in those dingy mines.

## NOTES

1. Antonin J. Liehm, *The Politics of Culture* (New York: Grove, 1973) 144, 146. Liehm's text in English has "Seduced Lyricism"; however, in May 1991, in conversation with me, Kundera expressed dismay at that translation from the Czech. He retrieved the Czech version from his library and went over his comment word for word. He said "Abused Lyricism" is the proper translation.

2. Kundera's speech can be found in Dusan Hamsik, *Writers against Rulers* (New York: Random House, 1971).

3. See his "Defence of Poetry," an essay that perfectly (and innocently) illustrates Kundera's joining of lyricism and politics.

4. *Life Is Elsewhere* (New York: Penguin, 1986) 31. Further references are noted parenthetically.

5. Later, in *Immortality*, Kundera will develop this interest in, and talent for, sloganizing into a commentary on the culture of our time, a time when the imagologue replaces the ideologue as a mover and shaker in the democratic West.

6. "Poetry is intoxication" (193).

7. This too is a theme that Kundera develops more fully in *Immortality*. In that book the great German poet Johann Wolfgang Goethe struggles for control of his reputation with Bettina Brentano, a young romantic poet who wants to link herself with him for eternity. Combining eroticism with history and literature, the Goethe–Brentano episodes echo themes from *Life Is Elsewhere*, a fact that Kundera calls attention to by having one of *Immortality*'s characters find that book left for him at a café.

8. For Kundera's discussion of the genesis of this section, see *The Art of the Novel* (New York: Grove, 1988), 85.

9. For these and other ideas I am indebted to an excellent study, "Narrative Voices in the Bildungsroman," a dissertation by Kim Lauren McKay, Lehigh University, 1990 (Ann Arbor: UMI, 1991; 9109576) Much of the material referred to here is derived from Jerome Buckley's *Season of Youth: The Bildungsroman from Dickens to Golding* (Cambridge: Harvard University Press, 1974).

CHAPTER SIX

# Man's Faith, Earth's Fate:
## *The Farewell Party*

*To bring together the extreme gravity of the question and the extreme lightness of the
form—that has always been my ambition.*
—Kundera, *The Art of the Novel*

In *The Art of the Novel* Kundera says that *The Farewell Party* is the novel
that is dearest to him because he had "more fun, more pleasure" in its composition than with the others. He calls it a "farce in five acts," without digression, narrated at a constant tempo, and "very theatrical." He also says
that it asks an important question: "Does man deserve to live on this earth,
shouldn't the 'planet be freed from man's clutches'?"[1]

The passage may strike the reader as odd because it combines the high spir-
its of joyful composition with a rather solemn philosophical quest. But the
very combination of light form and somber thought pervades Kundera's work
from *Life Is Elsewhere* onward, and with *The Farewell Party* he brought the
disparate elements of his style together in a new way, perhaps accounting for
the happiness he expresses about the writing. Following are some of the developments that occur in Kundera's work from the publication of *Life Is Elsewhere* in 1973 through the publication of *The Farewell Party* and the novels
that come after it:

1. In *The Joke* and *Life Is Elsewhere,* he concentrates, traditionally, on one
character and traces that character's development through thought and feeling. In the later novels his emphasis shifts to groups or pairs of people and
some philosophical ideas concerning them or people of their type. Character
still possesses importance, but not *a* character, not one central persona.

2. Kundera blurs the narrative line in unusual ways in the more recent novels, shifting back and forth in time, not an unusual technique really, but,
more important, letting the narrative eye dance in space, allowing the story
to proceed by idea or feeling rather than by logic, incident, or a geographi-
cally restricted point of view. In certain stories we can say he moves through
narrative passages by association, letting them follow the path his language
takes as he describes an incident or character, or "talks" to the reader about
some political or philosophical concern. Here the tone and mood of a novel

take on the special quality of the narrator's character—more and more obviously Kundera's as he progresses toward *The Book of Laughter and Forgetting* and the novels that come afterward.

3. We should remember Kundera's comment that he changed his style in favor of clarity once he started to write for a translator. That may account for the way his narrative voice evolves after *The Joke,* becoming that of a raconteur, someone who knows his audience, or tries to, because he knows he has a good story for them. He uses third-person narration, but in *The Book of Laughter and Forgetting* he begins to intrude with autobiography and personal commentary, becoming highly self-conscious by the time of *The Unbearable Lightness of Being* and *Immortality,* in both of which he uses his narrative presence to remind us we are reading fiction. (Perhaps this was Kundera's way of controlling the lyric impulses in his work, transforming them into narrative experiment. More likely, he would see the change as evidence of his evolving sense of the novel's formal possibilities.)

4. In many ways, as a result of Kundera's narrative intrusions, his storytelling becomes a form of philosophic discourse, almost the voice of nonfiction as he writes what he calls ''novelistic'' essays about music, art, words, and philosophic ideas. Certainly by the time he reaches *The Book of Laughter and Forgetting* and *The Unbearable Lightness of Being* he has decided to blend the two discourses, like one of his masters, Hermann Broch, and write novels that are part fiction, part philosophical speculation. However, the main purpose of his work still remains to entertain and charm the reader. But, always, somber ideas fill the vessel of light form. (See chapters three and seven of this study for further comments on Kundera's use of the narrative voice.)

5. Characters greatly multiply in the later books, and they are not always related, either by friendship or family. Increasingly Kundera resorts to accidental or incidental ties that become a part of a character's ultimate fate. For instance, Jakub, the bearer of the poisonous pill that kills Ruzena in *The Farewell Party,* has no relation to her except for a tragic accident of time and place that has nothing to do with their individual desires or faults. They hardly know one another, yet Ruzena's fate may be seen as a culmination of Jakub's own.

6. In the later novels Kundera plays different character types against one another, attempting to make comedy and, more important, say something about the human condition or about human individuals in a variety of conditions. It is a technique he developed in *Laughable Loves* (published in several formats at different times in Czechoslovakia, then gathered, edited,

corrected, and published anew in several versions from 1974 to 1987 in France, England, and America), particularly in one of its stories, "The Symposium." In these stories character relationships take on a thematic, almost symbolic, quality masked by humor, eroticism, and drama. Once again, grave questions sail on the uplift of form.

7. With *The Farewell Party* Kundera's novels begin to take on the qualities of romance. Their tone, admittedly artificial and fictional, lacks the nineteenth-century novel's attempt at realism. Theme and meaning carry more importance than the mystery of psychological motivation, and action defines self. As a result of these developments the idyll or, perhaps more accurately, its negation through parody becomes a primary narrative mode, with sets of characters compared and contrasted in a way that is similar to those in Shakespeare's *A Midsummer Night's Dream* or *The Tempest*. Starting with *The Farewell Party* the novels contain a more overt sense of fun, with parody, exaggeration, and humorous wonder at people with higher benevolent powers (their grand ambitions betrayed), leavened by an occasional sweetness that surfaces in the most unlikely circumstances, even in the face of death.

8. Finally, Kundera has settled on a narrative form that returns to his novelistic beginning. The spirit of the last section of *The Joke*, with its shifting geography, its canon of clashing yet oddly complementary voices and points of view, its harsh comedy mixing body functions with higher philosophic notions, and its amused exploration, almost anthropological, of a small town as an expression of human life in general, seems to inspire Kundera the narrator for the entire text of the novels that follow *Life Is Elsewhere*. So *Life Is Elsewhere*, a companion piece to *The Joke*, may be considered a completion of some sort, as well as a bridge to *The Farewell Party* and the later novels.

## "First Day"

A reading of *The Farewell Party* should begin with a consideration of its setting. Of all Kundera's works the setting for this novel is the least concrete, the least connected to political and social realities. After his attack on the dangerous union of politics and literature in *Life Is Elsewhere*, Kundera moves to a fictional setting completely divorced from national politics in order to write a tale that can have little or no political meaning. We are at an unnamed spa, near an unidentified small town situated in a nameless country probably somewhere behind the Iron Curtain in Central Europe. With no ties to the area, the characters live in an atmosphere of total exile, seeking health through the baths and medical ministrations or simply, as in the case of the doctors and staff, making a living. Autumn light colors the air as the book opens, and the reader must note with a little irony in this season of dying that some patients at the spa arrive to achieve fertility. The themes of birth and death combine to strike the opening chord, along with the narrator's reminder that the colors of the leaves make the town seem surrounded by hellish flames.

We learn of Nurse Ruzena's predicament immediately. Born and raised in this small town, she looks for a means of escape from provinciality, most likely a man, and feels imprisoned by her job, the infertile women she attends, and the valley. Kundera makes evident her alliance with the other nurses in her opening conversation with them. Jokingly, they tell her to telephone someone at his home, and she replies that she will call him at his rehearsal hall. The second chapter switches to Klima, a famous jazz musician, and we enter his consciousness as he reacts with fear to the phone call Ruzena has made. We learn that Ruzena has another problem in her life—she is pregnant, by him, she says—and we learn that while Klima will help her with an abortion, Ruzena has other ideas: "I'd never do such a thing, they'd have to kill me first," she says,[2] setting up the tensions that will move the plot and, ironically, resolve it all just as she plans. In the next chapter we learn that Klima had come to the spa to perform a few months before and, meeting Ruzena at a party afterward, had spent the night with her. Ruzena told her colleagues of her evening with Klima, and clearly they feel some attachment to the famous musician because of her. They discuss him familiarly, his picture appears in the staff room, and now that Ruzena is pregnant they feel a closer bond than ever. In fact, Ruzena's frankness about her night with Klima and the resulting pregnancy, along with her colleagues' comic excitement about him, sound very much like the ideas about published autobiography that Kundera satirized in the Tamina sections of *The Book of Laughter and Forgetting*. Here graphomania and the desire for fame are replaced by the wish to be near fame, to be familiar with it, and, most important for Ruzena, to use it to escape the confines of a small-town life.

The narration moves to Klima as he discusses Ruzena with the members of his band, and Kundera finds as much humor in the men's attitudes as he finds in those of the nurses at the spa. He tells of Klima's once receiving a phone call from a woman who had a sorrowful tone to her voice and his relief that the sorrow was over her mother's death and not a surprise pregnancy. The band members react just as insensitively. They deny that Ruzena's child can be Klima's and promise that if she insists on having the child, they will all say they slept with her. Finally the guitarist, who regards Klima as his idol, volunteers to solve the problem by driving to the spa, enticing Ruzena into the road, and running her over. Klima calls him "awfully decent" (11) for this thoughtfulness but decides instead to promise Ruzena a divorce and marriage as long as she will have the abortion. So through deceit and cruel disregard for Ruzena's feelings, the men show themselves to be happier with death than life—another theme that will be played out ironically at the end of the story—and underlining Kundera's question quoted at the beginning of this chapter concerning man's dominion of the earth.

Klima returns home, worrying about Ruzena and his wife, whose birthday falls on the following day. Wanting to settle matters, he calls Ruzena to say he will meet her at the spa the next morning. To excuse himself with his wife, he buys her flowers, and Kundera narrates the Klimas' evening comically by detailing their secret knowledge of, and doubts about, one another. Upon receiving the flowers, Kamila Klima knows her husband won't be home for her birthday; and, sure enough, he provides a lame excuse about socialism's need to take arts to the people, thus forcing him to leave her alone on her birthday. She knows he is lying, probably to cover a meeting with another woman; he knows that she knows. The tension colors their evening, but they leave it behind when Klima suggests they attend a Western at the local cinema. In that way a wandering American culture hero (like jazz, a particularly American art form) becomes Klima's model for success and escape. As in a Chinese puzzle, Ruzena's route to freedom, Klima, has its own confining box around it.

## "Second Day"

This section opens in the morning with Klima walking down a tree-lined lane to the Richmond House, where he will meet Bartleff, the rich American staying there because of an ailing heart. Providing more details of setting, the narrator places the Richmond House, the only building to keep its pre-Communist name, across from Karl Marx House, where Ruzena lives and where Klima passed his "two fateful hours" with her. Bartleff greets him in pajamas and announces his appreciation of slow, languorous mornings, which he conceives as bridges from night to day and hopes will bring him a miracle to show that his dreams may continue through the day. From those comments we conceive of him as an idealist and dreamer, and we understand the quality of his dreaming when Klima points to a painting, done by Bartleff, of St. Lazarus, who was martyred, not by pagans who wanted him to deny his

Christianity, but by Christian ascetics who wanted him to give up painting. Dramatizing the clash of aesthetics and ideology in a very Kunderan way, the incident also illustrates Bartleff's religious attitude when he says, approvingly, that St. Lazarus refused to stop because he regarded painting as his means of praising God. And when Klima brings up his problem with Ruzena, we learn something more about Bartleff's unusual nature. Surprised at Klima's coolness toward Ruzena, he recounts his own experience with a woman who said he fathered her child. Bartleff felt flattered rather than fearful, he says, and now he advises Klima to love Ruzena rather than doubt her. Also, in a very rich blend of optimism and confidence founded on a life of privilege, he urges "total acceptance of life" (26), especially the unplanned, saying that a child is the essence of the unforeseen. But Bartleff, although strong in his beliefs, almost to the point of having angelic innocence (as defined in *The Book of Laughter and Forgetting*), is really not doctrinaire. Reflecting Voltaire's famous pledge to fight to the death for the right of an opponent to speak his mind, he calms Klima's fears: Although he opposes abortion, Bartleff says he will help Klima because he is his friend.

Together they visit Dr. Skreta, a gynecologist and abortionist who represents another kind of idealism, that of the scientist. Perhaps a burlesque version of Goethe's Faust, Skreta regards women as a scientific field, seeing them solely as producers of children. At the same time he possesses a vision of universal brotherhood that he works toward accomplishing in a comically practical way by injecting his own sperm into the bodies of women who have had trouble conceiving. Unknown to them, Skreta has been prodigiously successful, populating the world after his own image rather than their husbands', and at several points in the novel we are made aware of his facial characteristics appearing on children. A dreamer like Bartleff, Skreta has scientific rather than religious values, making him oddly amoral in his attitudes toward birth and death.

Bartleff introduces Skreta to Klima, and we find that, to the doctor, playing drums with Klima has as much importance, if not more, as Ruzena's pregnancy. The three men discuss women and their motivations, revealing three very different attitudes. Klima is a sort of Everyman, bewildered and seeking help; Bartleff voices humane and idealistic views; and Skreta expresses a careless cynicism, essentially telling the others that the color of a woman's hair and skin determine her character. His attitude may be seen as a scientific parody of the ideas of Klima's colleagues in the band. Blondes are demanding and bitchy; dark-haired women make life pleasant for men. Skreta suggests that if dark hair became fashionable, the world would improve greatly. He confirms that his examination the day before showed Ruzena to be pregnant and agrees to help convince her to have an abortion, but not before asking Klima to play with him in a concert. Clearly he, like Ruzena's friends and co-workers, is more interested in association with the famous musician than in the problem of Ruzena's pregnancy.

Klima leaves the meeting to see Ruzena who, in her room, changes out of her work clothes while talking with her father. They argue about civic duty and pride, Ruzena's father accusing her of caring more about the right dress for her boyfriend than the social good of their community. But Kundera undercuts that seemingly honorable approach when we learn that Ruzena's father seeks to destroy all unleashed dogs in order to keep the town clean. Ruzena's father represents one of Kundera's pet peeves about the Communist government in Czechoslovakia: its urge for order and cleanliness at the expense of human life. In *The Art of the Novel* he has told how Communist Party leaders created an "organized massacre of dogs" throughout Prague after the Russian invasion of 1968, and he alludes to this in *The Farewell Party* to set the intellectual and spiritual climate of the times. In relation to those times the divergent idealism of Ruzena's father, Skreta, and even Bartleff, as we shall see later, have odd similarities. Although one deals with killing dogs and the others concern themselves with women and babies, all three tamper with life arbitrarily, with an aloof disregard for individual human consequences.

Klima meets Ruzena in a bar, drives her into the country to avoid autograph hounds, and there, while they talk, convinces her he truly loves her but that a baby would be in the way, especially with his "natural" doubts about its fatherhood. Ruzena agrees to go before Skreta and the medical board to receive permission for an abortion. Then as they return to Klima's car they encounter a young man on a motorcycle who shouts at them. Later we learn that this is Ruzena's boyfriend, Franta, a character who represents the boring, mundane limits to her life and who, at key points during the next few days, will function as Ruzena's naive, limited fury. Kundera practices an interesting exercise in diversion with this scene. While Klima, after speaking to Bartleff, drives back to the capital in the moonlight, we think of him as under a real threat—from his wife, from the pregnancy, even from Franta—yet it is Ruzena who will die, not because of Franta, not because of her pregnancy, but by means of a new character, Jakub, whom she does not know but whose past, as he escapes the valley (and the country), carries the accident that will destroy Ruzena and any chance she has for freedom.

## "Third Day"

In this section of the novel we meet two new characters, Jakub and Olga, his ward, who stays at the spa under Dr. Skreta's care. Jakub visits Skreta in his office, and once again we see the gynecologist's callousness toward women, in this case two patients whom he examines in Jakub's presence, conversing with Jakub while working absent-mindedly and at times jokingly, pretending that Jakub is a gynecologist too. Skreta's procedure is as unorthodox as his manner, and he regards women's bodies biologically, without a hint of eroticism, as he discusses their legs, their ovaries, their bone structures strictly in reproductive terms. Kundera underlines a theme about the nature of male eroticism here, especially when we consider a paragraph from the previous chapter: in the country Klima kisses Ruzena and, distracted by his worries about her pregnancy, senses "a *real* mouth, a busy opening through which passed loads of dumplings, potatoes, and soups," instead of a mouth made romantic by "a fog of desire" (47), as it had been when he met her several months before.

Kundera expands on this theme when Jakub leaves Skreta's office to talk to Olga, a young woman whose intelligence, thin, unattractive body, physical frailty, and desire for quiet mark her as a figure who contrasts markedly with Ruzena. Olga has modern ideas and, like many modern women, the narrator tells us, she divides herself into one woman who experiences and another who observes. Her character is marked by mental forces rather than physical ones, as Ruzena's is, and Kundera accentuates that when Jakub and Olga talk in the spa's dining hall.

Jakub looks at Ruzena, sitting near them, and mentions an observation from Hegel concerning the classic Greek profile. Hegel felt that the beauty of that profile occurs because it accents the upper part of the head, "the seat of intellect and spirit" (66). Although Ruzena is attractive, Jakub says, the force of her face is concentrated on the mouth and would disgust Hegel, while Olga's head would please him because the top part dominates the rest. But Olga explodes all this talk of character based upon appearance, calling it absolute nonsense. "I picture myself with a big chin and a sensuous mouth," she tells Jakub, saying that, knowing herself from the inside, "I am not at all the person I look like!" (66).

Summing up this series of passages, we might make the following statement concerning Kundera's theme: for women (Ruzena and Olga) the wished-for self is not always possible; for men eroticism and body parts are a matter of attitude (Skreta sees them biologically, Bartleff spiritually, and

Klima aesthetically). These are suspect ideas, especially from a feminist viewpoint, but in Kundera's defense we should add that, for everyone in his novels, men and women, appearances are false and inner feelings are profoundly suspect, turning us into prisoners, not only of a country or a provincial small town but of our bodies as well. If, as Kundera has said, the novel explores the possibilities of human existence, where does freedom for the human character lie? With science (through Dr. Skreta)? Romantic spiritualism (through the religious Bartleff)? Aesthetic sensibility (through the musician Klima)? Or the inner workings of the intellect (through the psychologist Jakub)? Probably Kundera would answer: Nowhere; freedom, like truth, is relative, lying partly in all of them, yet wholly in none of them. As a result, all we have to depend on is ourselves, our individual points of view, reputation, and memory. So Olga wonders about the character of her father, martyred by the Party; Klima worries about an adoring public that sometimes gets too close for comfort; and Bartleff and Skreta aim, in different directions, for a world made peaceful by universal love.

Through the next few chapters about this day the narrative follows the separate stories of Ruzena and Jakub, bringing them together in momentary clashes of themes and personalities that, although unimportant at the time they occur, lead inevitably to Ruzena's death. Ruzena meets her boyfriend Franta at the spa, and we now see him as less threatening, more a foolish victim of jealousy than an aggressor, a young provincial boy, fearful that fame and glamor will take his love away. He apologizes to Ruzena for his behavior the day before and, to make amends, gives her the gift of a blue nightgown. Unmoved despite his apology, Ruzena lies, telling him Klima is an old friend and that nothing exists between them. She promises Franta to see him after the weekend. Ruzena worries that her father will find them together, saying he would "kill her," and Franta replies that marriage would solve that problem. "We'd have a family," he tells her (74). Reacting strongly, Ruzena ignores her pregnancy, and, reversing her earlier comment to Klima, says she would kill herself before having a baby. The irony of the switch is compounded when she says several times that Franta will drive her to suicide. In reality, she seeks life rather than death, the baby inside her, as she tells herself, being her ticket to a larger, more interesting world. As in Kundera's previous novel, here too "Life is elsewhere."

Meanwhile, we learn more about Jakub and Olga, their opinions, and the past they share. Olga's father was a friend of Jakub's, executed by the Party in the 1950s and later politically rehabilitated. After her father's death Jakub took Olga on as a ward, wanting to experience fatherhood with no obligations. Free to pursue his own life, he has looked after her from afar, always thinking she harbored a secret love for him. Now, granted a visa to work in another country, he plans to leave his homeland permanently, and he has come, with mixed emotions, to say good-bye to her.

They discuss her dead father and the ambiguities of human character in relation to reputation. Olga asks if her father had really died with a clear conscience and should have been rehabilitated. When Jakub assures her that her father was a good man, Olga tells him she has received anonymous letters calling her father violent and cruel, a man who drove innocent people with different beliefs than his to execution. Jakub, who had been jailed by the Party himself, tells how Olga's father was beaten unconscious by other prisoners when he first entered a cell. Jakub calls it an act of revenge, which he says is "stronger than time" (70), and goes on to tell Olga that in his experience the victims are as bad as their oppressors, that they would be as violent if the roles were reversed, and he sees cruelty and revenge as innate in human nature. This grim assessment—Jakub calls it a "definition of hell" (70)—repeats the attitude of Ludvik Jahn in *The Joke* and leads the way to the story of Jakub's blue pill, given to him by Skreta, that would allow him to kill himself if life became unbearable in prison or in his country. His ticket to freedom, or at least the controlling of his own destiny, in the same way that Ruzena's pregnancy is, the pill is the novel's final concrete tie between Jakub's fate and Ruzena's. Both seek an escape from the prison of their existence, the hell of the lives they lead. And Skreta, the comic Faust, the abortionist and fertility expert, is the ironic means by which their two escapes occur (and by which Jakub tests himself morally).

Colored blue, the pill repeats a motif Kundera has referred to several times in the novel and picks up again in *The Book of Laughter and Forgetting*. In that novel Kundera discusses death while telling the story of Tamina. He refers to a Thomas Mann short story—"The Wardrobe"—about the man who has a beautiful naked woman in his wardrobe telling him stories. Kundera says the woman and her tales are death, and he follows with the idea that they represent the "sweet bluish death of nonbeing."[3] He adds that nonbeing is "infinite emptiness," which is blue, a color that comforts and beautifies more than any other. Continuing his meditation, Kundera cites the eighteenth-century German romantic poet Novalis, who believed in the mystic unity of all things and urged Europe to strive toward a new universal church that would reestablish the spiritual unity of mankind. Novalis's unfinished *Bildungsroman, Heinrich von Ofterdingen,* treats the life and development of a young poet during the Middle Ages and, in its time, established the Blue Flower as a symbol of German romanticism. Kundera responded to that novel in *Life Is Elsewhere*, making Jaromil's lyric narcissism and romantic longing for brotherhood a subject for satire, although he does not seem to have used color, at least the color blue, in any symbolic way. In *The Book of Laughter and Forgetting*, however, he tells us that Novalis "loved blue" and always sought it out. He refers to him as the "poet of death" and finishes his passage on nonbeing, emptiness, and color by saying, "Death's sweetness is blue."

The statement may be seen as a belated gloss on the usage of the color in *The Farewell Party*. First, there is the blue glow associated with Bartleff, especially when Klima accidentally barges in on him and sees a blue light in the corner. Bartleff says he was thinking, and when Klima mentions the glow he saw, Bartleff jokes, saying he must have hallucinated because of the tension over Ruzena's pregnancy (52). We again encounter the color later in the book after Ruzena spends the night with Bartleff and wakes, happy for the first time in her life, to a blue light that she attributes to the moon (163). Finally, there is the blue halo that Bartleff paints on his portrait of St. Lazarus because, as he tells Jakub, in reality halos have that color. Reflecting the passage from *The Book of Laughter and Forgetting*, Bartleff goes on to say that people with a saintlike love of God feel a radiant joy that is "mild and calm, and has the color of the blue heavens" (88). Asked by Jakub, the rationalist man of doubt, whether he believes halos to be real rather than symbolic, Bartleff replies affirmatively and without shame. While saints do not walk around with a glow like lamp posts, he says, they do at times feel "intense inner joy" (88), and at those times radiate a light that early painters accurately depicted in blue until the conventional colors of gold, yellow, and orange replaced it and expressed the Church's secular power and glory.

So, in the scheme of this book blue carries a sense of serenity and love that is both romantic and religious, appealing to the human spirit in moments of intense life as well as during the eternal calm of death. Thus, Jakub's lethal pill possesses the same external qualities (color and shape) as Ruzena's vial of tranquilizers that deliver moments of "death's sweetness" in the feverish hell of human life. In the same way Franta's gift to Ruzena of a blue nightgown must be "death's sweetness" too, a pseudo-romantic, pseudo-serene promise of the glow she will see, not in Franta's arms, but in Bartleff's room and experience only in taking Jakub's pill by mistake. Blue equals a way out, a life above and beyond the flesh, an escape from the color of blood, the red that licked the trees in Kundera's opening sentence of this book, making the town seem surrounded by flames. And when, in the middle of an important conversation concerning Herod and Jesus, and man's joy in life as well as his dominion over the earth, a young, angelic girl enters and offers Bartleff a dahlia before leading him out of the room, we reflect on Novalis's Blue Flower and see the color of the dahlia, normally a blue-tinged violet, indicating Bartleff's intense love of life, as the romantic joy that makes him saintly, providing the power that, along with his money, allows him to make people happy.

Along with this serene, romantic theme of blue, we must now consider a balancing theme that also occurs during the third day: the clash between Jakub and Ruzena over the capturing of loose dogs in the park. Ruzena's father works at rounding up dogs with other older men from the village, and we have seen from the argument Ruzena had with him that she has no enthusiasm for his job. But today, while she sits in the park contemplating Franta's gift of a blue nightgown, she sees Jakub strolling toward her, and her frustration over Franta and Klima, her anger at Olga, whom she saw dining with Jakub earlier, and, most important, her dislike of the look on Jakub's face, especially the irony she sees as always kicking her back where she came from (84), turns her against him and the dogs. Reminiscent of the combat of grimaces in Gombrowicz's *Ferdydurke,* Ruzena sees Jakub's ironic facial expression and, judging him by appearance as he judged her earlier, hates him on sight. She sides with the old men when they attempt to capture a stray dog Jakub holds by the collar, and, as he walks the dog into Richmond House, she shouts, as her father would, that dogs are against the house's rules. Jakub ignores her, making an ironic comment about her carrying a pole with a noose on it, and then, as Kundera describes it, their eyes "clash" with "naked hatred" (84). The contrast of these two themes is very important to an understanding of the book. On the one hand we have the serene color of blue promising a romantic, peaceful retreat from life; on the other we have glances of naked hatred denoting the reality of conflict over rules and the individual right to live. But if as sophisticated readers of literature, we tend to side with the intellectual Jakub here, we have to remember his admonition to Olga about victims and oppressors. He too, given the opportunity, would be cruel.

The following sections of this third day of the narrative raise this contrast of hatred and serene love to a philosophic level that goes beyond looks on characters' faces. In these chapters Bartleff, Skreta, and Jakub discuss issues concerning procreation and man's dominion over the earth. They speak of Jesus and Herod, with Jakub defending Herod, the destroyer of human offspring, as a leader with a reasonable hatred of mankind and the "noblest" motive to free the earth from man's dominion. Clearly Jakub's experience with political imprisonment influences his thinking here, but Bartleff reveals another possible response to oppression by revealing that a jealous lover denounced him to the Gestapo and, flattered, he regarded his consequent imprisonment as the result of passionate love. Surely Bartleff's response is cause for laughter, its inappropriateness a side of his naïve, romantic nature that we will see again, negatively, in later chapters. Yet Kundera intends him to be sincere, his opinion every bit as exaggerated as Jakub's is. Jakub will act cruel, but so will Bartleff, his insistence on the total acceptance of life, including unpleasant and unexpected events, preventing his appreciation of tragedy in human experience. The result is a shallow optimism that lacks pity for human individuals.

When Olga enters this discussion with her own academically earned opinions, she prompts Bartleff to discuss his favorite saints, especially Makarios of Alexandria and Simeon Stylites. He describes their lives as driven by a thirst for admiration and praises that quality as a motivation for human achievement. Whatever Olga, or the reader, thinks of Bartleff's opinion, his interest in holy men and the comparison he makes between them and the achievements of athletes calls to mind Kafka's famous story "A Hunger Artist." In that story the saintly artist starves himself in front of carnival crowds for weeks on end in an effort to break the world record for fasting. But his fame, his feeble nobility, and his Christlike rejection of material life come down to a one-line joke that makes up his last living statement. Asked why he, now a pile of bones and wrinkled flesh almost forgotten beneath the straw of an animal cage, has fasted so devotedly, the Hunger Artist replies that he couldn't help it; he couldn't find the food he liked. If he had found it, he assures us, "I should have made no fuss and stuffed myself like you or anyone else."

Kundera examines the motivations for human achievement with a similar Kafkan view throughout his work and especially in this philosophic discussion. Bartleff, Jakub, and Skreta center on what they see as God's disgust with mankind's failures, a disgust that led Him to cause the Flood. But, as Bartleff sees it, Jesus altered that disgust, suffering and dying on the Cross not for rational, intellectual causes, but because of love: He simply did not wish to see his Father's creation "turn out badly" (94). As a result, Bartleff says, he believes, with Jesus, that it is worthwhile being human.

However, the American philanthropist's thoughts do not end the section, and we should not accept them as Kundera's last word. That more probably occurs after Skreta and Jakub drop off Olga at her room and go for a walk, during which we learn of another scheme to promote humanity and save the world. Skreta tells of a sperm bank he has created in the hopes of making a world of brothers. He asks Jakub to join him in donating sperm so that, even after leaving the country, he will have children at home. As day three ends, Skreta the dreamer perceives a future country, and world, made better ("lovely," he calls it) by benevolent descendants of Jakub and himself. The narrator calls attention to the full moon in the sky at this juncture, bringing to mind the light Klima saw in Bartleff's room at the end of day two and the light Ruzena will see as the fourth day ends. About a land of dreamers, the novel, this part of it at any rate, truly can be called a "Lunar Adventure" and all that name entails. Once again we are in the fantasy world of one of Shakespeare's idylls.

## "Fourth Day"

The next section opens the following morning, in the apartment of Klima and Kamila, as he prepares to drive to the spa to attend the medical meeting with Ruzena and play in the concert with Skreta that night. Not believing he must go, Kamila arranges a day off from work and takes a train to the spa in order to surprise her husband at what she thinks of as his game. The next chapter switches to the spa, where Olga and Ruzena follow their usual routine, one as patient, the other as nurse, until a television crew arrives to shoot footage for the national news. Naked, Olga covers her body while the older women happily prance around in the buff for the camera. Ruzena, young but angry, sides with the older women and the camera crew against Olga, denying her right to privacy by saying the filming is officially approved, saying she disobeys her doctor's orders in leaving the pool too soon, and finally insulting her with a reference to her snobbishness and intellectual rather than physical beauty. The narrator excuses Ruzena's harsh attitude, her despair over her pregnancy and Klima's reluctance to love her forcing her on the side of the older women whose overweight, misshapen bodies prove the lie behind the ideal of feminine beauty. In the next chapter we see another lie as the point of view shifts to Jakub driving the dog he saved back to its owners, who are proprietors of an inn outside of town. They welcome the dog, feed Jakub, and discuss Skreta's work, which they see as miraculous. They have a child with a large nose, like Skreta's, and as the couple discusses the possibility of the latent features of ancestors appearing in their child, Jakub remembers Skreta's sperm bank. Comparing the spa town to Bethlehem, he thinks of the inn owners as a holy family with their son the product not of a mortal father, but a divine physician.

In chapter five of this section Franta, who works as a refrigerator repair-man, leaves his job and drives to the spa to follow Klima. Kundera picks up a theme we have heard before from him when he describes Ruzena's young man as suffering from the inexperience of youth. Again, naïveté causes un-intentional suffering, this time Ruzena's. Franta enters the concert hall to lis-ten to the rehearsal. The narrator describes Franta, in the back of the auditorium, as "turning into a shadow" that will not leave Klima that day (119). That attachment establishes the form of this day's narrative, and it may be useful to emphasize it here. Kundera has developed a pair of romantic axes in *The Farewell Party*—Klima, Kamila, Ruzena, and Franta, romantic and physical characters, on the one side, and Jakub and Olga, intellectual and dispassionate, on the other. Throughout most of this section he alternates points of view between members of these two axes, allowing them to con-verge at various points, particularly in the spa's restaurant where Jakub sees Klima with Ruzena, precipitating the moral crux of the novel's action.

As he awaits Olga, Jakub observes a man at a nearby table. The man hap-pens to be Klima, as we learn in the next chapter. He waits for Ruzena and, when she arrives, the first thing she tells him is that she won't have the abor-tion. In the following chapter Jakub studies them carefully, making a pro-found, but mistaken, moral interpretation of the scene by seeing Klima on the side of life and Ruzena on the side of death. Jakub conceives of her face as pretty but vacuous, the face of a proud executioner whom he has spent his whole life debating, and with poor results. As Ruzena previously saw his ironic expression "kicking her back," Jakub now sees hers as defeating him, accusing him of arrogance. Jakub associates the expression with all he dis-likes about his country, and he reflects with immense relief that tomorrow he will leave it behind.

In chapter nine Kundera switches to Ruzena's point of view again, and he portrays her as caught between two sets of allied, hostile eyes, Jakub's and Klima's. She sees a third set of eyes, Franta's, aiming at her "like the barrels of a gun" (123), and at that point we learn something important: She hasn't been sure whether Klima or Franta is the father of her child. Ruzena *feels* Klima is the father, knows it in an emotional sense because of her idea of the sacredness of motherhood, but she has no logical, rational proof. "Faith" may be the word to best describe her certainty about Klima. She takes one of her blue pills to calm herself and, tragically, sets the plot of her own death in motion. Under Jakub's hostile stare, she places the vial of pills on the res-taurant table, forgetting them when she and Klima leave.

Kundera handles the following scene masterfully. Jakub moves to Klima and Ruzena's table to get a better view of the park, its red-leafed trees compared to a pyre on which he will cast the first part of his life as he drives from the country. He notices the vial of pills, reads the label with an incomprehensible medical name and the prescription "3 X daily." He sees the pills' blue color and shape as almost exactly the same as the "escape" pill he obtained from Skreta, and in melodramatic fashion endeavors to see meaning in the similar appearances. What has Ruzena said? he wonders (not God, not Fate, not even meaningless accident, but what has Ruzena said). That she hates him, that he will still need blue pills, that leaving the country is another form of suicide? Clearly Jakub aggrandizes his exile in the same way Ruzena aggrandizes her pregnancy, forcing him to read too much into this chance occurrence. He opens the vial, takes out a pill, unwraps his own, and compares them, judging his as slightly larger, slightly darker than Ruzena's. He drops them both into the vial, his on top, just as Olga arrives, remarking with great jealously that she has just seen the famous trumpet player Klima with Ruzena. Jakub closes the vial, leaves it on the table, and rises to greet Olga when Ruzena, returning, interrupts them. She reaches for the vial on the table, but Jakub gets to it first. Ruzena demands her medicine. Jakub, caught up in their mutual animosity (and his melodramatic thinking about Ruzena as his country), asks for a favor, saying he takes the same medicine and could use one of the pills now. Ruzena refuses, saying she is not a mobile pharmacy, and grabs for the vial just as Jakub begins to open it. Her lack of charity, along with the accidental, and superficial, mutual hatred with Jakub, leads to her death. When she shouts for her pills and extends her hand, Jakub drops them into her palm.

Kundera works out the aftermath of that fateful exchange through shifting points of view, varied scenes, and an expanding number of players who gradually take in most of the characters of the novel. First we see Jakub wrestling with his conscience as he tries to understand his motivations in allowing the nurse to leave with the poison. Finally, after deciding that deep down he intended harm, he tries to find Ruzena. Meanwhile, she, left alone as Klima attends another rehearsal, enters a rundown restaurant where she meets the television crew and, without knowing her, Klima's wife, Kamila. A playful, somewhat decadent scene occurs as the women flirt and drink with the television crew. The point of view passes from Ruzena to Kamila and back again, with Jakub's moral anguish set in as background. Then Ruzena, with a cameraman's hand on her breast, recognizes Kamila from a picture that she had seen earlier and, in a series of stop action moments of narration made possible by shifting points of view (and Kundera's short chapters) we see her fall from a carefree moment of happiness. She throws the cameraman's hand off her breast; Kamila, the cameraman, the director, and his assistant make fun of her puritanical behavior; and Ruzena, out of her element and feeling the need for calm, reaches for her vial of pills, the first of which, we know, is Jakub's. The chapter ends as she feels a hand take her wrist. It is Jakub, we believe, but as the next short chapter opens, we find that the hand belongs to Bartleff, whose smile and firm grip convince her to drop the vial back into her purse.

The episode that follows carries echoes of the famous inn scenes in *Don Quixote* when the anachronistic knight takes on the soiled realists of his day, sees castles in dining halls, and falls in love forever with Aldonza Lorenzo, the local village girl whom he greets as a glorious lady and renames Dulcinea. Bartleff performs the role of knight errant for Ruzena, transforming the seedy restaurant into a gracious dining room despite the jeering attitude of the television crew. Ordering the best wines and cheeses, receiving excellent, polite service, he joins the company at the table and toasts Ruzena as a queen, a jewel against the provincial background of the town, a "butterfly over a plain of snow" (142). Mocked by the cameraman as overdoing his praise, Bartleff replies with uncharacteristic anger, saying the cameraman yearns to see the same ugliness outside himself that he carries within. When Bartleff offers the toast again, the crew refuse to drink with him. Undaunted, he invites the restaurant proprietor to drink, and he, surprised at first to toast Ruzena, agrees, saying she must be beautiful simply because she sits next to Bartleff. At this point Kamila, the real beauty at the table, laughs, relieving the tension and completing the episode's metamorphosis of Ruzena. The television crew laughs with Kamila, Bartleff toasts once more, and they all drink to "Ruzenka," a nickname of particular endearment. His triumph achieved, Bartleff rises and takes Ruzena with him to Klima's concert. After they leave, the narrative enters Kamila's mind as she realizes with regret that she too must attend the concert. Apparently, for one of the few times in her marriage with Klima she feels the urge for adventure, but, leaving the crew alone, she decides to follow her plan to surprise her husband.

The point of view switches to Jakub as he sits with Olga in the concert hall near Ruzena and Bartleff. Still melodramatic, he imagines that God, in whom he doesn't believe, has placed Ruzena near him to test him about the pill. He resolves to do something to save Ruzena, but she and Bartleff leave in the middle of the concert and he then imagines God not as a merciful tester but a destroyer. The narrative balances these theological ideas with two images of Skreta sitting behind the drums "like a Buddha" as he plays (148), and then switches to Klima's point of view as he watches Ruzena leave while Kamila appears to encourage an encore. He begins one, enduring his own melodramatic interpretation of events: playing trumpet behind his own coffin, the narrative says, Klima closes his eyes, letting "the wheels of fate" roll over him (150).

Kundera devotes the remainder of this speculatively theological fourth day to a variety of human resolutions. As Franta broods, walking back and forth alone in his own nightmarish version of hell—the road before the Richmond House—three couples pass through the night in other forms of symbolic afterlife. Klima and Kamila, suffering, engage in an unacknowledged sexual combat, she attempting to seduce him although she feels no desire, he trying to express love with his body in retreat. Jakub and Olga work through their own contradictions, she seducing him, feeling grownup and mature; he pleased and happy to respond until she utters a lascivious word. And between these two suffering couples Ruzena, in Bartleff's apartment, lies in heavenly ecstacy, seeing a blue glow after having made love with Bartleff. Happy for the first time in her life perhaps, she wonders at the source of the light, thinks it might be from the moon, and, as Bartleff strokes her face, closes her eyes and falls asleep. At the end of this fourth day, as Franta paces before the door of the Richmond House, three men go to bed with women as an act of sacrifice: Bartleff, a variation on the Don Quixote figure, has tried to transform and heal Ruzena; Klima, an Everyman whose story, as Bartleff tells him when they meet, is "the experience of all men who ever lived" (28), has attempted to save his marriage; and Jakub, a timid Raskolnikov, has endeavored to atone for the hell his pill has made for him. All their efforts gain results, but only temporarily.

## "Fifth Day"

The narrative of the final day continues to change points of view with each new chapter as we move from Klima, to Franta, to Ruzena (rising early to go to work), and then to Jakub and the other characters gathered at the spa while Kundera, at a steady pace, concludes his story. We find out that Ruzena has decided to proceed with the abortion, her decision set by her love for Bartleff and the evening she spent with him. We also experience Jakub's relief when he calls Ruzena at the baths the first thing in the morning and finds that she still lives. Remembering the label saying the medicine should be taken three times daily, Jakub assumes that by now she has taken his pill and survived.

But regret mixes with his relief because he realizes that the pill, if not poisonous as he thought, has supplanted, as if with a joke, the tragic sense of his potential suicide, thus changing the tenor and meaning of his past. Then, leaving Olga's apartment for a final walk in the park, he meets Kamila Klima, agrees to walk her to Skreta's office, and, moved by her beauty, experiences a different kind of transformation. About to leave his country for good, he begins to consider Kamila, rather than Ruzena, as representing it and realizes that, swept up with revenge and dissatisfaction in his life, he has never before known beauty. For him, Kamila merges the world of music and art with the red foliage surrounding them as they walk, and he no longer regards the burning landscape as fire or hell but "an ecstacy of beauty" (175) made real by her presence. He tells Kamila that he regrets leaving but must because "I am really no longer here" (175). He prepares to depart his former life as Ruzena is about to leave hers, with a new vision of life's possibilities. Unfortunately for Klima, Kamila has new visions too. When Jakub leaves her at the door to Skreta's building, they stare at each other a long time, underlining the importance of this chance meeting for both of them. Saying goodbye to Olga a few minutes later, Jakub remembers that look and is struck by Olga's shallowness in comparison. Filled with the notion that she has molded her own destiny rather than be a passive victim, Olga views her night with Jakub as "terrific" (178) and misses, according to his thinking, the greater significance of their good-bye. Showing no emotion, she bids him farewell and goes to her daily bath where she will witness Ruzena's death.

Jakub's attitude toward Olga, seemingly more profound, more sensitive than hers toward him, proves as false as his assumptions about the pill he has left in Ruzena's vial. In fact, the very foundation of their relationship lacks truth because, as Jakub tells Skreta just before leaving the spa, Olga's father did not try to save him but voted to jail him instead, knowing he would in all probability suffer execution. What's more, self-sacrifice may not have been Jakub's reason for befriending Olga. As Skreta says, Jakub, like Bartleff's saints, sought admiration. He wanted others to know he was noble enough to befriend the child of a man who voted to murder him. Jakub denies that interpretation (he merely felt sorry for her, he says) but he admits to himself his wish for nobility. Later, driving toward the border of his country, he sees a young boy looking at him through the frames of his eyeglasses as if through bars. In that moment Jakub has another vision of his homeland. From Ruzena's hatefulness and Kamila's beauty, he moves to the idea of the young boy as wearing his prison and thinks his pride and wish for nobility have made him indifferent to the humanity of his countrymen, making him see them all as murderers. Yet his knowledge of the pill he left for Ruzena levels his sense of pride. Ironically, he considers himself a Raskolnikov-like killer, although in name only, with no physical harm to the victim; and, as he drives toward freedom, he thinks, while leaving his past behind, that true nobility lies in "loving people even though they were murderers" (205).

Such easy sentiments would not work for Jakub if he knew the consequences he has left behind him at the spa. Ruzena is already dead as he drives. After appearing before the medical committee with Klima to have the abortion approved, Ruzena meets Franta. With the same faith in feeling that Ruzena has about Klima's paternity, Franta claims the child as his own and refuses to let her give it up. They argue in front of several patients. Franta threatens to kill himself if she aborts the child. Anxious, Ruzena reaches for her vial of blue pills, takes one, and, as Franta looks on, collapses.

In contrast with the serious, ultimately false moments of Jakub's introspection, Kundera turns the reality of Ruzena's death into farcical melodrama. The thistle-thin Olga and the pear-shaped other women, naked and dripping wet, push to look at Ruzena's dead body. Franta throws himself on his knees beside her, calling himself her killer, shouting for the police, and asking to be arrested. The narrative switches briefly to Skreta's office. As the doctor, involved in Jakub's story, tries to remember something he wanted to tell him, his phone rings and he receives a message calling him down to the baths.

Bartleff arrives at the baths just after Skreta and, displaying the same anger he showed at the restaurant the day before, denies Ruzena could have killed herself. She had experienced a wonderful night with him, he says, and describes her in his own romantic terms: an "ordinary girl" who had become "radiant" and full of love (199). Later, rather than let Ruzena's reputation go undefended, he will accept the police inspector's half-joking proposal that he must be her killer. But even Bartleff's dedication to goodness rings a little hollow, since he mourns her loss of reputation and his own idea of their beautiful night more than he mourns her loss of life. Like Olga's ideologically minded father, Bartleff regards principle as more important than individual life, and, by means of Kunderan irony, his attitude aligns perfectly with Jakub's self-serving epiphany about loving a murderer.

Finally, in the book's last chapters the shallowness of Bartleff's feelings becomes clear. As he and Skreta walk to the train station to meet their wives, Bartleff has all but forgotten Ruzena. His evident love of his wife and child turns Ruzena's dreams of happiness with him into tragic self-delusion even as other, perhaps less deserving, hopes for the future come true. Skreta asks Bartleff to adopt him so he can gain American citizenship and travel freely throughout the world. Bartleff agrees, and Kundera narrates the distinctly uncharacteristic happy ending with an ironic joke: As the two men meet their families at the train station, we learn that Bartleff's son has a birthmark on his lip exactly like Skreta's. The "mad" doctor, in all likelihood, will become a brother to his son. The idealistic Bartleff, however, regards the birthmark as a miracle and calls Skreta an angel who has left his "angelic sign" (209).

The novel closes on that ambivalent note. We think of Jakub, traveling in deluded freedom, a killer unknown to himself, and Olga, imprisoned by sickness in her room, aware that Jakub has poisoned Ruzena but feeling a secret pleasure in that knowledge. As the happy Bartleffs and Skretas leave the lamps of the platform behind, they may step into moonglow, but the other characters, including the penitent Klima and the newly free Kamila (already envisioning the end of their unhappy marriage), journey to their separate futures in the dark.

## NOTES

1. *The Art of the Novel* (New York: Grove, 1988) 93–95 passim.
2. *The Farewell Party* (New York: Penquin, 1981) 5. Further references will be noted parenthetically.
3. *The Book of Laughter and Forgetting* (New York: Penquin, 1981) 172.

# CHAPTER SEVEN

# Longing for Paradise: *The Unbearable Lightness of Being*

*That is why man cannot be happy: happiness is the longing for repetition.*
*—The Unbearable Lightness of Being*

The ending of *The Farewell Party,* almost theatrical with its closing emphasis on lights, shadows, and the players walking off the platform into the dark, may remind some readers of the end of *The Tempest,* where Shakespeare, through the character of Prospero, is said to bid farewell to his art. In certain ways the ending of *The Farewell Party* is also a good-bye of sorts: to Czechoslovakia and, according to Peter Kussi, one of Kundera's translators, to Kundera's former style of writing fiction.[1] After this novel he will no longer wear the mask of an anonymous third-person narrator. Instead, Kundera will step forward into the new world as himself, a created, fictional self to be sure, a raconteur, telling stories of the old world as well as the new. That narrative stance begins with the opening paragraphs of *The Book of Laughter and Forgetting,* continues into *The Unbearable Lightness of Being,* and reaches for a new subject and sensibility in *Immortality,* Kundera's first completely Western novel. By the end of *The Farewell Party* Kundera has become like Shakespeare's Prospero, as well as his own character Jakub: Having made his peace (perhaps under false, or painful, circumstances), he is ready to go home, not to Czechoslovakia, but to France, the center of European culture in the Modern Era. With that move he will finally realize for himself the potential for Czech literature that he voiced at the Fourth Writers' Congress in 1967: to move beyond provincialism, to transcend borders instead of guarding them, and to make European culture, not just Czechoslovakia, one of its central targets of concern.

Along with the move to France would come Kundera's new realization of the role the narrative voice could have in his fiction. The character with that voice, an invented Kundera, would be intelligent and rational, like Jakub and Ludvik, but with flaws and weaknesses not usual in narrative personae, especially third-person ones standing in for authors. He would lack knowledge, insight, and power, standing equal with, not superior to, the other characters and the reader. Despite obvious intelligence, despite his acknowledged authorship of the events each novel tells (in *The Book of Laughter and Forgetting,* remember, Kundera confesses that he invented Tamina, a character with a name "no woman has ever had before"), he will not have complete control. Instead, he will puzzle over life as his characters do; and he will, like the reader, try to make sense of the complex personalities, actions, and fates of the characters he creates. In effect, Kundera's concept of the narrator after *The Farewell Party* can be compared to an eighteenth-century deist's concept of God: a clockmaker who sets the world in motion and then, no longer involved, sits back to watch, with a mixture of interest, happiness, and fear, whatever happens next.

In that manner Kundera's personal narrative voice implies human limitations and constantly reminds the audience of a blurred line, or border, that tradition has erected to separate fact from fiction. He can wonder at the actions and antics of the world he sets in motion, musing with the reader over probable outcomes, possible meanings, particular alternatives in parabatic passages (a technique discussed more fully in chapter three) that are at once comic, human, and philosophical, reflecting Kundera's playful yet serious attempt to understand the world we live in through the model of the world he imagines in his story. Storytelling becomes an act of philosophic inquiry, therefore, an attempt, as Kundera has said about novels in *The Unbearable Lightness of Being,* to understand "human life in the trap the world has become."[2] That approach makes the act of narration at least as important as the story itself, turning the aesthetic and thematic spotlight of the novel onto the narrator's mind and voice as well as the characters' actions and fates. Giving himself the role of raconteur, Kundera encourages his readers to understand in the way he does: by sympathizing with the characters, identifying with their experiences and emotions while never losing sight of their true ontological nature. They are people who exist as compilations of words and thoughts—fictions, in other words—who do not die, feel pain, or cry real tears, yet provoke allied feelings in us and, by extension, help the narrator and his reader to better understand the world. Such a technique encourages Kundera's audience to maintain objectivity while urging greater intellectual involvement in his characters' lives. With that goal in mind, a notable aesthetic advance over the impersonal approach practiced in many modern experimental novels, the reader may better appreciate the narrative voices in the novels following *The Farewell Party.* They are voices that, as Peter Kussi has pointed out, essentially take Kundera's career as a novelist in a new direction.

## "Lightness and Weight"

When he begins *The Book of Laughter and Forgetting* with a joke about his country's history (Vladimir Clementis's hat photographed on Gottwald's head), Kundera does so to set the tone of his new novel. It will be historical, philosophic, filled with tragic, often true, events, but at the same time ironic in tone and manner, its power derived from the sense of play in the narrator's thought and tone. In one parabatic passage after another Kundera will undercut our identification with the characters of the story, work to dilute purely political interpretations, and attempt to reason with us about the historical and philosophical meanings of events. Meanwhile, he will move the stories of his fictional characters forward so that we are never quite sure, as we read, whether his interpretations will prove themselves correct or not.

He broadens the narrative perspective enormously in *The Unbearable Lightness of Being,* moving from the relatively narrow confines of twentieth-century Czech history, striking though it may be, to the broader, more airy philosophic issues he originally touched upon in the first "Angels" section of *The Book of Laughter and Forgetting,* where he discusses the necessity of balance between good and evil in human life. In *The Unbearable Lightness of Being* he opens with a comment on Nietzsche and his "mad myth" of eternal return: that all things we experience happen again, not once but infinitely. This idea adds great weight to experience, Kundera tells us, but the inverse also applies: If things happen only once, as we in fact experience them, no matter how serious, tragic, or painful they are, they have no weight and therefore no meaning. From that perspective Kundera can ask the reader to consider a monumental event such as the French Revolution in the same light as a war between two fourteenth-century African kingdoms. The stories of both contain great human suffering and pain, yet we can pass over the horror of such times, even glorify some awful aspects of them (Kundera points to the French historians' admiration for Robespierre, whose inclination to behead his enemies made him one of the most bloodthirsty tyrants in European history) simply because they occur only once.

Proceeding by association, as he did so frequently in *The Book of Laughter and Forgetting,* Kundera introduces an autobiographical anecdote. A short while ago, he tells us, he leafed through a book about Adolf Hitler and, instead of experiencing the horror of those times, found himself nostalgic for his youth. Several members of his family died in German concentration camps, but their suffering is minuscule compared to the loss he felt for his boyhood in the 1930s. Puzzled by that, Kundera goes on to make a point about the transitory nature of our experience; because it happens once, "everything is pardoned in advance . . . everything cynically permitted " (4). But while doing that, he also levels himself with the reader and the characters in his story, saying that all of us, even the narrator, have limitations and no one, including the invented Kundera who "speaks" the words of *The Unbearable Lightness of Being,* can know or understand everything. As a result, this parabatic introduction to the novel has a clear effect: It reminds us once again that we are reading fiction, not fact; it shows a narrator reaching out to his audience on a very human level, as if his listeners (or readers) were a company of thoughtful friends; it encourages us to speculate, along with Kundera himself, on the meaning and nature of his characters' lives in the context of real experience; and it urges us to escape, not *from* the world, but *into* it through an imagined one, the world of the narrator's story. That story functions as a model, and through it Kundera asks us to think about the meaning of human life as he does, in the context of his characters' suffering.

After another parabatic essay on lightness and weight, during which he mentions the division that Parmenides (a Greek philosopher in the sixth century before Christ) made between positive and negative poles, much as Kundera divided the world between angels and devils in *The Book of Laughter and Forgetting,* he goes on to ask which is positive in the division of things between lightness and weight. Parmenides made lightness positive, but like a good rationalist Kundera does not accept that judgment, calling the lightness/weight division the "most ambiguous" (6) one in human life. This philosophic review completed, Kundera continues his discussion as a novelist normally would, through the more concrete forms of characters, action, and fate.

He opens chapter three of this section by introducing Tomas as a character he has thought about for years but has come to "see," or imagine, clearly only during his reflections on the myth of eternal return and the values of lightness and weight. In a scene that Kundera says is a key to his character's life, he sees Tomas staring out his window at a wall, thinking about Tereza. He works as a surgeon in Prague, she as a waitress in a small provincial town. After spending an hour with her some three weeks before this thoughtful moment, Tomas finds himself uncharacteristically wanting her in his life and, more intriguing since it implies a sense of real emotional weight and extra burden, pictures himself dying at her side. He doubts the validity of these feelings, annoyed with himself for not knowing what he wants until he realizes that, experiencing life just once, all human beings find it impossible to know what they want. Dismissing his quandary as nothing, Tomas goes about his business without making a decision until Tereza calls him to say that she has just arrived in Prague.

Tomas agrees to meet her at his apartment the next evening. Thirty-six hours later she enters with Tolstoy's *Anna Karenina* under her arm and, after they make love, Tereza fulfills Tomas's greatest fears: She has no hotel room, so she will have to stay with him, and she has left her bag, a suitcase Tomas imagines as containing her whole life, at the train station. Conceiving of her as a child who, like Moses, has drifted in a basket downstream to enter his life by fate (and chance), Tomas spends nights in his office while Tereza sleeps in his apartment alone. When he finally spends the whole night with her, he feels she has offered her life to him and he cannot let her go. Kundera reflects on the abandoned child as a motif of civilization's important myths, mentioning Oedipus as well as Moses, and ends the chapter with a comment on the "danger" of metaphors. They are not to be trifled with; they can give birth to love, in a sense making the language of life more weighty than the experience.

Kundera provides some background on Tomas's life. Divorced, he has a son whom he has not seen in years, principally because his former wife made meetings difficult and demanded gifts and money in exchange for time with the boy. As a result, Tomas has no family ties, his parents having become sympathetic to his former wife because he gave up his son, and he has developed a series of erotic friendships with women, the most important being an artist named Sabina, who provide him company with no obligations. The rule of threes applies: Tomas sees women three nights in a row and then never again, or he continues their friendship for years but only for meetings at least three weeks apart. Most important, until Tereza brings her suitcase full of fate into his life, he has never slept overnight with any of them. Tomas decides that love asserts itself not in the desire for sex, which might include any number of partners, but shared sleep (or death), which applies to only one. Extending Kundera's rumination on lightness and weight, we can place the desire for sex (Eros) on the side of lightness and the desire for love (shared sleep and death—or its personification, Thanatos) on the side of weight. Lightness implies movement and energy; weight implies stillness and falling. In an interesting combination of those two themes Tomas lives on both sides of the balance by means of his two principal lovers: Sabina, the artist with whom he shares sex and no obligations, and Tereza, with whom he shares love and a desire for rest. Like Klima in *The Farewell Party,* he is both a conservative husband and a rake, a romantic lover as well as a libertine, Everyman as well as Don Juan, one who lives life under the swell of pears as well as the roar of tanks. And once again the world of pears carries the greater weight, the greater emotional significance.

Giving in to his fate, and hers, after two years, Tomas marries Tereza and gives her a puppy, a mongrel with a German shepherd body and a Saint Bernard head whom they call Karenin, after the dull but faithful husband in the book Tereza carried into Tomas's life. The dog takes to Tereza immediately, becoming child and husband to her in an *Oedipus Rex* motif that Kundera will call upon frequently in the novel. The dog also frees Tomas somewhat since he cannot, as he admits, cope with Tereza alone, and it provides an orderly pattern to their daily lives. Tomas still carries on affairs with Sabina and other women, and so Tereza cannot be happy with him until, as Kundera explains, the Russian tanks roll into Prague in August 1968. A staff photographer for a magazine now, she enters the historical moment to record it with pictures that she hands over to Western media. Tomas perceives her to be truly happy for the first time since he has known her, and when she urges that they emigrate to Switzerland after Alexander Dubcek's public humiliation at the hands of Soviet officers, he agrees to go, realizing that despite marriage, Karenin, and his own modest efforts at loving her, Tereza has not been happy with him. He accepts an offer from a hospital in Zurich, and they leave Prague for what seems like a new beginning to life.

But Sabina has gone into exile too, and, although she lives in Geneva rather than Zurich, she and Tomas manage to see each other, affairs without obligation being Tomas's "life-support system" (28). Aware of his continued meetings with other women, Tereza takes Karenin and leaves Switzerland for Prague again, just a half year after their arrival. She leaves Tomas a note, blaming herself for not being strong enough or mature enough to live abroad. Staggered, but happy at first, Tomas revels in his renewed freedom and lightness until three days later the compassion that drew him to her in the first place reasserts itself: "Russian tanks were nothing compared with it" (31). When Tomas tells the director of the Swiss hospital that he must return to Prague, Kundera refers to the famous *Es muss sein* (It must be) theme in Ludwig van Beethoven's last quartet, a phrase that Beethoven introduced as the "difficult" or "weighty" resolution (33) of fate. Following that fate, Tomas leaves Switzerland, and as he drives toward the Czech border, Kundera adds a touch of musical humor to lighten the melancholy note of Tomas's imminent imprisonment. Speaking in his narrative persona, he imagines a cartoon-figure Beethoven, "gloomy, shock-headed," leading a firemen's brass band in a march to the usually somber *Es muss sein* theme. Tomas himself wonders if it really must be—if he has no choice, in other words—but because he cannot test the possible results of either returning to Prague or remaining in exile, he follows his emotions and crosses the border irrevocably. At their apartment in Prague, instead of falling into Tereza's arms, he stands apart and imagines the two of them outdoors, in the snow, shivering. They have not spoken for days, but we learn in the next section, mainly about Tereza's experiences, that she shares this imagined experience with him.

The section ends with Tomas in bed beside Tereza, tortured by the fact that he has returned to Prague despite himself. Thinking about their marriage, he calculates that six chance occurrences, each potentially yielding a different result, brought them together seven years before and became his fate. The story of their love could easily have been otherwise, he concludes, and so could the story of his fate. Tomas lies awake in bed while Tereza snores, his stomach churning because of difficult thoughts.

## "Soul and Body"

Kundera begins the second section of the novel with a parabatic introduction that picks up the theme of the rumbling stomach that closed the previous section. Saying that an author should not even attempt to convince the reader that his characters once existed, he tells us that the German adage he quoted earlier, *"Einmal ist keinmal"* (What happens but once might as well not have happened at all [8]), gave birth to Tomas. He goes on to say that a rumbling stomach gave birth to Tereza and explores the dichotomy between the two characters by returning to the story of Tereza's entrance into Tomas's apartment. She had not eaten since getting on the train in the morning, and that bodily neglect created the hunger that led the compassionate Tomas to take her into his arms, and life, moments after she arrives. So if cultural voices heard through the words and philosophy of an adage speak for Tomas, then the "ventral voices" of the body speak for Tereza. Appropriately, we may say that the world of the mind and the soul gave birth to Tomas, while the world of the body and heart gave birth to Tereza.

Kundera continues the analysis of his two characters with a philosophic discussion. Saying that the "fundamental human experience" (40) of body and soul duality (growing out of a rumbling stomach) gave birth to Tereza, he describes in four very moving paragraphs the progression of humanity's understanding of itself from fear and amazement over the body's separation from the imagined seer, thinker, and believer trapped inside it, through the scientific understanding of the physical self as a collection of technological instruments (the nose, for instance, is a nozzle on a hose taking air into the body), and finally to a linguistic appraisal where naming body parts gives an illusion of understanding and unity. In actuality, Kundera says, the essential mystery of duality remains until a crisis of love (manifested by Tereza's rumbling stomach) exposes the fiction of such scientific thinking.

But we see a third pattern to this human confusion over identity that Tereza represents in *The Unbearable Lightness of Being,* and that is personal history, a theme that Kundera treated thoroughly in *The Book of Laughter and Forgetting.* Here we learn that part of the mystery of Tereza's self, the difficult part, stems from her mother. In a comment that suggests an interpretation without the usual authorial insistence, Kundera says that he "sometimes" feels that Tereza's life merely continues her mother's, as if there were a human fate or theme that crosses the border of generations, fulfilling itself in spite of individual attempts to resist. Tereza's mother, Kundera tells us (and we know this is a fiction, because he has reminded us how the character of Tereza evolved), was a beautiful, vain young woman of the provinces who gave birth to Tereza as a result of a chance pregnancy, settled into an embittered marriage with Tereza's father, and when she noticed signs of age on her face, took up with another man. Downcast, Tereza's father began to speak openly about the faults of the political system, was arrested, tried, and sentenced, and died after a short time in jail. The mother moved in with her lover, gave birth to three more children, and, further embittered by her aging body, sought revenge on her daughter, whom she regards as a "fateful second . . . named Tereza" (44) that has ruined her life. Left alone by an increasingly unfaithful husband, Tereza's mother turned coarse and cynical. Removing Tereza from school so the young girl could take a job, she forces her daughter to tend the children and do housework as well, shaming her with gross displays of her overweight, aging body as well as its "ventral" functions. Yet Tereza aspired for a better life, "something higher," not anchored to the body. She had been the brightest student in her class at school, and now even while working and tending children, she reads constantly—thus the copy of *Anna Karenina* under her arm in Prague—and perceives life with Tomas as a step upward. A surgeon, he views the body objectively, understanding its mechanical parts both inside and out, and yet has the compassion to respond to the emotions it displays. And he too reads. The first time she sees him in the restaurant, he has a book open in front of him. The fact that Tereza hears a Beethoven composition on the radio while serving Tomas confirms her sense of him as representing a higher destiny in her life.

So escape from provincial life for Tereza leads to "fate" in the person of Tomas surrounded by literature, Beethoven, and a journey to Prague. If Tomas reads the events around their love as a scientist obsessed with the mathematics of catastrophe and chance, Tereza reads the same events as an aesthetician obsessed with the search for form. When Tomas speaks to her in the restaurant, Tereza feels the soul within her body ascend "through her blood vessels and pores to show itself to him" in a blush that unifies body and soul (48). When Tomas thinks of the six coincidences that brought him to Tereza, his stomach rumbles to assert its separation from the internal calculator of the odds. Both characters feel their soul's assertion in the body. Tereza's inclinations make her perceive the event as magical, unforgettable, unifying; Tomas, on the other hand, perceives the event scientifically, in terms of accident, with the stomach's rumble affirming body and soul separation. We can say, therefore, that just as Tereza needs Tomas to ascend to a higher level of living, so Tomas needs Tereza to assert unity, beauty, and form in his life. Unlike Freud, Kundera the narrator speaks of an aesthetic dimension to human psychology. People compose their lives, he says, "like music," seeking form, following "laws of beauty even in times of greatest distress" (52).

But even though Tereza possesses unity of body and soul, we soon learn of another division in her experience, the one between night and day, between the life of dreams and the life of reality. Kundera describes Tereza's dreams during her years with Tomas and analyzes them as expressions of an inner search for identity. The most prominent dream has feminist connotations, featuring Tomas in a basket hanging over a pool, forcing naked women to march around the pool while they sing and do occasional kneebends. If one of the women does a poor kneebend, Tomas shoots her. She falls into the water while the rest continue marching and singing. The horror of the dream begins before the first shot, the narrator tells us, commencing immediately with the vision of the naked women and Tereza among them. Nakedness levels the women, especially before Tomas's critical eyes, obliterating their individuality in the same way that nakedness denies the individuality of the sad characters on the nude beach in the final episode of *The Book of Laughter and Forgetting,* and as it denies individuality among the naked women at the baths in *The Farewell Party.* Tereza's dream is a variation on a theme Kundera has touched upon several times, but here he develops it in greater, almost martial, detail. A poor kneebend takes a woman out of lockstep, individualizing her before the background of regimen, and the shot Tomas fires not only confirms but erases that uniqueness as a flaw. The fall into the pool, accompanied by shouts of joy from the marching women, renders her "sameness absolute" and, the narrator says, makes futile Tereza's attempt to make her body "unique, irreplaceable" to Tomas (58).

The dream also becomes Tereza's way of telling Tomas that his affairs with other women deny her individuality, making her the same as they are, even though she reasons during the day that she is, in fact, different and special. Torn by the contrast between her reasonable daytime self and her nightly terrors, she also exposes an impossible division in Tomas's life. He fears that Tereza wants to die, and the fear fills him with guilt. He cannot be both Don Juan and Everyman, libertine and husband. His compassion, a sign of his longing for unity, will not allow it, and at some point he will have to choose. But in certain respects, as with the adult character among adolescents in Witold Gombrowicz's *Ferdydurke,* Tomas really cannot choose because outside forces, such as chance, social roles, and destiny, make the choices for him. Thus, Tomas's retreat from Geneva to Prague, an act of individual compassion, also represents a surrender to unity and fate, or what Kundera might call fate's long aesthetic curve—from Tereza's mother's destiny, to Tereza's, and now his. What's more, the shape of the curve, beautiful though it may be, turns downward, like the plunge of the naked women in Tereza's dream. So it is attractive, powerful, dangerous. No wonder Tomas's stomach rumbles while he lies beside his wife in Prague that night.

The aesthetic dimensions of destiny, its shapeliness and form, lead directly to Sabina, the third important character in this novel and the other important woman in Tomas's life. A painter, she appeals to Tomas's need for beauty, as Tereza does, but not to his need for unity, allowing him the freedom of his Don Juan impulses, placing no claims on him, having other lovers and pursuing her career as an artist by herself. When Tereza first comes to Prague to live with Tomas, Sabina helps her find a job developing and printing photographs on the staff of a magazine. She also instructs Tereza on the principles of graphic art, and Tereza, talented and ambitious, responds rapidly, becoming skilled with the camera, and is soon promoted to staff photographer. But while the two women talk about principles of art, we learn of a technique in Sabina's work that illustrates her own divided vision. All Sabina's paintings, Tereza discovers, illustrate a convergence of two views, one on the surface plane, "an intelligible lie," Sabina calls it, and another, beneath the surface, which she calls "the unintelligible truth" (63). Developing this technique by way of an accidental drip of paint on a realistic paining she did as a student, Sabina has expanded it to encompass a vision controlling all her paintings, exposing the socially (or politically) approved version of life's meaning to the criticism of the mysteries of reality, likely less formed, more chaotic, and certainly less comforting to the ordinary citizen. Her openness to these absurd, threatening views derives from the spontaneity of her artistic nature, and in one very important scene that spontaneity and openness to dual vision play off her relationship with Tereza.

In another variation on the theme of nakedness and individual identity, Tereza visits Sabina's studio to do a series of photographs of her. They discuss Sabina's paintings at first, then, after an hour of taking shots, Tereza asks Sabina to pose in the nude. A gulp, a glass of wine, and a conversation about a bowler hat belonging to Sabina's grandfather follows. Again, we must think of Clementis's hat on the head of Gottwald and Papa Clevis's hat sliding into Passer's grave in *The Book of Laughter and Forgetting*. Both provide humorous touches for solemn situations, both relate to moral borders, both remind the reader of memory and loss, especially lost individuality. In this variation Kundera has Sabina keep the hat on a model head usually meant for wigs, and he reports with humble, arresting details what she tells Tereza about its former owner. Her grandfather was mayor of a small town; he left just two things behind, the bowler hat and a photograph of himself with other dignitaries standing on a platform for some unknown ceremony. With that sketch of her past completed Sabina enters the bathroom to disrobe.

The scene that follows, short, not very graphic, but memorable because of its latent sexuality, becomes more powerful because of the hat preceding it and the horror of the Russian invasion that Kundera introduces immediately afterward. These elements provide a double exposure in words like those Sabina reveals on canvas. But within that double exposure Kundera places another. The camera, he says, is Tereza's eye to see as well as a veil to hide behind. She can observe a portion of Tomas's life by photographing Sabina, and she hides a part of her own by being the photographer. But then Sabina heightens the situation by issuing Tomas's command to "Strip," a seduction technique with which they are both familiar. Sabina takes the camera as Tereza disrobes. In a variation on the Narcissus myth that we have seen before ("Mother" in *The Book of Laughter and Forgetting* and the last scene of *Life Is Elsewhere*), the two women, wife and mistress, become united in their nakedness. Reflecting Tereza's dream, they lose their individuality even as they temporarily and without his presence unify Tomas's life. Their laughter and embarrassment, however, show how impossible that unity would be on a permanent basis. After Sabina takes a couple of pictures, both women laugh at themselves and then get dressed.

From the theme of nakedness and loss of individual identity Kundera moves to loss of national identity by opening the next chapter with the invasion of Russian tanks in August 1968, and the fact that of all the crimes by Russia against its neighbors, the one against Czechoslovakia was the most photographed. Czech cameramen, he says, knew they were the best equipped to record this act of national violence for history. Tereza joins them, passing her undeveloped rolls of film to Western journalists who smuggled them across the border. When she goes to Zurich with Tomas, however, she tries to sell some fifty prints she has left over from the days of the invasion and finds editors no longer interested. They have forgotten the invasion, much as the world might forget the mythical fourteenth-century African war Kundera mentions in the opening paragraphs of the book. One editor is more interested in printing photographs of naked families on a nude beach. Underlining the similarity between lost individuality and national shame, Kundera has Tereza, reminded of her mother's shameless nudity around the house, tell the editor that her pictures of Czechs among the Russian tanks are the same as those of the naked families. Shame, vulnerability, and obscenity are the key similarities here, with loss of identity, public and private, the paramount theme.

Kundera goes on to show us that Tereza's photographs grew out of passion, not for the art of photography, but over her anger at the invasion and the shame it brought to her country. Other subjects do not inspire her. With no need for money, she has little incentive to pursue photography. As a result she feels weak, limited, and when she receives a phone call for Tomas from a woman with a German accent, she feels her weakness doubly exposed by jealousy and decides to return to Czechoslovakia, the country of the weak. Kundera calls her return an example of Tereza's vertigo, which he defines as the "heady, insuperable longing to fall" and "the intoxication of the weak" (76). Tomas, strong, yet too weak to resist her or his compassion for her, then follows her back, as we know. By the end of the second section, a variation on the ending of the first section, Tomas has finally fallen asleep as he lies beside Tereza. She awakens shortly afterward, concerned that he has changed his destiny for her. Something fundamental has altered in this variation. Now Tereza feels responsible for Tomas's life and fate. In the country of the weak, she has become the strong partner in her marriage (much like Kamila Klima at the end of *The Farewell Party*). But, despite the burden of responsibility for Tomas that she now fears, the last paragraph of "Soul and Body" shows a heartened Tereza. She remembers that the church clock struck six just before Tomas walked into the apartment, just as, back in her village some years before, the clock had struck six as she began talking to Tomas after work. Seeing this numerical coincidence as meaningful, Tereza feels confident again because beauty and form have returned to the love of her life.

116

## "Words Misunderstood"

Kundera does five new things in this third, critical, section of *The Unbearable Lightness of Being*. He introduces an important new character, Franz; he turns the focal point of the narrative on Sabina to provide us with yet another variation of viewpoints on his themes (telling us, by the way, that Tereza and Tomas have died in an automobile accident); he introduces an Oedipus motif that has lain dormant in his references to *Anna Karenina* throughout the first two sections (let us not forget that Anna, already in love with Vronski after meeting him at a dance, refers to him as "that officer boy"); he moves the story and his characterization forward by means of a clever narrative technique, "A Short Dictionary of Misunderstood Words"; and, finally, he provides a variation on his thematic linkage of public and private concerns, elements of Tereza's dream being further developed through Franz's political liberalism and the idea of the European Grand March.

The section opens with a description of Geneva and the relationship of Franz and Sabina. Franz works at the university, a professor of philosophy who has spent his life "marching in step"; that is, doing the right thing, with a home, a wife, and a child, supporting the right liberal causes, lecturing, publishing papers, achieving enormous success no matter what he does. In his affair with Sabina he wants to continue that march of correctness, and he works to keep his love for her separate from his family life. As Kundera describes him, he accomplishes this separation out of guilt for having married someone other than Sabina (83), and we come to see that Franz bears a heavy burden of responsibility toward women that limits his freedom and establishes his thematic position within the quartet of lovers now situated at the center of the novel. We learn that, because he felt responsible for his mother's misery after her husband left her, Franz behaves weakly, dutifully, like a good son, toward women, seeking his mother in every woman he loves (90). With that situation Kundera lays bare the Oedipus theme that I see, along with the four lovers, at the heart of the novel. To this point he has pursued the Oedipus theme by means of Tomas and Tereza, with Tereza gradually gaining ascendance in her marriage to Tomas; he has referred to the theme obliquely with Tereza's dream about marching in step (Oedipus's lame foot, from being tied to a stake and abandoned in the woods as an infant, is a sign of his inability to march correctly, or in step); and he continues in this "Words Misunderstood" dictionary by exploring the characters of Franz and Sabina in pointedly Oedipal ways.

Kundera contrasts the two couples in other ways as well, founding a consideration of their characters on the "marching in step" motif that clearly signifies obeying authority, or at least following the rules of the social game. Tereza must march in step, for instance, in order not to be like her mother, while Sabina absolutely cannot. On the other hand, Tomas can't march in step despite his compassion for Tereza, but Franz absolutely must despite his love for Sabina. In fact, Franz's allegiance to what Kundera calls Europe's Grand March, ultimately leading to his death from a violent blow he receives while defending himself in Bangkok, Thailand, is a variation on the theme of Tereza's nightmare—we can see the Grand March as the public, historical version of Tereza's women marching in step. Drawing a further comparison, and another variation on the theme, we can say that in this novel the Grand March compares to the circular dances Kundera described in *The Book of Laughter and Forgetting;* it joins hands (and feet), isolating individuals; it asserts the historically "light" world of tanks over the "heavier" world of pears. As narrator, Kundera says, "It never occurred to [Franz] that . . . the parades he imagined to be reality were nothing but theater, dance, carnival—in other words, a dream" (100).

Kundera explores other motifs of the Oedipus myth in this section, but none more clearly than the idea of blindness. In Sophocles's play, Oedipus, seeking the murderer who has caused the plague in Thebes, consults the blind soothsayer, Tiresias, who experienced life as both a man and a woman and was struck blind by the gods because they were jealous of his knowledge. Ironically, when Oedipus finally discovers that he has caused the plague by killing his father and having children with his mother, he plunges his mother's brooches into his eyes, striking himself blind, choosing punishment for the truth rather than acceptance of the horror the truth contains.

Kundera plays on the idea of chosen blindness in this section, first, in describing Franz's closed eyes while he makes love to Sabina, underlining his blindness to the Oedipal nature of their love. Less obvious, perhaps, is the idea of linguistic blindness, when Kundera offers the dictionary of misunderstood words to explore the gulf of differing visions and experience dividing Franz and Sabina. As a result of this dictionary, really an exploration of attitudes regarding basic life situations, we can also reflect on the differences between Tomas and Tereza that Kundera has explored in the first two sections of the book and from there make comparisons with Franz and Sabina. If Tomas analyzes his return to Tereza as a result of chance occurrences, Tereza perceives it in light of beauty and form ("the birds of fortuity" twittering around her shoulders at the end of part two); if Franz closes his eyes while making love in order to float in the heady space of oblivion, Sabina keeps her eyes open and likes the light of day in order to see—and understand. If Franz sees the private life of books (his world of pears) as false, Sabina sees public life (the world of tanks) as flawed and, in her paintings, attempts to cut through that surface to find an internal meaning. Similarly, if Tomas, as a compassionate surgeon or as a libertine Don Juan, seeks the truth by entering the privacy of other bodies, Tereza has sought it in public through photographing tanks.

Kundera incorporates an aesthetic dimension into his use of blindness by developing Sabina's thoughts about chance and intention in art. First, during a visit to New York with Franz, she sees European cities representing planned, intentional beauty, while America, at least the America she experiences in New York, represents accidental beauty or, as she says, "beauty by mistake" (101). Still, she feels attracted by the city (Franz merely feels homesick), and Kundera further explores the relationship between the aesthetics of chance and intention in the story he tells about the emergence of Sabina's painting style. She discovered her double-layered vision by accident as a student, having painted a realistic scene and, by mistake, dripped some paint from her brush onto the canvas. Perceiving that line of drops metaphorically, she saw them as an incision in the canvas and worked to open the incision further until she laid back the surface plane, revealing another, opposing scene, a second level of reality that belied the first.

That breaking through, by means of a mistake or accident, to another vision of reality mimics exactly the experience of Sophocles's *Oedipus Rex*. At the beginning of the play the audience sees the proud, commanding, public figure of Oedipus; but gradually as Sophocles, an aesthetic surgeon cutting through layer after layer of meaning along the way, moves the plot forward by means of accident, mistaken belief, and then full, ironic display, we come to see a second Oedipus hidden beneath the first: the blind, vulnerable child, as man, stumbling into the future, more susceptible to accident than ever before. The image Sophocles unearths at the end of the play is powerful, disturbing, yet the audience perceives it, in the context of tragic form, as beautiful. Thus we might say that Sophocles, attracted by the randomness he saw in the myth of Oedipus's experience, wrote a controlled, meaningful dissection of his character, a laying back of the public for the private self, combining a history of life's accidents with his own artistic vision. Similarly, Sabina creates meaning, intrigued by the shapely form of paint drops on her canvas. Comparing life to art (and a scientist to a painter), if Tomas, because of his compassion, fails to overcome chance in his life with Tereza, Sabina's artistic objectivity allows her to take advantage of it, pursuing accident further into meaning. Many people read Tomas, because of his intelligence and womanizing traits, as the Kundera surrogate in *The Unbearable Lightness of Being*. But very clearly Sabina functions as the author's persona. Her views on accident, art and society, public and private values, match those Kundera has expressed, and the linkage between her artistic methods and those we perceive of Sophocles in *Oedipus Rex* makes the comparison doubly appropriate, especially when we remember Kundera's beginnings as a playwright and poet.

Kundera explores the Oedipus theme throughout this third section, finally using the motif overtly as an explanation of the demise of love between Franz and Sabina. Before going to Rome with Sabina, Franz tells his wife, Marie-Claude, of his affair, which has been going on for nine months. When Sabina finds out, she regards the public knowledge of their love as a burden, feeling she must now play the *role* of Sabina the mistress rather than be herself. This public role functions as preordained behavior, as if it were written in a script, providing another example of Witold Gombrowicz's aesthetic in Kundera's work.

For Sabina the former privacy of her affair with Franz contained more meaning, more possibility for accident and life, making her time with Franz susceptible to chance and, important for her, choice. Immediately after describing the change in Sabina's attitude, Kundera provides several Oedipal images that haunt the ending of their love. Of course, the nine-month length of the affair has obvious significance; in a sense, a new Franz has to be born. But then, in Rome, Sabina turns off the light in their hotel room when they make love, leaving them both in the dark, or "blind," but with a difference: for Sabina darkness means the "refusal to see, " or choice not to (95); for Franz it means infinity, space without borders, experience without distinctions. Kundera reports Sabina as sickened: "The idea that he was a mature man below and a suckling infant above, that she was therefore having intercourse with a baby, bordered on the disgusting" (116). Immediately after that chapter Kundera moves to Franz's thoughts of his mother, this time as he returns home contemplating the image of her in his wife.

Kundera continues to use the Oedipus motif thereafter, but with some changes. When Sabina leaves Franz, he finds himself abandoned, Marie-Claude having declared their marriage finished, and he moves into his own apartment. Soon he buys his own desk, hires carpenters to build bookshelves and decorate his apartment, and Kundera describes him as grown up at last.

He begins an affair with one of his students. Thus, Kundera presents an inverted image of the Oedipus theme, a variation that, because of their difference in age, we can see as a second layer of the one Sophocles dramatized. But Sabina, though physically absent, has not really left Franz's private world. He thinks of her frequently, conceiving of her as a golden footprint in his life, so that his memory of her is a form of beauty whose shape is yet another variation of the marching in step part of the Oedipus theme.

In the following chapter Kundera switches to Sabina. We find her in Paris now, free but depressed with the burden of the unbearable lightness of her existence. She has spent her life betraying, she thinks, first her father, then her party and her country, and now, without Franz or Tomas, she feels she has nothing more to betray. Moreover, Sabina wonders what purpose her life serves. Is the unbearable lightness of being her one true goal? While thinking those things (after four years in Geneva, three in Paris, Kundera notes), she receives a letter from Tomas's son, Simon, (a name we learn in part six [270]), telling of the deaths of Tomas and Tereza. Simon thinks of Sabina as his father's closest friend, she learns. Moved, she walks to a cemetery, where she wonders at the vanity of the tombstones, some in the form of chapels and houses. Sabina feels depressed by the sight of the stones because to her they mean the living refuse to let the dead get out. Remembering her father's grave with flowers and a tree, their roots yielding a path of escape for the dead, she notes that in Montparnasse Cemetery she sees stone only, and therefore no means of escape, the weight the dead bear being the very antithesis of her life. She pictures Tomas as if he were in one of her double-layered paintings: Don Juan in the foreground but Tristan in the layer of truth beneath the opening. Kundera describes the scene in the painting as like a stage set, reminding us of the double vision of Oedipus Rex, both statesman and the wanderer burdened with guilt. As a result of these reflections, Sabina misses Franz and realizes she will have to move on in order to maintain the freedom, and lightness, of her existence.

At that point Kundera closes the "Words Misunderstood" section by rounding out the story of Franz. Although loving the woman he lives with, he becomes passionate about the plight of Central European countries because of Sabina. He attends lectures and conferences, closing his eyes, Kundera says, in blissful remembrance of his former love. In the dark about Sabina's fate, as well as her emotions and politics, he still shares her search for destiny. Unlike him, however, she wanders, open to chance—and choice—while he follows the drumbeat of Europe's Grand March.

## "Soul and Body"

In his essay "The Structural Study of Myth," the French anthropologist and philosopher Claude Lévi-Strauss compares variations on the myth of Oedipus as they are found in several contexts, including his study of origin stories among tribes of Pueblo Indians in North America and the Oedipus complex of Freudian psychology. Comparing specific elements of the myth such as names of characters, slaying of monsters, and deviations within blood relationships, Lévi-Strauss concludes that the Oedipus story holds in opposition two theories about humanity's origins: whether mankind sprang from the earth like a plant (alluded to when the infant Oedipus is tied to the stake in the forest) or whether humanity is born of itself (so Oedipus begets children by his mother). By contrasting those two origins without necessarily resolving the contradictions, the Oedipus myth offers opposing views of human essence: *Animal or vegetable* is one set of essential possibilities; *born from earth or elsewhere* is another. So the Oedipus story raises fundamental philosophical as well as biological questions about the essence of humanity. In *The Unbearable Lightness of Being* Kundera raises similar concerns, developing the theme of human essence in "Soul and Body" that he treated in another variation in the second section of the novel, also entitled "Soul and Body" and also about Tereza's search for identity.

Along with the philosophical themes of identity and essence, the section raises the political-social issues of privacy and spying, with the modern world likened to a concentration camp, a comparison developed by Kundera to link the political imprisonment of his country by Russia to his ideas about the imprisonment of modern man caused by the pervasive influence and intrusion of the mass media. In Kundera's fiction privacy and isolation make up, in a Parmenides-like social opposition, positive and negative poles of twentieth-century life: one, privacy, is a route to self-definition and possible fulfillment; the other, isolation, is a form of impotence before large historical and social forces. The threatening of either, but particularly privacy, as we have seen in *The Joke, Life Is Elsewhere*, and *The Farewell Party*, diminishes our humanity by increasing the effect of the other. As Kundera says "A concentration camp is the complete obliteration of privacy" (137).

In "Soul and Body" Kundera makes spying the political and social motif of these two human conditions, and he begins by describing Tereza sniffing Tomas's hair while he sleeps for the odor of other women. Generalizing the condition, he also describes Tomas and Tereza listening to the radio and hearing broadcasts by the secret police of Czech dissidents' conversations. Apparently the Czech police tried to embarrass dissidents through these broadcasts, their ordinary conversation reducing them from heroic status by exposing their petty concerns and ambitions. Thus, the secret police publicized privacy, according to Kundera, and he compares the political act to the private again when he calls to mind Tereza's mother. He ties her behavior to her daughter's by describing her as "sniffing" out Tereza's diary and reading it at the dinner table while everyone laughed. On her way to a health spa, Tereza looks at Old Town Hall in Prague, left in shambles after World War II and not yet rebuilt. The scene reminds her of her mother parading her nakedness before her family to show, especially to Tereza, the true misery of the human condition, and she reflects that Prague under the Communist government has done the same thing with its buildings. In that way, she thinks, by exposing its private misery, the whole world becomes a concentration camp.

At the same time, through Kundera's narration we do a bit of spying on our own. We observe Tereza at the health club and in her home, struggling with her identity by looking at her body in the mirror, wondering if she would still be Tereza if she had a different body, a different nose. In the absence of a rational answer Tereza's emotions make a statement for her. Having smelled another woman's presence in Tomas's hair, she cannot control her jealousy, feeling that her body has failed her, as if it were the essence of her identity. She tries to dismiss the notion, but the "hidden seer" inside her provides yet another reaction, and statement, by means of a dream. She dreams of Tomas taking her to a park with red, yellow, and blue benches in it. The park lies at the foot of Petrin Hill in Prague, and Tomas, sitting on one of the benches, tells her she will find what she wants if she walks to the top of the hill. Tereza does and when she reaches the top, she finds men who fulfill people's wishes to die. Carrying rifles, the men escort them through a forest until they find a tree they like. There, the men blindfold them, stand them by the tree, and shoot them. This dream is a variation of the one Tereza had earlier, of course, the element of choice replacing the missed kneebend as a sign of individuality deserving of death. But the dream is also a variation on the Oedipus story, the tree comparable to the stake Oedipus is tied to as an infant, and the blindfold a clear variation on his blindness as a mature man. And Tereza's character has changed as well, her stronger inner character illuminating her dream by allowing her the right of refusal. While in her former dream Tomas had absolute authority over life and death, here she must take responsibility herself. When the men tell her the rules, saying she must have walked up the hill of her own free will and that she herself must choose to die, she tells them someone else made the choice, and they respond by freeing her, saying they cannot kill her under those conditions.

Kundera renders another variation on the Oedipus theme in the next few chapters, when Tereza decides to test herself by going to the apartment of a customer she serves in the bar where she works. She tells herself that Tomas sends her to the man (called "the engineer"), but clearly she wants to try other possibilities, perhaps test her independence, perhaps experience sex without love, which is Tomas's explanation of his affairs outside their marriage. In any case, when she enters the engineer's apartment, she feels great confusion and doubt. But the shelves of books on the walls overcome her hesitancy (she has always thought books imply a higher kind of life). She spots a copy of *Oedipus Rex* and, remembering that Tomas had given her a copy of the play, responds to the engineer when he embraces her. As they undress, however, her soul, Kundera says, resists, even though she feels her body's excitement. Looking at a birthmark just above her pubic hair, she perceives it as her soul's mark on her body, and as the engineer physically enters her, Tereza's soul and body respond in self-contradictory ways. While her sexual excitement mounts, she swings her fists and spits in the engineer's face.

If we think of Josef Stalin's definition of the writer as "an engineer of human souls,"[3] we can see this scene as Tereza's rejection of manipulation, not only by the engineer but by the teller of her story as well. In that light, the various games, sexual, philosophic, and narrative, that Kundera plays throughout *The Unbearable Lightness of Being* come together at this moment, with Tereza rebelling against the man she has sex with, her fate, and the narrator of her fate (Kundera, the object of characters' disdain in *Jacques and His Master*), in order to affirm her soul, her self, and her own version of her destiny. Through the rest of the novel she gradually, sometimes painfully, gains increased independence and strength as her soul asserts its power against her body and the world around her.

Continuing with that theme, the following chapter contains one of those poetic meditations on a taboo that unite the philosophic with the comic in a typically Kunderan way. While Tereza sits in the water closet of the engineer's apartment, Kundera compares the toilet to a white water lily floating on a Venice of defecation, the very image, with its emphasis on beauty and spirit on top of physical waste, bringing together the themes of this section of the novel, Tereza's life, and the Oedipus myth. Becoming absolute body, she voids her bowels and leaves the water closet ready to throw her arms around the engineer in desperation, the way she threw her arms around the tree in her dream, until she hears the engineer's voice and feels her soul reject him. She leaves the apartment immediately. On her walk with Karenin not long afterward, Tereza finds a crow buried up to its head by two young boys. She frees it from the dirt, takes it home, and, laying it on a bed of cloths, stares at the bird as if it were a "reflection of her own fate" (159), that is, soul weighed down by body, or spirit coming from, and limited by, the earth in a variation of the Oedipus theme as Claude Lévi-Strauss interprets it. Completing the motif of soul and body, Tereza keeps "vigil over a dying sister" (160), but when she steps away for a moment to eat (that is to feed the body), she returns to find the crow has died.

The section ends with Tereza and Tomas driving to a country spa they went to some years before and discovering that the names of streets and buildings have been changed to commemorate Russian, rather than Czech, history. On the public, political side of the soul and body theme, we perceive that the Russian names indicate two things for Czechoslovakia: the privacy of its land, or body, has been violated, while its history and language, its soul, have been forced to flee. Parallel to this public experience we see Tereza in some private ones. She realizes that the engineer probably worked for the secret police and that they may have photographed her in bed with the man in order to compromise her and force her to spy. In the final chapter, written as if it were real, although it just as well could be a dream, Tereza walks down to the Vltava River and sees park benches floating by in the water. Remembering that she first spoke in a flirtatious way to Tomas while he sat on a park bench, and that he sat on a bench in her dream when he told her to walk to her death on Petrin Hill, we can see this experience as a sign of Tereza's past, like her country's, flowing away. "What she saw was a farewell," Kundera says (171).

Not completely negative, the dream bids farewell to a part of herself. Something inside Tereza has changed because of her experiences with the engineer, the crow, and Tomas. In addition, a literary inversion has occurred: Vronski no longer controls Anna; Oedipus no longer dominates Jocasta. Since Tomas plays no role in this dream experience, we can say it shows Tereza no longer lives within his power.

## "Lightness and Weight"

This part of the novel returns to Tomas and his perceptions, showing him as much weaker and less weighty than he has been up to this point, an ironic narrative change since the story of this section consists primarily of Tomas's professional and psychological descent, a situation requiring some symbolic weight.

Kundera begins with the story of Tomas's essay about Oedipus's acceptance of guilt for the crimes that destroyed Thebes, although he in fact spent his entire life trying to avoid his fate. Comparing Oedipus to his countrymen, Tomas asks, How could all those people working in the government before Dubcek came to power look on the results of their acts and not feel guilty? He writes an essay, submits it to a journal and has it printed, in abbreviated, oversimplified form, on the "Letters to the Editor" page. The abbreviation offends Tomas, but he says nothing, mainly because he does not regard the issue as important. But after the Russian invasion, the Husak regime, governing Czechoslovakia in place of Dubcek, uses the essay as a reason to attack him after he returns to Prague.

Tomas's friend, the chief surgeon at the hospital, a job Tomas would probably step into upon his friend's retirement, asks Tomas to retract the letter in order to preserve his position. At first Tomas perceives the issue as completely unimportant, but in a classic manifestation of Aristotelian *hubris* he says he cannot make a retraction. He would be ashamed if he did. When the chief surgeon tells him that he would not have to publish a retraction but would simply need to write a note for the government saying he holds nothing against them, Tomas agrees to think it over; but the pitying, commiserating looks of his colleagues signal that they know his situation, and he refuses to write the note. Dismissed against the chief surgeon's better judgment, Tomas becomes a medical functionary dispensing aspirin at a clinic outside of Prague until he meets a man from the Ministry of the Interior who flatters him and tries to elicit information about the editors of the journal that had printed his essay. Tomas names no one, but the man again encourages Tomas to retract the Oedipus essay. He provides a model letter to be published that is more servile and false than the one the chief surgeon had suggested. Tempted, but only momentarily, Tomas promises to think over a possible statement of his own but ultimately refuses, resigning his post and becoming a window washer because he knows that in that lowly position the regime will forget about him and his letter.

In a parabatic comment following this incident, Kundera contemplates the forces in Tomas's life, saying that although Tomas himself interpreted his life's events in terms of chance, Kundera perceives necessity, or *Es muss sein*, in his commitment to medicine, which occurred as a result of compassion and a "deep inner desire" (193) to know that led him to surgery. Making the best of his new work as a window washer, Tomas sees himself as on vacation from his career and resumes his former libertine life, taking advantage of sixteen hours a day without Tereza. Kundera links this libertinism with

Tomas's desire to know the individuality of his lovers, seeking the "millionth part dissimilarity" (199) that separates one woman from another and gives a clue to her *I* (just as Tereza seeks the clue to her *I* by staring at her image in the mirror and by imagining herself with a longer nose). So Tomas's pursuit of women does not stem from a wish for pleasure, Kundera tells us, as much as it comes from his wish to possess the world (200). Such a wish lies very close to the comic desire of Dr. Skreta in *The Farewell Party,* who seeks to populate the world with his illegitimate children. But either wish—Skreta's or Tomas's more serious, philosophic one—must be recognized as impossible and a sign of unreasonable human ambition.

Tomas's pride remains politically neutral, however, and Kundera demonstrates it at work in other directions, not just against governmental intrusion. On one job, when Tomas enters an apartment to wash windows, he finds he knows the people. They are his son, Simon, and the editor of the journal that published his essay on Oedipus. Simon has renounced his mother and her politics and idolizes his father from afar. He and the editor are circulating a petition requesting amnesty for political prisoners in Czechoslovakia, and they have arranged this meeting with Tomas in order to obtain his signature. Tomas, reluctant at first because he thinks the government authorities will use the petition as an excuse to lengthen prisoners' jail terms, almost signs because his son's presence embarrasses him. But before he picks up the pen, Simon compliments the essay on Oedipus, and as they discuss it, Tomas wonders aloud why he wrote it in the first place. He recalls Tereza who, upon entering his life, made him think of abandoned children such as Romulus, Moses, Oedipus, and he remembers that those thoughts prompted the article. Then he envisions Tereza again in a mythlike image of her holding the injured crow against her breast, and, with that picture of her kindness in mind, he refuses his son's political and moral call. He must do nothing to hurt her, he thinks. So when Simon says it is Tomas's duty to sign the petition, he replies that to dig a crow out of the ground is more important. Immediately, he feels a dark, heady excitement, like vertigo, similar to the emotions he felt upon refusing to retract his Oedipus essay. We can call it the emotional and physical equivalent of the downward spiral of his fate. Tomas realizes his career will suffer further, but he also knows he must follow his preferences. He has crossed a watershed once again, and Kundera underlines the occasion by disclosing that later, when the government publishes a slanderous attack on the signers of the petition, Tomas looks at a wall across from his apartment and tries to remember why he did not sign. That moment brings the reader back to the beginning of the novel and Kundera's original conception of Tomas and what we might call the original image of this novel: man facing a wall and trying to understand (6 and 221).

After a meditation about the history of man on earth being a tale of inexperience and lightness—*"Einmal ist Keinmal"* (What happens once might as well not have happened at all [223])—Kundera performs a different variation on the Oedipus theme with another of Tereza's dreams, this one given in her narration. Buried alive, like the crow she saved, Tereza waits until Tomas comes to see her every week. Knocking on the grave to awaken her, he tries to remove the dirt from her eyes after she sits up, but she tells him her eyes are holes, like the eyes of Oedipus after he puts them out. Tomas suggests another month's rest in the grave, but Tereza understands that suggestion as his bid to have a longer time free of her. Miserable as he listens to the dream, Tomas holds her and gradually soothes Tereza to sleep. Imagining himself entering the dream in order to calm her, he comes to a highly personal, torturous understanding of death: Tereza living in nightmares, he not able to bring her back from sleep.

In the following series of passages mixing public and private misery, Kundera narrates the next great step in Tomas's fateful downward spiral. He attends a funeral, seeing the mourners filmed by police and, back home, becomes physically ill with a stomach ailment as he tells Tereza about it. They both say how spiritually and physically ugly Prague has become, and Tereza suggests they move to the country to escape it. Tomas agrees, although he realizes that a rural life will effectively end his pursuit of women. But if he could give up surgery, he realizes, he can certainly give up women, the other necessity of his life (234). Completing the role reversal hinted at in the progress of Tereza's dreams, she comforts him as he tries to sleep despite his stomachache.

In a parabatic meditation that follows, Kundera discusses the difference between love and sex, calling sex a mechanism invented by God to amuse himself, while love, he says, remains a human trait, something beyond our *Es muss sein*. In a dream Tomas meets a woman who, in a bland and undefined way, seems perfect for him. If he were to live in paradise, he thinks, he would have to live with her; in fact, she would be what Kundera calls the *Es muss sein* of his love. Tomas ponders the conflicting demands of two classical myths of necessity—the one from Plato's *Symposium* about the lover compulsively seeking his other half, and the biblical one about the abandoned child who, like Moses, comes floating into one's life in need of care. Awake from the dream, Tomas realizes that he would abandon the perfect other half of himself for Tereza no matter how many times the choice arose. Beyond experiment, his love and his compassion would force him to follow her. As he thinks of these things, Tereza stirs and half in a dream asks what he is staring at. In fact, Tomas looks at Tereza, but he tells her they are in a plane and he is gazing at the stars. Satisfied, she sleeps again, an accident of stars having become his fate, his constellation, his astrological destiny. It is a lovely moment, resonating with romance and poetic lightness, but we must not forget that they fly in a plane and, even in a dream, what goes up must inevitably, humanly, return to earth again.

## "The Grand March"

Almost entirely parabatic, "The Grand March" concerns Kundera's discussion of kitsch and his playful use of the term as a metaphor for certain kinds of ideas, social causes, and memories. Primarily he discusses the lies we tell ourselves about life and its meaning, especially as we try to deny the limitations and demands of the body to follow higher, "lighter" principles, or ideals. As a result, the "Grand March" of Europe that Kundera relates to kitsch, referring to the history of political and social events that have motivated human beings to band together in a group (or form circular dances, as in *The Book of Laughter and Forgetting*), becomes a metaphor for social and intellectual exclusion banning individuals as well as individualistic thinking. As a political formula the Grand March requires good intentions (it is the "march from revolution to revolution, from struggle to struggle, ever onward"[99]), along with narrowness of perception, an unwillingness to accept alternate views of reality, and a need to see things only in optimistic terms. Needless to say, in aesthetic and moral matters kitsch requires similar limitations. So Kundera, keeping to his image of the commode as a white lily floating above a sewer, opens the "Grand March" segment with a story about the bowel habits of Stalin's son, Yakov, and the embarrassment over them that led to his suicide in a concentration camp during World War II. Referring to Yakov Stalin's death as the "sole metaphysical" one of the war (apparently because it was due to his soul's shame over the behavior of the body), Kundera uses the suicide as a foundation for a broad philosophic discussion, eventually centering on kitsch, a system of values that he defines as an "absolute denial of shit," allowing us to praise life and, in a religious sense, express our "categorical agreement" with God's creation (248).

In his discussion Kundera targets theologians generally, followers of social causes on the right and the left, and, most of all, politicians and media personalities in search of attention as he develops the subject of kitsch along with the background of Franz's participation in an international protest march to Cambodia. Referring to kitsch as the realm where the "dictatorship of the heart reigns supreme" (250) over reason, Kundera fills the "Grand March" section of the novel with events that belie its optimistic title. In addition to Yakov Stalin's death at the beginning, we learn about Franz's useless, violent murder in Bangkok after the march accomplishes nothing but a few publicity photos, the accident that kills Tomas and Tereza, and Sabina's aging, lonely trek westward to California where, resigned to her rootless end, she draws up a will asking to be cremated and have her ashes tossed to the winds.

By contrast, we read of the triumph of Marie-Claude, Franz's estranged wife, who welcomes her husband's return and plays the grieving, forgiving widow before a credulous Parisian society. The section ends with an ironic coupling of kitschy epitaphs: Of his father, Tomas, the religious Simon writes, "He wanted the kingdom of God on earth," while Marie-Claude composes for Franz, "A return after long wanderings."

In a world that reduces complex events to simple, catchy images—Beethoven's frown of genius, a photo of an actress (or politician) lovingly embracing an Asian child—such epitaphs carry the ring of appropriateness, but certainly not truth. In a civilization that obsessively denies death and the waste of the body, Kundera tells us, kitsch is an oasis in the desert of memory, a brief, illusory rest stop on the journey we all take toward oblivion.

## "Karenin's Smile"

In this novel, as well as in *Immortality* and *The Book of Laughter and Forgetting,* Kundera explores storytelling as a function of self-definition; personality becomes a manifestation of storytelling (rather than vice versa) and, by extension, the character of humanity in general becomes an expression of the stories of ancient myth and their residual variations in the practices, ideas, and stories of modern life. Thus, the classical theatrical device of parabasis influences Kundera's form, while structuralism in general, with particular reference to Lévi-Strauss's "The Structural Study of Myth," underpins the intellectual, thematic content. As a result *The Unbearable Lightness of Being* contains playful commentary on human behavior through such devices as "A Short Dictionary of Misunderstood Words" (Part Three), encyclopedic definitions and discussions of philosophic ideas (Part One) and cultural concepts such as kitsch and the Grand March (Part Six).

Having taken care of human concerns (while disposing, briefly and casually, of the lives and destinies of the four major characters), Kundera moves to animal life in the final section and writes about it in a way that loses none of the seriousness or wit of the previous pages. In so doing, he hints at an animal's conception of man (the cow parasite, as Tereza imagines it) and discusses from that point of view the injustice in man's biblical claim to dominion over animals. As a result, the major emotional event—and climax—of this section becomes the illness and death of Karenin, Tereza's dog, while in a turnabout of the usual narrative logic Kundera merely hints at the tragic accident ending Tomas and Tereza's existence.

He performs this inversion for several reasons. First, he provides a happy ending to the love story of Tomas and Tereza, having put their deaths somewhere off in the distant, unknowable future; second, he subverts the man-centered notion of existence by investing importance and emotion in the loss of an animal; and, third, through Karenin he confronts the fragility of bodily existence and the inability of the human mind to accept death of the body as an end for the mind and spirit as well.

At the same time Karenin embodies some of the thematic notions of *The Unbearable Lightness of Being,* alternately living as male and female, like the soothsayer Tiresias in the Oedipus myth. In addition to those mythic variations, Kundera humanizes the dog's ordinary, daily character, portraying him as a happy and central part of village life. Also, while narrating Karenin's death, Kundera elevates our conception of him to rather noble heights: (1) we see him diseased with cancer, operated on, and then revived, waking in the middle of the night with full joy at having been reborn; (2) we are moved that Karenin, apparently in pain, still walks with Tereza and Tomas to make them happy; (3) we witness his continued decline and can contrast Tereza's tearful sense of loss with the local farm woman's pragmatic attitude about animals; and (4) we sympathize, with a bit of ironic distance, when Tomas and Tereza argue about Karenin's death in the same way they would a human's.

To be sure, Kundera places some larger intellectual context around Karenin's death, discussing in extended passages of parabasis human beings and their relation to animals. He writes about Descartes's naming of humanity as "master and proprietor over nature" (288), coupling it with the fact, as we have read already in *The Farewell Party,* that after the Russian invasion, Czech Communists, in an act of civic kitsch, ordered all stray dogs killed in order to keep streets clean. After that litany of human egocentrism and cruelty, Kundera says, "Mankind's true moral test . . . consists of its attitude towards those who are at its mercy: animals" (289). He continues in that vein, commenting that he loves Tereza when he thinks of her with Karenin, because she reminds him of the time Nietzsche threw his arms around the neck of a beaten horse. In their sympathy for animals both Tereza and Nietzsche step aside from the road mankind normally follows in yet another Grand March toward progress, toward some unknown but eagerly anticipated future.

From that comment, with its implied criticism of change, Kundera meditates on an opposite obsession, the idyll, a perfect, unchanging condition that he defines as monotony breeding happiness instead of boredom. Humans, who live in the hope of improving life's conditions, need change; yet at the same time they long for stasis, a preeminent condition in one of the envisioned ends of human life: paradise, or heaven.

"The longing for Paradise is man's longing not to be man," Kundera says (296), using that sentence as a transition to discuss the life that Tomas and Tereza lead after abandoning Prague for the country. Karenin, completely at home there, revels in daily repetition, and Tereza realizes that, now more used to repetition herself, she could tolerate her mother more easily here than in Prague simply because she would no longer want to improve her and would no longer fear being like her. But even in the country this idyll evolves. Karenin's cancer returns, and in a moving, delicately written scene Tomas puts him to death with an injection. Burying him in their garden beneath two apple trees, Tomas and Tereza give Karenin an epitaph that reflects a dream Tereza had about the dog: *"Here lies Karenin. He gave birth to two rolls and a bee"* (303). The two rolls refer to the game Tomas and Karenin repeated each idyllic morning of their country life, the bee to the inevitable yet dreaded idyll, the sting of death.

The emotional climax of the novel reached (and with the emotion of the death of Tomas and Tereza denied us), Kundera winds his story down, preparing for a dissonant ending with a veneer of resolution and harmony. After Karenin's burial Tereza dreams of death in a recapitulation of most of the dreams in the novel: Tomas receives a letter summoning him to the airfield of a neighboring town. Horrified, she leaves for the airfield with him; they board a plane, fly through clouds for a short while, and land. As they descend from the plane, two hooded men with rifles await them. One raises his rifle and aims. Tomas slumps over, dead; Tereza, ready to fling herself on top of him, sees that Tomas's body is shrinking before her eyes. In quick order, he transforms into a rabbit, the men chase and catch it, returning it to Tereza. She finds herself walking through Prague, where she reaches the apartment she lived in as a child with her parents. She enters, taking the rabbit to the room she occupied as a girl. There a lamp burns, as if awaiting her. On the lamp sits a butterfly, its wings outspread, with two large eyes painted on them. "Tereza knew she was at her goal" (306), Kundera says, underlining the idea of repetition in her return. But she has progressed personally as well, at least in her dreams, for she has Tomas under control and can love him better ("Better, not bigger") because she thinks the "love of man and woman is a priori inferior" to love between humans and animals (297). Lying on the bed, Tereza presses the rabbit to her, and we see in the childish, fairy tale image another variation of the Oedipus theme.

In the final chapter of the book Tereza sees Tomas as an aging man and, with a tinge of regret and guilt at the change, feels responsible. Her weakness, "aggressive" weakness, Kundera calls it (310) has destroyed his strength, effectively turning him into a rabbit. They descended from the heights of his profession, Tereza thinks, to make him prove his love. But that night, at a country dance some distance from their home, while Tereza voices her doubts, Tomas reassures her by saying that he, no longer Don Juan but Everyman, feels happy. More important, perhaps, he also feels "free, free of all missions" (313) at last. In their room that night, the last that they will spend together since we know they will die next day on the road homeward, they see a butterfly ascend from the lampshade and hear the sounds of music from the dance hall beneath them. Another lovely moment: The spirit ascends while the music of death sounds from below.

The moth in flight is lightness weighed down by death; the music is heaviness, or fate, lifted by art. If we perceive the music as form, we can interpret the moth as content. Art and nature: they comprise the possibilities as well as the limits, as Kundera sees them, of the joys and sadness of the human condition.

## NOTES

1. Peter Kussi, "Essays on the Fiction of Milan Kundera," PhD. Diss:, Columbia University, 1978 (Ann Arbor: UMI, 1978; 7819373) 162–63.

2. *The Unbearable Lightness of Being* (New York: Harper, 1984) 298. Further references will be noted parenthetically.

3. See Josef Skvorecky, *The Engineer of Human Souls* (New York: Knopf, 1984). The acknowledgments page says that, according to political indoctrinators, "As an engineer constructs a machine, so must a writer construct the mind of the New Man." The New Man is the Stalinist Man.

# CHAPTER EIGHT

# The Possibilities of Human Existence:
## *Immortality*

*The basis of the self is not thought but suffering, which is the most fundamental of all feelings.*

—*Immortality*

Kundera's frequent use of parabatic passages serves to remind us not only of the many types of fiction that concern him, but the many types of truth as well: the ordered truth of novels and short stories; the manipulated truth of historical and political language; and, most worrisome, the mysterious truth of self that humans constantly work to solidify, and clarify, into language only to have it undermined, in a Kafkan, Gombrowicz-like manner, by the accidents of history, gesture, and external event. In the two masterpieces of his post-Czechoslovakian period of writing, *The Book of Laughter and Forgetting* and *The Unbearable Lightness of Being,* and in his latest novel, *Immortality,* Kundera explores storytelling as one means of self-definition, using his own voice and life as narrative conceits, freely mixing fact and imagination until the novelist's own character and opinion become as much of the imagined texture of the work as the characters he has created on the page. If *The Unbearable Lightness of Being* is a modern love story, perhaps two love stories, told against the background of classical myth and contemporary experience, it is also an author's very personal meditation on the crossed purposes of historical destiny and individual desire, along with the influence of creativity on the individual's fate. In the same way, *The Book of Laughter and Forgetting* recounts not only the struggle for personal freedom against ideological tyranny on both sides of the Iron Curtain, but also Kundera's own attempts to understand himself and the forces that molded him into the man (and writer) he has become. In a sense, therefore, it can be said that in his novels Milan Kundera is exploring self as well as world.

In that self-exploration his special ironic sense of humor joins some of the darkest questions about existence with the frivolous, ignominious side of human behavior. In particular we may think of his satirical portrait of Czech writers in "Litost," the fifth part of *The Book of Laughter and Forgetting,* or his confession, in the first "Angels" story of the same book, that he felt the urge to rape a woman editor. We can frown on that latter scene, wonder if it is true, and despise the character of the man Kundera portrays himself to be as well as the embarrassment he causes in writing so intimately about a friend who helped him. But we must also admire the courage of the novelist who dared to admit his frailty, include it in his story, using himself as an example of just how low "the possibilities of human existence" can sink. In this incident Milan Kundera is the example of base human possibilities; and human character, not the Czech Communist Party, is one of the world's primary evils.

In that same challenging mode, but with a lighter, perhaps less savage touch, *Immortality* continues the investigations of the earlier novels, linking up with Kundera's first exploration of the relation between creativity and politics, *Life Is Elsewhere,* as well as the contrast between public form and private feeling demonstrated by the characters of *The Farewell Party.* In *Immortality* the provincial spa becomes a health club, most likely at the top of the Montparnasse Tower in Paris, while the issues of birth and death receive the same philosophic analysis of his earlier novels, although this time in relation to Parisians, not Czechs, caught in the trap of love problems and mid-career crises. Part of the novel's humor derives from the persona of Kundera himself, stepping on the stage once again, but this time to act as well as deliver parabatic asides. Where before he told stories (presumably true ones) about himself, letting autobiography mingle with fiction thematically, in *Immortality* he himself mingles with the fiction in the person of his created characters, especially Professor Avenarius, named after a German positivist philosopher of the nineteenth century.[1] This character functions as Kundera's metaphoric link between the two mirrored worlds of fiction he has created in this novel: the "real" world of Paris inhabited by the character Milan Kundera, whom we listen to and read about on the page, and the "fictional" Paris (within that other "real" Paris) narrated by the Kundera existing in the story as well as the one who, living and breathing in "reality" with the reader, sits at his computer and, presumably, punches keys.

In addition to that bit of fictional gamesmanship, Kundera narrates *Immortality* against the background of the biography of a famous lover and writer of love stories, Johann Wolfgang von Goethe, whose career and experience may be said to have marked the transition between the traditional European world and our modern age, the epoch marked by the anti-heroic characters and absurdist style of *Immortality.* Goethe had romantic as well as classical leanings; he wrote poems, plays, and novels as well as scientific treatises; he embraced the classical harmony of the Mediterranean in his later years despite a Northern (perhaps Gothic) European temperament in his youth. The quintessential eighteenth- and nineteenth-century literary artist as well as politician, Goethe possessed at the same time a self-centered artist's egotism and a healthy respect for the people of his time who served in public life. With such a broad range of interests and character traits he represents European culture, especially European culture of the Modern Era, more than any other historic figure; and in placing Goethe's personality, streamlined and simplified, to be sure, at the center of *Immortality,* Kundera makes clear that he aims at a criticism of contemporary life, and of the place of literature and the literary artist in that life. Thus his latest novel presents analyses of twentieth-century media, modern love, the idea of truth in media as well as literature, and above (or beneath) them all, the limned figure of Kundera himself, the contemporary novelist making, or trying to make, sense of it all through his storytelling and the game he plays of interspersing historic reality with the fancy of fiction and comic books.

## "The Face"

The novel begins with an anecdote about its sources, an experience that, Kundera as narrator tells us, inspired his conception of the principal character, Agnes, and led him to the obsession that became this book. He sat in a deck chair at his health club, observing the people in the pool while awaiting a friend, Professor Avenarius. His friend being late, Kundera observed a woman, sixty or sixty-five years old, taking swimming lessons from the club lifeguard. She grasped the edge of the pool and, breathing in and out, created the "idyllic sound," Kundera calls it, of a steam engine[2] while her comically earnest motions charmed and captivated him. But an acquaintance began talking to him, and by the time Kundera turned to observe the woman again, he saw that the lesson had ended. She walked around the pool, passed the lifeguard, then turned and waved to the young man, the gesture moving Kundera with its mixture of charm and pathos because the woman's movement and her smile had the stamp of a twenty-year-old. The young lifeguard laughed, while Kundera felt a pang in his heart because somehow the woman's gesture lived outside the time so evident in her body. Some part of ourselves, our essence, our being, "lives outside of time," he offers as explanation, and we remember our age "only at exceptional moments" (4) of awareness, otherwise existing in an ageless realm of gestures. Moved by these thoughts, intimations of the novel *Immortality* we might call them, Kundera tells us that the word "Agnes" entered his mind, even though he never knew a woman by that name.

He provides a second incident accounting for the genesis of the novel in the next chapter. Mixing the realities of Paris life with the invented city of this book, Kundera delivers Agnes as a dramatic character instead of just a name and provides some details of her daily existence. Yet he begins by describing an ordinary (imagined) morning of his own: Kundera lies in bed, passing in and out of wakefulness and dream while listening to a pair of radio announcers chatter about themselves, the weather, and some recent French medical scandal in between the music and song of their station's advertisements. Drifting into sleep, Kundera dreams he attends an opera where two tenors sing about the weather and a choir of women celebrate a sale of furs. He wakes, turns the dial, hears other voices chatter about themselves, the weather, and some recent scandal and feels happy (ironically) that all the stations have people saying the same things at the same time. With the themes of drama, human repetitiousness, and public self-consciousness established, Kundera adds the key topic of an author as public figure. The announcers discuss a new biography of Hemingway that accuses the novelist of lying about his war wounds and sexual exploits. Further blending fiction and biography, Kundera tells us finally that he awakens fully at eight-thirty and immediately thinks of Agnes, whom he imagines lying in bed "sweetly swinging," as he does, between life and dreams (6). Asking who Agnes is, he lists a few details of her life—a husband who has left early on a Saturday morning; a daughter who sleeps in another room and whom Agnes, for some reason, avoids seeing; a planned day full of chores she does not really enjoy. And he also reminds us that she sprang from the gesture of the woman at the pool whose smile and wave moved him to nostalgia, giving birth to the Agnes of his imagination.

Pondering the meaning of that birth, Kundera wonders how the gestures of one woman can metamorphose into those of another. Are not people, especially fictional ones, individual, inimitable, he wonders, and then he answers himself by saying that with eighty billion people on earth it is impossible that each have unique, individual gestures. Mathematically, therefore, gestures in and of themselves must have more originality than human individuals. He adds that we cannot consider a gesture as the expression or creation of an individual; rather, the gestures create us, making us their "bearers and incarnations" (7). With that musing complete, Kundera describes the rest of Agnes's time at home. She leaves her apartment, duels with a stuck elevator, walks down the steps to her car, and begins her day. It is an ordinary Saturday, but one with a certain pull in Agnes's life: five years ago today her father died, and she remembers him, alive, in a particularly difficult moment. He sits before a pile of photographs that he has torn. Most contain his wife's image. Agnes's sister shouts at him for tearing the photographs, but Agnes defends him. The sisters quarrel in a rush of intense hatred, Kundera says, but he does not report their words. Instead, he ends the chapter with Agnes, in the present, entering her car.

The next few chapters take us through Agnes's Saturday, with the roar of her automobile's engine commencing a chorus of grating, almost operatic, city sounds, scenes of pressing, steamy bodies, and alienated, empty faces, with mouths agape, forming a nightmare vision of modern urban life that Agnes travels through with intense distaste. She enters her health club, presumably the same one where Kundera saw Agnes's prototype, endures a crowded sauna filled with overweight women and loud rock music, listens to one woman passionately (and comically) proclaim her need for steam, her detestation of modesty, and her love of cold showers. After a swim Agnes enters the streets again, the cacophony of traffic and jackhammers combining with the press of crowded sidewalks and fast-food restaurants to make her wish for the deaths of two strangers and admit to herself that she no longer loves her world. Throughout this difficult day she continually returns to thoughts of her father, his gentle, retiring character operating as an antidote of sorts to the aggressive, assertive habits of Paris. During her ruminations we learn that Agnes's father separated himself from his wife and daughters by spending most of his time in his study, and that after his wife's untimely death he arranged to live alone in an apartment. Agnes now sees that apartment as her father's lifelong dream, an expression of his intense desire for solitude, and she realizes that now, after years of her own marriage and family, she shares his desire to live alone, his wish for quiet and privacy, his dislike of being too close to other human bodies.

We also learn of her father's love of Goethe's poetry, an idea that provides transition to the second part of the novel, the section entitled "Immortality," which introduces Goethe as a character. For years Agnes has dreamed of returning to Switzerland to live alone and has actually looked at apartments she might rent or buy. Secretly, her father left her most of his money when he died, and she has taken his gift as a sign that he understood her preferences to be like his. As a result, he has become a "seductive voice" (29), Kundera says, intruding upon Agnes's marriage from the past and inviting her to join him in his world of solitude. After a short chapter about the similarity of human faces, and a conversation about those faces between Agnes and Paul, her husband, Kundera intrudes on the narrative with yet another parabatic aside, this time describing himself as he writes about Agnes. He tries to imagine her, he says, and so he sends her through her day: at the health club, in the streets of Paris, at home leafing through a magazine. He reminds us that he has not yet spoken of the elderly woman's gesture that gave birth to Agnes, and he reassures us that he has not forgotten it. Agnes has not used the gesture for years, he tells us by way of explanation. In fact, the wave and smile formed part of her behavior as a young girl, and Kundera recounts an experience at sixteen with a young boy when, after a couple of awkward attempts at kisses, they walk home. She, in her mixture of disappointment and compassion over his timidity, walks away from the boy, turns, smiles, and, as if she were the woman Kundera saw at his club pool, waves good-night, her right arm moving lightly, "as if she were tossing a brightly colored ball" (36).

Kundera works further back in Agnes's life, saying that she observed a forty-year-old woman wave that way to her father when she was younger. Agnes knows little about the woman, except that she was her father's departmental secretary and that she caused tension whenever she visited him at the family home. But the woman's wave of good-bye to her father, which Agnes saw just once, affected her deeply, awakening a feeling very much like the one Kundera experienced upon seeing it at the pool. He does not know how long the gesture kept "using" Agnes, as Kundera puts it, but when she saw her younger sister wave with the same motion while bidding a girlfriend good-bye, Agnes stopped it herself. And in fact she began to distrust all gestures in order to hold on to her sense of self. Finally, visiting her sick father she feels a strong desire to say something important as she leaves. Not able to find the words, she walks to her car, turns, and, smiling, raises her arm in the wave she used to bid good-night as a sixteen-year-old. At that moment Agnes puts herself in the departmental secretary's place and thinks that she and the secretary may be the only women her father ever loved. So the gesture, like the tossing of a brightly colored ball, speaks a moment of sweetness and regret (in youth and age), of love and friendship, of a parting with acknowledged but unmentioned importance, a moment of emotion not quite fulfilled.

Part One ends with Agnes and Paul home from their dinner party, Agnes feeling increasingly isolated from "two-legged creatures with a head on their shoulders and a mouth in their face" (39). Unable to sleep, she fantasizes that a man from another planet pays them a visit. The man represents another world or life and, in Agnes's fantasy, offers another possible fate for her. He informs Paul and Agnes that faces exist only on the planet Earth and that in the opinion of beings of other worlds life on Earth is horrible. He tells them that they will not return to Earth in the next life and asks if they want to remain together or never meet again. After some hesitation Agnes gathers the courage to reveal her feelings: they never want to meet again, she says, speaking for both of them. Kundera describes her response as "the click of a door shutting on the illusion of love" (42); the illusion is that love can last forever.

## "Immortality"

With the introduction of Goethe's poem and the description of Agnes's fantasy about the visitor from another planet, Kundera has cleared the way for the new subject matter and themes of Part Two: biographical material concerning a woman in Goethe's life and the two principal meanings of the word that give this book its title. While "immortality" primarily denotes everlasting life or existence, Kundera possesses too much twentieth-century doubt to take that meaning literally, and so the word's secondary meaning—everlasting fame with implications concerning memory, nostalgia, storytelling (fictional or nonfictional), and, ultimately, human culture—concerns him more. While the spiritual connotation of the word resonates throughout the novel, especially with the narrative's sad, Zenlike sense of the emptiness beneath human gesture and the cartoonlike fantasy conversations between Goethe and Hemingway, Kundera retains the quintessential European novelist's concern for the issues of real human life. Thus, "immortality" 's secondary meaning of fame and memory eradicates the primary afterlife sense, with fame and memory existing as ironic, problematic throwbacks to an essentially outmoded religious concept.

But as if they too were merely gestures, fame and memory provide implications of unspoken meaning that, upon closer inspection, as with the wave of the arm that reminds Kundera of someone tossing a colorful ball, really denies individuality. Here Kundera, like Witold Gombrowicz in *Ferdydurke*, emphasizes the general, external formulation for motivation in behavior, thereby denying originality and power of human intentions. In other words, as Kundera ponders the smile and peculiar toss of the arm that moved from the woman at the pool to his character Agnes, back to her father's departmental secretary and Agnes's sister, the gesture proves to be more individual, and immortal, than the women using it. In fact, "it is gestures that use us as their instruments" (7) rather than vice versa, and with his idea of a finite universe of gestures expressing themselves through a limitless number of human bodies, Kundera can introduce us to this section entitled "Immortality," a world of historical fact, gossip, and fabulation, so that he can speculate on the nature of fame and its relation to the contradictory human need (as with Agnes and her father) for privacy and retreat.

The section begins in history, September 1811 to be precise, when a young poet and writer, Bettina Brentano, newly married but infatuated with Goethe, visits the aging poet with her husband and stays with him and his wife for several weeks. The visit ends badly when, at an art exhibit, Bettina and Goethe's wife, Christiane, a loyal but uneducated woman, argue about the quality of the paintings. Christiane, upset that Bettina has contradicted Goethe's opinion about the paintings, and more upset because she has flirted with Goethe despite her new marriage and the great difference in their ages, swipes Bettina's glasses from her nose. Naturally the incident ruffles everyone's feelings, and when Goethe hears about it, he bans Bettina and her husband from his home. The episode, small but famous in the poet's biography, concludes with Bettina's comment. Calling Christiane a "fat sausage," she says that Goethe's wife "went crazy and bit" her. Kundera calls the remark immortal. Referring to the word's secondary meaning of fame, he says Bettina's words circulated throughout Weimar and caused "immortal laughter" that resounds in our ears to the present day (47).

In the next three chapters Kundera muses on the meaning of the word "immortality," commencing with one of those brief parabatic comments he has sprinkled throughout his novels. He refines the secondary definition of "immortality" by giving it two applications: the "minor" application, living on in the memories of people one has known in life, and the "great" application, living on in the memory of people one has never known. Poets and statesmen walk on a path toward "great immortality" (49). He illustrates those ideas by recounting a famous meeting between Goethe and Napoleon as if it had occurred before television cameras, complete with dramatic poses and "sound bite" comments from the quintessential politician, Napoleon (*"Voilà un homme!"*). Kundera makes fun of political attitudes toward literature, having Napoleon, misinformed by his aides, mix up Goethe with the playwright Friedrich Schiller and tell him in a sound bite statement that "theatre should become the school of the people" (55). The idea, at least as old as Plato's *Republic* (where the only poets allowed are those who sing praises of military heroes and civic leaders), reflects a Stalinist attitude toward the arts and complements Napoleon's dictatorial ambitions. He mentions Voltaire's play *The Death of Caesar* and, missing its point, says Voltaire should have shown the audience how Caesar's short life prevented him from fulfilling humanistic goals. With a point made about political attitudes toward the arts (and the political art of immortality), Kundera portrays Napoleon as suddenly distracted by his aides. Left to himself, Goethe politely awaits the emperor's renewed attention. It does not return, and finally informed that the audience is over, Goethe leaves, having played a quiet part in one of the principal images, or gestures, comprising Napoleon's immortal fame.

For the next few chapters Kundera continues with the story of Bettina and Goethe, filling in a few more biographical details and emphasizing the child-like qualities of Bettina that appealed to Goethe and gave her a sense of innocence, "as if childhood were her shield" (57). He discusses their meetings (only about three or four times alone, apparently), their correspondence (many long, passionate letters from her, a few kindly, reserved responses from him), and Goethe's realization, at least until Bettina married, that love, not sex, lay at the root of their relationship. What's more, ambition fueled her love, Kundera tells us, because as a young writer Bettina sought "great" immortality, and like Napoleon she sought it through association with a figure already on the road to that kind of fame.

Kundera sorts through various episodes in Goethe's life, evaluating the records we have of them and, in particular, analyzing those that come to us through Bettina Brentano's account. In Kundera's view the issue of control of posthumous reputation motivated their relationship, and he describes them as competing throughout the years for the right to the final word about it. He recounts the legendary scene where Beethoven and Goethe, strolling together at a spa in Czechoslovakia, encounter the empress and react with two different gestures that have marked their characters in immortality: Goethe removes his hat, bows, and steps aside; Beethoven tugs his hat lower over his eyes and strides boldly forward, forcing the empress and her entourage to step aside. As a result, the image of Goethe catering to royalty comes to our minds today, while we see Beethoven as a man of the people. But the only source for the story, Kundera reminds us, is a letter written in Bettina's hand after both Goethe's and Beethoven's deaths, and he speculates that she invented the story to spoil the writer's reputation and explain his rejection of her love.

The last four chapters of this section explore the relationship between art and life, particularly the motivations behind aesthetic passion. Do people love the forms and techniques of art or the ideological musings art stirs in them? Did Bettina love Beethoven's music or the romanticism his music conveyed to her? Kundera moves to the relationship between the artist's life and his reputation, and in three comically fanciful chapters portrays Hemingway and Goethe conversing in the afterlife. First, Hemingway complains that people are more interested in reading about his wives and his war wounds than they are in reading his books. Goethe, with more experience in the afterlife, calls that immortality. "Immorality means eternal judgment," he says (81) and tells Hemingway about the last dream he ever had. During a puppet performance of his *Faust*, where he recited the words as he manipulated the figures on stage, he looked up and found the audience sitting behind him rather than in the theater. Apparently they were more interested in him than in the play. When he returned home he found the audience now surrounding his house, their noses to the windows, driving Goethe to retreat to a corner with a blanket thrown over his head—a farcical image of his death.

Finally, in a gesture of completion, Kundera ends this section with a playful parabatic aside excusing himself for putting Hemingway and Goethe together in immortality. Out of "sincere love" for Goethe, he says (85), he dreamed up the meeting between these two literary icons. America always fascinated the German author, he informs us, and besides, like Agnes, Goethe really did not like his contemporaries. Joining the themes of his fictional and historical stories, Kundera tells us that just as Agnes did not want to spend her next life with Paul, Goethe did not want to spend his with the writers of his time. So Kundera chose Hemingway as an "immortal" companion for Goethe, and we can reflect on the reasons: Hemingway wrote classical, restrained prose; his personal life, like Goethe's, has become the stuff of gossip and legend, commanding more attention than his work; finally, Hemingway, like Goethe, is a writer who, by general consensus, embodies his era more than any other author.

## "Fighting"

In Part Three, the longest section of the book, Kundera restates the novel's themes, develops some ideas about the gesture of good-bye that has motivated his narration, and complements the meaning of that gesture with an allusion to Agnes's death. He also introduces a new major character, Laura, Agnes's younger sister, whom Agnes argued with when their father tore up their mother's photographs. Laura followed Agnes to Paris, studied music at the Paris Conservatoire, and, when she met Agnes's husband, Paul, felt he was the only man she could ever love. Seeing that love as impossible, she found another man to marry and became pregnant so that Agnes's daughter could have a cousin. But Laura miscarried, and doctors warned her of serious complications if she became pregnant again. As a result Laura feels specially marked. She carries sadness and tragedy like a mask, wearing a pair of dark glasses to cover them up and, at the same time, accent them, Kundera says.

So *Immortality* presents a pair of sisters, one mathematical, secretive, and retiring, the other musical, extroverted, and ambitious, as two characters responding to twentieth-century conditions in divergent ways. Agnes withdraws into quiet, contemplative, intellectual experiences, while Laura, though seeming to copy Agnes, embraces the noise, the media, and the publicity of our times, her body both a means to and expression of her acceptance of modern culture. An example of this is her love affair with Bernard Bertrand, a radio journalist whom she meets through Paul. From a very well-connected political family, Bernard, younger than Laura, becomes Kundera's primary means of evaluating electronic media and their influence on contemporary behavior. We might also say that he and Laura make up Kundera's twentieth-century variation on the relationship of Goethe and Bettina Brentano: their ages reversed, the classical poet who raises metaphysical questions becomes a youthful electronic journalist who demands answers, and the adoring, admiring younger poet becomes an older woman and failed diva.

In the seventh chapter of this section, "Imagology" (an invented term, the narrator says) Kundera explains the central idea in his critique of contemporary culture. The thinking of the world has changed, he tells us, so that the reduction of ideas from logical systems to isolated slogans and suggestive images has diluted the power of ideology and increased the importance of those who publicize and manage public opinion—ad agencies, campaign managers, fashion designers, in short those who specialize in images rather than ideas. Mindful of the importance of imagologues in the past (Hitler had one as advisor, for instance), Kundera points to the public nature of image purveyors now—how they discuss their work openly, often speaking for their clients, revealing the advice they give, reveling in the power they possess as a result of the victory of the image over thought. As Kundera sees it, his grandmother could grasp the world she lived in. She could understand it and manage it simply because less information, less technology, existed and fewer abstractions surrounded what she knew: baking, carpentry, butchering, sewing, and politics, for her purely local, palpable events. But mass communications have transformed the world into a global village, and as a result contemporary life holds experience, real experience, at a distance because, for example, the ordinary citizen works in an office for eight hours, drives home in a car, and sits before a television to find out what has happened that day. Sound bites replace personal conversation, and public opinion polls become a form of knowledge, a "higher reality" that allows the imagologue to control and project truth, or live with it in "absolute harmony" (115).

Ideology could affect history, overturning governments, starting wars, but imagology creates alternatives instead of revolutions so that change has a new meaning. Instead of development, change means a shift in position, front to back or one side to another, a switch from one system of short duration to another. To use a form from one of Kundera's own methods of composition, we can say that change operates like the musical term "variation": the basic melody line remains, but its presentation may be (among other things) slowed down, speeded up, turned over, or reversed, creating different effects but with the original structure intact. As a result, "Imagology organizes peaceful alternation of its systems in lively seasonal rhythms" (116), and history as we know it effectively ends. So, according to this idea, another form of human memory weakens and another form of organizing human experience disappears. If we return to the opening chapters of *The Book of Laughter and Forgetting,* with the story of the airbrushing of photographs and the ironic reminder of Vladimir Clementis's hat on Gottwald's head, we can see a thematic variation at work in *Immortality.* The propagandist has yielded to the imagologue in the East and West, but the struggle over lost individuality, the validity of human relationships, and private control of faith in the face of public manipulation of truth continues. When Paul's friend Bear discontinues Paul's radio program because imagologues find it boring, we have, in a minor, less discordant key, a variant on the theme of betrayal Kundera has treated in all of his novels. As Ludvik Jahn says, no one passes the test; everyone raises his hand—out of fear or conviction—to condemn a friend or colleague (*Joke* 65).

Kundera next develops the story around Paul and Bernard for a few chapters, switching perspectives from his opening character, as he does so frequently in his novels. Paul receives a letter from Bear informing him that he has lost his program at the station; at the same time Bernard receives a visitor, a tall man with a huge stomach, who hands him a diploma declaring Bernard a "complete ass" (125). The man (we later find out he is Kundera's friend Avenarius) congratulates Bernard, and leaves. Now both Paul and Bernard behave correctly, although each feels foolish and somehow wounded by the insulting news he receives that day. They meet for lunch, commiserate, and decide, feeling sad but philosophic, that as individuals we humans are nothing but our images in the eyes of others. What's more, we have no control over those images since, as Paul says, a well-turned malicious comment can transform us "forever into a depressingly simple caricature" (127)—a laughable one, we might add. Kundera follows them through the next couple of chapters as they relate to the women in their lives: Laura, Agnes, and Paul and Agnes's daughter, Brigitte. Laura, uninformed about Bernard's "diploma," upsets him by asking him to marry her—a blunder, Kundera says, as large as Mont Blanc because at that time Bernard's face smiled from his station's publicity posters all around Paris. Fame increases his self-consciousness, and he begins to retreat from Laura, feeling ashamed of her age and extravagant personality. Meanwhile, Paul perceives his release from the station as a sign of his advancing age, and he begins to cling to his daughter's opinions in order to feel younger and, presumably, more amusing.

Kundera describes Paul's youth, his fondness for Rimbaud, frankly comparing him to Jaromil, his main character in *Life Is Elsewhere*. Jaromil and young Paul consider themselves revolutionaries; both admire Rimbaud's phrase, "It is necessary to be absolutely modern"; and both face a situation where modernity undermines their own interests. Both respond by embracing the changes that make them obsolete. Jaromil writes poetry according to the tenets of socialist realism, and the mature Paul encourages his daughter's philistine values, values that he fought against in 1968 when the students of Paris revolted against their parents. Paul and Jaromil may be seen as variations of a character type, the "progressive," found in several of Kundera's novels. First, in *The Joke,* there is Zemanek, always following the latest fashionable ideas and openly admiring the youth who reject his own generation's values; secondly there is Franz, in *The Unbearable Lightness of Being,* who tries to do good and follows Europe's Grand March to his life's conclusion; and finally, in *The Book of Laugher and Forgetting,* there are all those innocents dancing in Prague while the poet Kalandra hangs, unaware that another change may cast them from their own victors' circle. So, in *Immortality,* filled with Kunderan irony, Paul decides that to be absolutely modern means to be an "ally of one's own gravediggers" (141).

Developing that theme, Kundera continues with the story of Laura's affair with Bernard, concentrating on her attempt to break down his increasing distance from her. While he withdraws, she demands more time and attention, being one to whom offering the body is a gesture of love. They argue constantly, yet the passion of their lovemaking increases because, as Kundera describes it, competition now fuels their sexuality. Laura fights to keep Bernard; he fights to maintain his independence from her. When they separate, Laura contemplates suicide, telling Agnes at one point that she will go to Bernard's family home in Martinique and kill herself so Bernard can find her when he arrives. In that way she will force herself (and her body) on his life forever, achieving that "minor" immorality that Kundera discussed in Part Two, thereby reinforcing the idea that the love story of Laura and Bernard works as a variation on the story of Goethe and Bettina Brentano.

Kundera underlines that variation on a theme by describing a gesture that Laura makes in her conversation with Agnes. Touching two fingers to her breast, she throws her hands upward, inclines her head, and smiles. Bettina made the same gesture, Kundera tells us in the next chapter, when defending herself against selfishness and neglect of her children. The gesture, repeated through Laura, means she wants to make large sacrifices, not small ones, intending to give herself to the world and thus achieve a form of immortality. In short, both women seek to be remembered, and so Kundera names their gesture *"the gesture of longing for immortality"* (164).

The next few chapters concern the gradual end of Laura's affair with Bernard and the increased intimacy she shares with Paul. Kundera portrays her as a child-woman (as he has Bettina) who acts in a motherly manner toward Bernard but who also seeks to sit on Paul's knee at a party. She complains to Paul of her unhappiness. Paul takes her side against his friend Bernard, in character with his tendency to turn the way the wind blows, and in a powerful moment of silence brother-in-law and sister-in-law feel a moment of intense closeness. Laura wonders what would have happened if had they met sooner, and Paul touches her. Laura puts on her dark glasses, proclaiming her misery, and the gesture, Kundera tells us, makes the "mist lift" between them (177).

Soon Agnes returns from work and accuses Laura of selfishness because of her threatened suicide, while Laura accuses Agnes of not loving enough. Their comments, accusations of egotism, mirror one another, but Kundera turns away from any psychoanalytic interpretation. Instead, he underscores the melodrama of the situation by asking us to consider the room a stage and describing the following events as if they were a set of tableaux, with the characters shifting positions as if for a set of publicity stills. As they pause in mid-action, Agnes stands against the fireplace, Laura takes up the center of the stage, with Paul a few steps to her left until he retreats to the wall opposite Agnes and leans against the bookcase. Confused, he tries not to look at the women. Agnes picks up the dark glasses that her sister left on the mantel, while Laura, in retreat, backs away from Agnes until she presses against Paul. The section ends with the following scene: Purposely, Agnes drops Laura's glasses, "symbol of her sister's sorrow . . . metamorphosed tears" (182), and they break. Meanwhile, Laura, child-woman as Kundera has described her, clutches Paul's thighs. More metaphysical and dramatic than psychoanalytic, the final image of the scene reverberates as an inversion of a story we have already read: Laura-Bettina, her glasses broken, has caught the loins of her new love, Paul-Goethe, in her hands while Agnes-Christiana stands separate, abandoned by her weak husband.

## "*Homo sentimentalis*"

This section, one of the most interesting and innovative in *Immortality,* mixes fantasy with some of Kundera's most playful yet trenchant cultural and historical thinking. First he returns to the story of Goethe and Bettina, telling us that in the eternal judgment immortality has brought to him Goethe has had to face countless evaluations of his actions in response to Bettina. Kundera provides outlines of three principal ones: those of Rainer Maria Rilke, a great German poet; Romain Rolland, French novelist, historian, and biographer of Beethoven; and Paul Éluard, French poet and one-time Stalinist sympathizer, the poet Kundera portrayed in *The Book of Laughter and Forgetting* as leading crowds in a circular dance while his friend Kalandra was executed. Rilke sees love as the important issue in the story and says Goethe should have humbled himself before it; Rolland regrets Goethe's political and aesthetic caution in choosing Christiane, a woman he describes as having no spiritual strength; and the revolutionary Éluard says Goethe should have allowed his passion to sweep away his conservative leanings. Kundera analyzes the three judgments and then, by means of quoting her letters, analyzes Bettina as well. His conclusion: She did not love Goethe so much as she, a confirmed romantic, loved love.

In the next few parabatic chapters Kundera develops some ideas about love and people of feeling (*Homo sentimentalis*), saying that Europe, normally thought of as rational and intellectual, might equally be a civilization of sentiment since on the Continent love and feeling have taken on a moral value. Kundera traces his ideas about sentiment back to the fourth-century Catholic bishop and writer Augustine of Hippo. In his *Confessions* Augustine censured himself from being "in love with loving" as a young man, yet his comments as a mature man reveal he still felt love had great moral value in and of itself. His seventh homily on the First Epistle of Saint John contains perhaps his most-quoted sentence: "Love, and do what you will." Historically the remark has justified the use of force in doing God's work and the church's bidding. Professor John Burnaby, editor and translator of *Augustine: Later Works,* calls the sentence a defense of "compulsion in the service of love— the sad monument of an uneasy conscience, seeking to assure itself that the end justifies the means" (257).

Kundera uses a more widely quoted but less accurate translation of the original Latin, "Love God, and do as you wish" (192), but clearly he intends the political, as opposed to religious, applications of St. Augustine's sentence. Bettina Brentano expressed similar sentiments in one of her letters to her husband, echoing St. Augustine by stating that love in and of itself frees us of guilt. We may say that for Bettina, in love "the end justifies the means." We might also say she agrees with Kundera's estimate that the "originality" of European law and its theory of guilt depend upon the idea that love automatically implies innocence. In other words, if we kill for money, we have no excuse; but if we kill out of passion or jealousy—that is, for love—the jury will consider our passionate feelings and, as Kundera says with irony, accord the *victim* the "severest possible punishment" (193).

So Bettina's surrender to the emotion of love makes her innocent in the eyes of Rilke, Rolland, and Éluard; but Kundera reminds us, through a discussion of Cervantes's Don Quixote, that the desire for love, the effort for love, and the decision to love may turn *Homo sentimentalis* into *Homo hystericus* ("hysterical man")—an appropriate label for Bettina Brentano when she relates to Goethe, and perhaps the label for Laura as well when she relates to both Bernard and Paul, two twentieth-century figures whom Kundera uses thematically to fill Goethe's shoes.

After another short chapter analyzing European love (it is "precoital," or "extracoital," accounting for the exile of Christiane from the usual list of Goethe's great loves), Kundera discusses the words "soul" and "heart," equates them with the "feeling self," and goes on to turn Descartes's great philosophic principle, "I think, therefore I am," into "*I feel, therefore I am*" (200) which he ironically calls more valid.[3] Conceiving human behavior playfully, as he did while commenting about gestures in the first part of the book, Kundera says we all think in similar fundamental ways, often borrowing and stealing thoughts from one another ( just as gestures are passed on from one person to another, even from generation to generation). But we endure pain alone, and through suffering we understand the uniqueness of our selves because "Suffering," Kundera says with irony, "is the university of egocentrism" (200).

While pursuing that line of thought, he also moves the plot, primarily to illustrate and reinforce his comments. First, he informs us very casually that Agnes suffers a terrible death and that Paul and Laura, devastated by their own loss, gradually fall in love, feeling "no sense of betrayal" toward Agnes (203). The incident, along with the manner of its telling, underlines Agnes's isolation without condemning Paul and Laura for self-centeredness. Kundera develops the relation of pain and egocentrism further with comments on European music, defining it as "a pump for inflating the soul" and saying it taught "richness of feeling" as well as worship of the "feeling self" (204). His ideas about music and progressive thinking are illustrated by describing

Paul and Laura's life together after Agnes's death. They encounter difficulties, primarily because Brigitte and Laura do not like one another. Each woman is self-centered, and each reveals her self-centeredness through musical preferences: Brigitte for rock, Laura for the romantic grandeur of Mahler. At last Laura demands that Paul choose between them; he cannot, loving each woman deeply but liking neither one's music. Finally Brigitte leaves the apartment on her own, and Laura, moved by Paul's pain, Mahler's music, and her own need to make a bid for minor immortality through sacrifice, decides to risk having a child with him.

The concluding chapter of the section shows Hemingway and Goethe together for the last time, and their conversation reiterates, in comic form, the issues that Kundera has raised about self, feeling, and immortality. Once again Hemingway complains that people will stop reading their books yet continue to gossip about their lives. Goethe replies that the subjects of the gossip have nothing to do with the two authors themselves. "I am not even present in my books," he says (214), adding that when he died he ceased to exist, vanishing even from his work. Obsession with image is a sign of human immaturity, he tells Hemingway, a denial of nonexistence, claiming that even after death men think about their image. But Hemingway smiles because, one hundred and fifty-six years after his own death, Goethe still wants to leave a good impression. He has dressed as a dandy, appearing to Hemingway as handsomely dressed as when he earned his reputation as a lover. However, Goethe excuses his vanity, pronouncing eternal judgment, or immortality, false, and announcing that he will soon sleep, enjoying "the delights of total nonexistence" (216), which he says Novalis, the romantic poet Goethe calls his enemy, described as "bluish." Kundera has used the color blue ironically before, especially in *The Farewell Party,* where Ruzena's blue pill is death as well as serenity, and blue haloes, blue moonlight, and bluish flowers contribute a sense of romance to an otherwise hellish vision of life. Here the ironic tone of Goethe's reference, along with the comic-book depiction of Goethe's meetings with Hemingway, trivializes an equally bleak vision. Death leads to "total nonexistence," but blue lends a serene, romantic (and, for Kundera, ironic) glow to an otherwise difficult concept. A bitter pill, like the one Ruzena swallows in *The Farewell Party,* it promises peace, quiet, and calm retreat, while in reality it delivers oblivion.

## "Chance"

The major themes of *Immortality* have been laid out; its plot, at least in outline, essentially concluded; yet there remains more than one third of the novel to read, and Kundera moves through the chapters that follow by deepening his portrait of Agnes. At the same time he adds a new dimension to her story by developing the "nonfictional" portion of the novel—the relationship between Kundera the character and Professor Avenarius, the friend he awaited while witnessing the gesture that evolved into his principal heroine.

The beginning of "Chance" complements the ending of "*Homo sentimentalis*" by extending the sleep theme from Goethe's farewell to Hemingway into Agnes's Sunday afternoon in Switzerland during a weekend away from Paul and Brigitte. She lolls on a bed after lunch, reveling in the space and privacy, the peace of two nights devoted to herself and her sleep, and prepares for the journey back to Paris, the last she will take in her life. Agnes has made a momentous decision during this weekend; she has decided to leave her family and realize her years-long dream of returning to Switzerland to live alone. By way of explaining her decision, Kundera meditates on the differences between highways and roads, calling highways a "triumphant devaluation of space" where islands of beauty are connected by one long line, while roads offer continuous, changing beauty and pay tribute to space. Presumably France, with its broad expanse of plains and agriculture, is the land of highways, and mountainous Switzerland, with its vistas of sky, pasture, and stone, is the land of footpaths and roads. Kundera also makes the point that, for Agnes, the world of highways is the world of husbands, while the world of roads is the world of fathers. The story of her life has come full circle with her weekend decision: a young woman, she left the world of roads for the world of highways and Paul; now, mature, she returns to her father's world of roads, walks, and, ultimately, the retreat of death.

Playing with the interstice of his novel's fictional and "nonfictional" worlds, Kundera returns to his meeting with Professor Avenarius for a discussion of fiction and four important novelistic ideas: coincidence in real events and imagined events; chance meetings between the "real" Avenarius and Kundera's two invented characters, Bernard and Laura; the mathematics of coincidence in general (existential mathematics, Kundera calls it); and the limitations on the fulfillment of love, especially in Agnes's experience. By means of a pair of fantasies we learn that Agnes's mother did not love her father very much and that, in relation to her mother, Agnes felt less loved than Laura. For her whole life she has felt as if her sister was chasing her in a race, and since the episode nine months before when she threw Laura's glasses to the floor and banned her from the apartment, she has felt her sister gaining on her. Now, she feels Laura will pass her.

151

Against Agnes's sense of defeat and loss, Kundera presents another scene between himself and Avenarius, during which they discuss an event Kundera heard on the radio. A young girl sits down in the middle of a country road one night, and three cars, swerving to avoid her, crash, causing injury and death to the occupants. As the chapter begins, Kundera tells us that Agnes drives on such a road, but instead of dramatizing the event, a clear foreshadowing of her death, he recounts his conversation with Avenarius, a conversation that centers on novels, the foundation for literary characterization, and an idea Kundera has for Part Six of *Immortality*. He says that today writers should construct novels so that they cannot be adapted or retold in any other medium. He calls dramatic tension the "real curse of the novel" and tells Avenarius that, rather than have the quality of a bicycle race, speedily moving toward the conclusion, a novel should enter the reader slowly, like a "feast of many courses" (238).

Avenarius, a pot-bellied idealist despite the fact that he bears the name of a nineteenth-century German positivist philosopher, worries that Kundera works too hard and advises him to jog at night. Unbuttoning his jacket, he reveals a complicated harness of belts and a scabbard with a kitchen knife in it, telling Kundera that as he jogs through Paris in the evening he fights "Diabolum" by slashing tires of parked cars because their presence eclipses the city's cathedrals. Playing Sancho Panza to this eccentric Don Quixote, Kundera changes the subject, savoring the wine along with his roast duck—presumably entering his body the way he intends his novel to enter us. He asks about Avenarius's meeting with Laura in the subway station (significantly, Avenarius saw her trapped between two drunken beggars, the way Don Quixote saw Dulcinea among the rabble at the inn) and seeks information about the events that occurred afterward in her apartment. Evasively, Avenarius describes the mathematical pattern he uses in slashing tires while he jogs and encourages Kundera to join him in his mission.

In the following chapter Kundera returns to Agnes, who is driving back to Paris. In a highway restaurant she muses on the causes of shame, seeing it as the first response to an awareness of the necessity of bodily form, and considers physical beauty as the "unpoetic average" (248) in humans while ugliness bespeaks true individuality. Remembering her father, a handsome man, she recalls that on his death bed he told her not to look at him, and she conceives of the world of the dead as one without faces. Recognizing him as her only love, she leaves the highway after some motorcyclists pass (reminders of her husband, who took her on motorcycle trips when they were young), and decides to follow a country road. Presumably it is one her father would have chosen to travel, but it will also lead, by means of a series of insignificant events and coincidences, to her death when she swerves to avoid hitting the girl who sits on the pavement.

The narrative switches back to Kundera and Avenarius, speculating, as they walk on a Paris boulevard, about the girl who attempted suicide. Kundera tells Avenarius that he understands human character as bearing what the Germans call *Grund*, meaning "cause" or "foundation"; he calls it an "internal code," in the nature of a metaphor, that determines our fate. He perceives the suicidal girl as one who, before the night of the accidents, could not get the world's attention. Her voice and character are too weak and so, despite her suffering, she could not make the world hear. Thus she threw herself away, Kundera says, as if the one throwing were different from the one thrown, and she would have no conception of the injury she caused others because to her the outside world did not exist. Suffering has made her that self-centered. Impatient with Kundera's philosophic absorption, Avenarius encourages him to take up jogging, but Kundera, careful and conservative, refuses, walking home as his friend, the tire-slashing campaigner against Diabolum, drives off in his car. Returning to the suicidal girl, Kundera meditates on her attempt to die. She, and the event, have become his fiction now, and so his thoughts take on narrative form, concluding the chapter with an analysis of her suffering: "Her only world was her soul" (254).

The following chapter begins with a variation of Kundera's meditation, making a transition from his fictional speculation concerning the girl's suffering to a dramatization of her actions and her state of mind as her fateful journey intersects so terribly with Agnes's. In a brief chapter, we witness the girl's retreat from the city, her despair at bearing the weight of her suffering, and her frustration at the world's indifference when she attempts to hitchhike and no one stops for her. She leaves the highway for a side road, the very one Agnes drives on, we know. In the following chapter, we follow Agnes's thoughts about her own discomfort with the world. For her, living is insufferable because living means "carrying one's painful self" (259) instead of simply being. Agnes sees love or the cloister as the only two possible means of avoiding the burden. Love has not worked for her; now she prepares to try the second option by retreating into her own private apartment in Switzerland—much as the girl tries to retreat by seeking her death on a walk away from the city. The next chapter, told from the girl's point of view, provides details of the event that ends Agnes's life so suddenly. Tired, with feet aching, the girl sits in the road with her back to traffic. Two cars swerve around her, spinning her and knocking her to her side before crashing off the road.

Triumphant, the girl stands because she senses the world finally recognizes her, its attention striking her as so beautiful that she tries to scream. She cannot, until a third car (with Agnes in it, although we don't know that until later) swerves around her. The resultant crash frees the girl so that she can finally give voice to her emotions and answer the scream of those injured in the cars. This awful, terrifying image of mirrored yet unshared suffering ends the incident, and the girl runs from the scene to find a phone, her voice finally achieving effect on the world.

It is the critical moment in this section, undoubtedly the most dramatic in *Immortality,* but also the thematic center of the ideas Kundera has raised concerning feeling and being, suffering and knowledge of the self. The young suicidal girl finally matters, but tragically. The third car contains Agnes (it is the third because, when Kundera returns to her point of view, she sees the girl standing in the road like a ''ballerina''), and we can only speculate that Agnes's is the scream that, in her dying, gives the young girl an audible voice. At the same time we must not forget that Kundera's conversation with Avenarius has underlined the fictional nature of the scene, and so we know our emotions have responded to nothing more than carefully rendered fabrication. Yet even knowing that, and even at several removes from Agnes's experience, such is Kundera's art that we feel her suffering powerfully, as though it were real. The value of art, its ability to build and destroy, to expand and deepen our sensibilities while doing so, has rarely been so finely rendered.

The final four chapters of the section present the denouement to the incident from three distinct points of view. First, as a form of comic relief, we witness Professor Avenarius on his tire-slashing mission; however, this night a woman, seeing the knife in his hand, shouts for help, claiming that he intended to rape her. A policeman, discovering the knife beneath Avenarius's jacket, arrests the professor. At that moment Paul walks by, dazed because he has just found out about Agnes's accident. He offers to help Avenarius. As the policeman takes Avenarius away, Paul finds that his car's tires are slashed, preventing him from driving to the hospital where Agnes lies dying.

Kundera switches to Paul's point of view as he returns to his apartment to call a cab. But he can find no driver to take him on such a long trip, ''a few hundred miles from Paris'' (265). Brigitte returns. She and Paul leave in her car, but arrive too late to see Agnes alive. She dies just fifteen minutes before they reach her room. So the farcical accident of Avenarius's nightly mission prevents the couple's final meeting. However, there may be other factors to consider in the irony of that failed farewell. We have learned already that

154

Agnes intended to leave her family. Now, with her death near, we also learn she has no desire to see her husband. She feels too tired. She senses that someone is chasing her, and she tries to hurry her death in order to maintain her privacy, to keep her freedom, to avoid the performance she sees her life with Paul as having become. Once more we observe Witold Gombrowicz's theatricality and emphasis on external forces in Kundera's interpretation of events and character: "They don't have faces there," Agnes thinks (269), meaning that in the land of the dead, individual roles do not exist. Kundera makes those words the last we know of her living thoughts, and when he portrays Paul staring at his dead wife's face, she wears an expression, a smile, he does not know and cannot understand. The smile calls to mind the gesture of good-bye that inspired the book, the lightly tossed orange ball, imaginary, already having left the real raised hand that gave birth to the character of Agnes in the first chapter.

## "The Dial"

Metaphor, not only in literature as words, but in life as gestures, has always been important to Kundera. In *The Unbearable Lightness of Being* he reflects on the abandoned child as a motif of civilization's important myths, mentioning Oedipus and Moses, and commenting on the "danger" of metaphors, warning that they are not to be trifled with. They can give birth to love, Kundera tells us, in a sense making the language of life more weighty than its experience. If chance and intention underline the different means by which the members of the principal couples in *The Unbearable Lightness of Being* react to love and beauty, these differences are not mechanical or mathematical, but rather a result of Kundera's metaphorical characterization. As a photographer, for instance, Tereza finds beauty and meaning in the accidents of real life, just as she sees form and destiny in the accidents that brought her and Tomas together. Similarly Sabina, through the accident of a drop of paint on a canvas, develops a style of painting that evokes her attitude toward life, ultimately becoming a statement for the way she lives. She looks for cracks in things, seeking deeper meaning in the layers beneath apparent surfaces. In *Immortality* Agnes's metaphor is the gesture of good-bye, an image of ephemeral beauty elevated by the figure of the tossed ball, a kind of sad yet joyful moment signifying a playful game as well as a farewell, a happiness made poignant by its brevity, and by its association in this book with the ironic moment of Agnes's decision to withdraw from the world of her family, only to find privacy in the dark, mysterious chamber of her sudden death.

Taking off from the mystery of self in Agnes's estrangement, "The Dial" presents a passage of digression that, as Kundera promised Professor Avenarius, introduces a new character in the book, makes up a "novel within a novel," and, when it ends, sets the new character free without bringing him back. At the same time this section provides another view of Agnes, revealing a woman with more adventure, more sensuality, and more mystery and passion than we have experienced in seeing her with Paul, Brigitte, and Laura. Here we see her as younger, self-centered and physical, similar to Laura in her sexuality, a characterization appropriate to her role in this section as a woman having a years-long casual affair. Once more Kundera dramatizes the mystery and variety of self that we do not ordinarily perceive in the traditional "realistic" novel, based as it usually is on the Freudian, or some other psychological, principle. As a result Kundera does not offer this section on Agnes in order that we may "understand" her behavior. Rather, he offers it to explore the complexity and mystery of her "self," the fractured, many-faceted character evolving from the single gesture that introduced her as a theme.

So we might say that "The Dial" works as a novelistic essay on human character, opening with the image of a newborn suckling its mother's breast, working through the ruminations of the fictional Rubens, a failed artist and Don Juan–like sensualist caught in a mid-life crisis as he contemplates the infinite variety and mystery of the women he has known, and concluding with Rubens's imagined picture of Agnes's body in cremation, a hellish image, more painful than the one in the previous section about the accident that took her life. Also on the metaphorical level the image of the title, "The Dial," functions as the primary figure of this section of the novel, an invented device that Kundera uses as a metaphor for the passage of individual human life. Describing the dial as a clock in the form of a horoscope, Kundera gives the device nine hands (the sun, the moon, and the seven planets) that turn on a clocklike face divided into the twelve signs of the zodiac. As the hands traverse the zodiac's signs at different speeds, they effect in different ways and in different periods "the various elements of your life's theme" (274), as if the passage of an individual's years were a musical composition such as a theme with variations.

Within Rubens's lifetime composition Agnes performs the theme of "the lute player," a side musician who presumably picks away at one variation on his life's melodic line. Also described, from Rubens's point of view, as the "princess of episode," Agnes moves him in ways that he cannot precisely understand, yet in the main outlines of his life's external form, fate, or composition, she hardly plays a part. From those fundamental conceptions Kundera develops the section into an exploration of Rubens's memory and its relationship to the larger issue of human understanding of life. In addition, as a variation on a chapter in his third section, "Fighting," he dramatizes some of the issues he developed on imagology. A failed painter, Rubens gave up his art, Kundera tells us, in order to pursue life through experiences with women. Yet now, suffering from the crisis of middle age and a knowledge of Agnes's death, he finds that at most he can remember her by means of only two or three unconnected images, with even fewer images making up his recollections of the other women he has known. Of what use, then, he asks, has been his quest for knowledge, his life's chosen mission? He conceives of his memory as a camera with a few still photos in it (a mere seven, we learn, encompass his whole erotic life); but he possesses no animated film, no sense of the fluid movement and energy of existence. From this thought he comes to understand that the reality of people he has known has been lost behind the images he has kept. He remembers that as a boy in school he drew caricatures of a teacher; although he drew her from life, Kundera tells us, Rubens came to realize that, even while looking at her, he saw only his own drawn caricatures, that is "fictions," and no longer the real teacher who walked and breathed in front of him.

Similarly, he can remember only three clear images of Agnes. Although they represent significant moments he spent with her (a first meeting, the first touch of her body, an erotic experiment with a third party), he finds he has no sense of her apart from them, that in fact he can grasp nothing of her internal self, nothing of her kinetic, living character. As a result he sees his attempts to learn about life through women as fruitless and, by extension, conceives of his own years of experiment as having come to nothing. Once imagining his life as a dial upon which the stages of love are expressed in varied forms, Rubens sees a significant and disturbing change: Recently he has sought passion through the women he knew in the past rather than any women he might encounter in the future. But after learning of Agnes's death, he perceives another, yet more troubling, internal shift. An image of Agnes sitting up in the flames that consume her body accompanies each of his sexual experiences, in effect blotting out the three images he has of her from life. The situation leads Rubens to postpone further sexual adventures, and gradually he comes to feel he will never pursue women again. Finished with sexual passion, with his chosen research into life, Rubens has essentially finished living. Like the figures at the end of *The Book of Laughter and Forgetting*, he has become morally and physically exhausted, a modern man with no biological imperative, no passions, no future except in his highly fragmented memory of the past.

We might remember at this moment that, according to Agnes's husband, Paul, "imagology begins where history ends" (116) and that, in much of Kundera's work, history and memory are frail human attempts to hold on to experience. Although we may disagree with the idea, Rubens's story illustrates it on a personal level and at the same time underscores the reader's own frustrated sense of ignorance in relation to life, life as metamorphosed in Agnes's character. Paul and Brigitte did not know her, certainly Laura did not; yet we may expect all three, at least in real life, to have thought they did. Rubens is the only character in a position to know his understanding of Agnes has failed. Each of the others has an idea, or an image, of her based on an intimate relationship and daily experience. Yet, as Kundera says in his comments about Rubens's memory of women, she has lost herself behind her image with the result that she remains mysterious. On the general level, meanwhile, history begins to wind down, become static. Withdrawn from the world by choice and the accident of her death, Agnes remains, but as a puzzle for the living to ponder—and, as they will with their own lives, make sense of as best they can.

## "The Celebration"

The final section of *Immortality* contains the celebration of two events, the fictional Kundera's completion of the novel he began upon seeing a woman of sixty or sixty-five take swimming lessons at his health club some two years before, and the gathering together of Paul's family when Brigitte returns with her child to live with him, Laura, and their own three-month-old daughter. Thus, in many ways a circle has been completed, or, to use a figure from the previous section, the dial of life has turned and a new stage has begun, with the novel, its characters, and narrator aligned to begin a new variation on the theme of the possibilities of human existence.

Before handling the human events, Kundera opens the section with references to several of the novel's themes. He describes the three walls of newly installed mirrors surrounding the pool along with a window on the fourth wall overlooking the famous rooftops of Paris. Saying the imagologues have insisted on the mirrors, Kundera will count up the images they make and tell us later that twenty-seven Pauls stand up to make a toast. But before he reaches that moment he reports a conversation he and Avenarius have as they lounge beside the pool. Avenarius proposes a survey of men, asking each to choose between one night alone with a famous, beautiful woman such as Brigitte Bardot, with the stipulation that no one would know of it, or a walk down the main street of a city with an arm wrapped intimately around the woman's shoulders, but on the condition that he must never sleep with her. The idea of the survey, of course, has to do with whether men prefer the experience of the beautiful woman or the reputation, and image, that goes with standing by her side. Kundera wonders whether he should ever take his friend's projects seriously, and the two discuss the issues of seriousness and humor, with Avenarius saying that humor can only exist when people recognize the border separating the important from the unimportant: "And nowadays this border has become unrecognizable," he says. Kundera raises a corollary issue, but Paul arrives, "attractive . . . between fifty and sixty" (333), and the discussion follows other tracks, still calling up themes the novel contains.

In introducing the two men, Avenarius refers to Kundera as a novelist, saying his wife thought *Life Is Elsewhere* outstanding. Paul says he doesn't read novels, finding memoirs and biographies far more interesting. He mentions a biography of Hemingway he has just read, calling that novelist a liar, sadist, and misogynist, and goes on to discuss Laura's favorite composer, Mahler, recounting the agonies he went through to perfect his Seventh Symphony before its premiere and betting that no one, not even musical experts, could separate the corrected from the uncorrected version upon hearing them in sequence. The symphony's perfection "surpasses . . . our memory," he says, so that no one can grasp more than one-hundredth of it. Referring to Mahler's symphonies as "cathedrals of the useless" (335) and then lumping them together with all art, Paul, absolutely modern and progressive (like Zemanek in *The Joke*, the dancers in *The Book of Laughter and Forgetting,* and Franz in *The Unbearable Lightness of Being*), denounces the inequality of reducing European culture to fifty immortal names. He stands, raises his glass, and with twenty-seven mirrored images joining him before the rooftops of Paris, drinks to "the end of the old days" (336) just before Laura enters the pool area.

She blushes, and, Kundera notes, Avenarius remains very guarded. Paul introduces the men to his wife, but she enters the pool immediately, leaving Paul to tell about his three-month-old daughter and the return of Brigitte with her own child. Surrounded by four women, he repeats a line from the Communist French writer Louis Aragon about woman being the future of man (339). Avenarius calls the phrase stupid, while Kundera bemoans such sound bite sentences, saying they will remain (like images) while literature (like history) dies out. Repeating Aragon's line, Paul says the world will be transformed into the image of woman. But after referring to Goethe's famous last statement from *Faust* about the "eternal feminine" drawing us on, Paul sinks into melancholy and, hinting at the chaos his life has become since Brigitte returned, says Laura and his daughter fight more than ever: "Maternity has made both of them more pugnacious" (339). Trapped by the conflict, Paul wishes for the end of all music and musicians, an aesthetic judgment ironically reflecting his comic hell and strikingly opposite to Rubens's desperate longing to hold on to Agnes, whom he imagined on the dial of his life as a lute player.

With the two sisters so neatly posed and contrasted, it remains for Kundera to resolve his themes in the last two brief chapters. He does so by taking Aragon's phrase about woman's being the future of man and dramatizing it through Paul as he performs a burlesque imitation of the gesture of good-bye that inspired Kundera's persona, that is, Kundera the narrator and fictional character. Laura leaves the pool, and, with the men drawn to watch her walk, stops before the doors to the locker rooms, making Agnes's (and the novel's) signature gesture so brilliantly, so lightly, that the tossed ball seems to hang in the air permanently. Kundera calls the gesture "exceptional" and "full of significance," saying Laura must have made it for Avenarius, although Paul, innocent, describes the gesture as typical of Laura and saying that she made it for him when he took her to the maternity ward to deliver their daughter. Lonesome for her while he waited at home, Paul made the gesture over and over for himself, he says, studying his image in the mirror, becoming subject and object at the same time, until he realized finally that the gesture was meant for women and he simply could not fit into it. He lacks women's "unsubstantiated hope" and cannot, as he says women can, invite others into a "doubtful future." Joining Goethe's words to that gesture, which he had earlier described as expressing a wish to be remembered, Kundera imagines the phrase as a myth, calling it a "proud white goose" flying above the pool. But he demystifies it too, in describing Paul's actions at the locker room doors: He stops, reflected in the mirrors beneath the bright, still-hanging ball (now an image, more real than the characters) that Laura has tossed, and waves, cheerful for the first time, Kundera informs us, making a "clumsy male imitation" (342) of the gesture of Goethe's eternal woman.

After Paul leaves, Kundera tells Avenarius that, although Paul spoke eloquently about the gesture, his ideas were unrealistic because Laura really wanted to let Avenarius know she had come to the club because of him. Acknowledging the interpretation, Avenarius excuses himself for cuckolding the man who helped him when he was accused of rape. Reality means nothing to Paul, he tells Kundera, as it means nothing to most men, who care more about appearance than reality and more likely would choose to walk down the street with a beautiful woman than to sleep with her. He goes on to say that Paul thought him guilty of attempted rape and yet still defended him. If he had told Paul the truth about the tire-slashing, Paul would have lost interest in the case. Moved because his friend risked jail rather than tell the truth, Kundera suddenly sees Avenarius's tire-slashing adventures in a new light. They work as a game—not a Quixotic mission or cause, the way a progressive like Paul would conceive of them—nevertheless a game with meaning.

The perception helps him understand Avenarius at last: He will not accept the importance of the world and has turned it into a toy. ''You play with the world like a melancholy child who has no little brother,'' Kundera says, and at the moment he feels he has found the right metaphor, or internal code, for his friend's character. Not having a brother, Avenarius declares he has Kundera instead, thus acknowledging their kinship: novelist and comic explorer, comic writer and serious man of action.

Leaving the club, they change in the locker room and separate, Avenarius driving off in his Mercedes, Kundera walking along a street filled with the sound of cars and motorcycles. The scene recalls the one Agnes encountered upon leaving the health club when she recognized the world as one she no longer loved. Kundera thinks of her immediately, informing the reader that exactly two years have passed since he first imagined her while waiting for Avenarius beside the pool. The reflection completes two primary figures in *Immortality*: Agnes, wanting to be remembered, carrying a forget-me-not and staring at it while walking on an ugly street; Kundera, imagining her while following the very same route. One focuses on life, the other on art. The characters support and feed each other, both heeding the call of beauty, delicate yet eternal and, as Goethe wrote about one image of it, always drawing us higher.

## NOTES

1. Richard Avenarius (1843–1896) founded a school of philosophy, empiriocriticism, that sought to develop a view of the world based on pure perception and devoid of the metaphysical inclinations and prejudices humans may carry into epistemoloy (the study of knowing).

2. *Immortality* (New York: Grove, 1991) 3. Further references will be noted parenthetically.

3. Personal letter to the author, August 20, 1991: ''Certainly it is a thesis made rather ironic in the novel.''

# CHAPTER NINE

# Amid Chaos, the Survival of Form: *Laughable Loves*

*The only thing I consider important of all that I ever wrote, the only thing that I allow to be republished are my novels.*

Kundera has begun to publish his collected works in Czechoslovakia. Following is an essay he wrote for that publication.

Publish my books. Yes. But which ones? There are two conceptions of an author's work, or "oeuvre." Some consider as oeuvre everything the author wrote; writers in the celebrated French Pleiade editions, for example, are edited from this point of view: namely, with everything: with each letter, with each journal entry. Or, the oeuvre is only that which an author, on balance, considers valuable enough to include. I have always been a vehement partisan of this second idea. To me, it is immoral to offer readers something the author knows to be imperfect and which no longer gives him any pleasure.

According to my thinking, that which one might call my "oeuvre" has nothing to do with (1) work that is immature (juvenile); (2) work that was not successfully completed; (3) work that is solely a product of circumstance.

(1) Work that is immature: all my musical compositions (until I was twenty-five, they were much more important to me than literature); all the poetry (published or not): around my twenty-eighth birthday my poetry displeased me—suddenly, radically, and totally (even that which is interesting among my verse, but which, otherwise, later becomes "motivational material" in my novels); the theoretical monograph on Vladislav Vancura (published under the title *The Art of the Novel*), that I wrote between my twenty-fifth and twenty-seventh years and that is probably excellent as a "school assignment," but certainly nothing more. And I consider as a school assignment handed in very late (I was already thirty years old), the play *The Keepers of the Keys*. Its form has

virtuosity (even if, perhaps, a slightly labored virtuosity) and the story of an absurd narrow-mindedness cracking open its head while knocking against history always seems interesting to me. Two years after the premiere of *The Keepers of the Keys*, I had the opportunity to read Ionesco's play *Frenzy for Two*, and I said to myself with sad recognition: "This is what I wanted to write when I began *The Keepers of the Keys*." My cardinal sin was that I set the story in the concrete situation of the German occupation. That situation, described a thousand times already, contained such strong moral stereotypes that they smothered the originality of the play despite all my efforts. For seventeen years, I have not allowed anyone in the world the right to perform *The Keepers of the Keys*.

(2) Work that was not successfully completed: the play *Ptakavina* (*A Farce*). I wrote it, I guess (I guess, really: I have never kept a journal, and all my dating after the fact depends on my feeble memory) around 1966 during a single happy week in the little spa town of Trancanske Teplice. Contrary to *The Keeper of the Keys,* I like this play enormously, but nevertheless, it is a draft, or sketch, not a fully completed work. I returned to it often to relieve it of its flaws, but I always ran aground. Maybe I'll try again. I don't know. As work that is not successful (or: not entirely successful) I also consider the three stories of the original *Laughable Loves* that I later eliminated from the collection.

(3) Work that is strictly circumstantial: excepting those that I wrote in French and collected in the book *The Art of the Novel*, all my essays and articles. That is, for example, all my politico-cultural writings from the sixties, including the speech "On the Nonevidence of the Nation" that I delivered to the Czech Congress of Writers in 1967. In addition, all that I wrote in French (in *Le nouvel observateur, La quinzaines litteraire, Le debat, L'infini* or prefaces) on Broch, on Fuentes, on Voltaire, on Kafka, on Roth, on Bacon, on Fernandez, etc. (these reflections later served me as preparatory studies for *The Art of the Novel*). And also all those essays meant to explain to the foreign public the essence of the Czech situation: "The Wager of Czech Literature" (1979); "Prague, Poem that Disappeared" (1980); "The Kidnapped West, or the Tragedy of Central Europe" (1983); the prefaces for books by Czech authors, for *The Miracle* by Skvorecky (1977), for Havel's plays (1980), for *The Ceiling* by Reznicek (1983), for the novel of

Sylvie Richterova, and all the French articles on Janacek, Forman, Skvorecky, Seifert, Sabata, Skacel, Hrabal, Kral, Vaculik and once again on Havel; all those essays say exactly what I think, but I wrote them more to serve my countrymen's cause than to discover and say anything new; with those essays, I did not wish to join in the Czech literary debate and therefore I do not intend to translate them into Czech or republish them. (I could also place among my occasional writings about one hundred interviews, but I refuse to consider these interviews as my texts. An interview is the work of a journalist who, in a free fashion, often scandalously free, reproduces a conversation with the person interviewed. For that reason, since 1985 I give no more interviews.)

And what, after all, do I consider worth publishing? When I retreated into my solitude after the Russian invasion, I began to realize that the only thing I took to heart (if I speak of my work) was the novel; I have stopped thinking of it as a genre like all the others; for me it is a unique art with its own ontology, next to music the most European of the arts (it is the art that helped found the Modern Era). I expressed that attitude later in the final words of the essay that opens *The Art of the Novel:* "To what am I attached? To God? Country? The people? The individual? My answer is as ridiculous as it is sincere: I am attached to nothing but the depreciated legacy of Cervantes." The only thing I consider important of all that I ever wrote, the only thing that I allow to be republished are my novels.

Following the example of composers, I would designate them by opus numbers. Opus one: *The Joke.* Opus two: *Laughable Loves.* Opus three: *Life Is Elsewhere.* Opus four: *The Farewell Party.* Opus five: *The Book of Laughter and Forgetting.* Opus six: *The Unbearable Lightness of Being.* Opus seven: *Immortality.* Beside this cycle of novels I have written two more books that I like without reservation and that I wish to continue to publish. But even these two non-novels are tied to the art of the novel: in first place is the play *Jacques and His Master, An Homage to Diderot in Three Acts,* the free variation on Diderot's novel, *Jacques le fataliste,* that had for me as a novelist an extraordinary importance (I wrote the play in Prague during the years after the Russian invasion and published it in Paris in my own translation in 1981); and then the collection of seven essays written in French and published in 1986 under the title that I borrowed from my "school assignment": *The Art of the Novel.*[1]

■ ■ ■

It is difficult not to see the present epoch as a period of summation in Kundera's career, preparation for another point of departure as, apparently, was *The Farewell Party* and Kundera's emigration from his native country in 1975. It is now 1992. The wheel of life has revolved to another position, not only for Kundera but for Czechoslovakia and Europe as well. He and his wife may now visit their native country at will; Kundera's works will again be published there, after a period of more than twenty years; and, if we look at his evaluation of his work quoted above, we see that he has begun looking back, checking the balance of his accounts, and attempting, through controlling the contents of his oeuvre, what he shows Goethe attempting in *Immortality*: to stamp his reputation in his own particular way on the long and public memory of literary history. On a somewhat less intellectual, but also important, level Kundera has reached the number seven in his fiction. As he admits in *The Art of the Novel*, the number seven feels right to him in assembling the parts of his novels, in all but *The Farewell Party* that is, and we see that as he evaluates his work in the passage that opens this chapter, he perceives nine books as particularly worth publishing, seven novels, with a play and a collection of critical essays as companion pieces. Perhaps he has reached some kind of closure, having composed seven chapters to his fiction-writing life. The self-reflexive nature of *Immortality*, with its obvious authorial intrusions, references to *Life Is Elsewhere* and *The Unbearable Lightness of Being*, along with its subtler references to the rest of his novels, may indicate that he also, on a less than conscious level, perceives the need for pausing, coming to terms, preparing for something new.

In the second chapter of this study, we saw how Kundera's one play published in English, *Jacques and His Master*, reflects his interest in novelistic form and narrative voice, containing as it does playful references to an "author" who is not visible but whose presence is felt simply because of the play's existence and especially because of its homage to a famous novel that makes a game of the voices telling stories. The play also makes use of parabasis with its characters' addresses to the audience, their comments on the stories within the play and the relation between the "fiction" at the back of the stage and the "reality" down front, and, of course, Jacques's pseudo-philosophical recitations of his former captain's comment about the author of it all, the one dozing over the inkwell above everyone's head. Emphasizing language as a form of reality, playing with the narrative voice and the comic, self-reflexive comments about the author of the drama, Kundera makes of

*Jacques and His Master* an important segue into his later novels, accomplishing a smooth transition between the dramatic farce of *The Farewell Party* and the virtuoso game with variations and narrative forms that became *The Book of Laughter and Forgetting*. *Jacques and His Master* helps shape that transition in four ways:

1) In his introduction Kundera makes an important critical point about the novel, saying that Diderot created a "space" that never before existed in the history of the form; as a novelist Diderot rejected "realistic" illusion and psychological motivation, declining to give the emotional background of his characters; as a result Kundera, following Diderot, can make his characters notably less "rounded," in the traditional realistic novelist's sense. With *The Book of Laughter and Forgetting* metaphor and action, rather than psychology and physique, become his guiding force;

2) Kundera calls attention to the unusual structure of Diderot's *Jacques le fataliste;* its coherence arises from the technique of polyphony and variation, he says, rather than from character and plot (its polyphony delivers three voices telling three different love stories, its variation derives from the interplay of the narratives' details; each story in the novel works as a variation in theme and technique on the others); *Jacques and His Master*'s dramatization of those three stories as they are being told develops an intense counterpoint between fiction and reality, one of the most important narrative techniques in Kundera's later novels, while the narrative intrusions on the part of the characters anticipates the parabatic spirit of everything that comes afterward: *The Book of Laughter and Forgetting, The Unbearable Lightness of Being,* and *Immortality*. We can say the techniques of polyphony and variation are the fruition of a decades-long interest that the composition of *Jacques and His Master* fulfilled;

3) In fact, Kundera calls his play an homage not only to Diderot but to the "technique of variation" as well; all of his novels exist with similar impulses toward variation behind them, but those that come after the play work more powerfully, more skillfully, more obviously toward that end;

4) Finally, in *Jacques and His Master* Kundera begins the gradual process of introducing himself into his narratives through the technique of parabasis; his jokes about the writer of the play (Jacques calls the writer an imbecile for having rewritten the story without including horses, the master calls for death to all those who rewrite what has already been written) lead immediately into the frank authorial commentary that marks his three most recent novels and, ultimately, the full emergence of the author as a character in *Immortality* (along with the interesting comment by the fictional Kundera to his friend

Avenarius that an author should compose a novel so that it cannot be adapted, or rewritten, for another medium).

This interest in ironic play, polyphony, and thematic variation as the basis of his concept of the novel's form has led Kundera to regard *Laughable Loves* as a novel in seven parts, although it began as a collection of ten separate stories published in three separate volumes in Czech. In *The Art of the Novel,* while discussing how frequently he resorts to seven-part structures in his novels, he says he eliminated three of the original ten *Laughable Loves* stories and "the whole thing became very coherent, in a way that prefigured *The Book of Laughter and Forgetting*: the same themes (especially the hoax) make a single entity out of seven narratives, the fourth and sixth of which are further linked by having the same protagonist, Dr. Havel. In *The Book of Laughter and Forgetting,* too, the fourth and sixth parts are linked by the same character: Tamina."[2] So *Laughable Loves* might be appropriately titled as *The Book of Laughable Loves,* and in fact, according to Kundera, at his request the work carries just that title in its German and Spanish versions.[3]

If, as he says, the hoax works as a principal theme in the book, we can extend that idea by conceiving of it as a novel about mistaken beliefs: in the self, in relationships, in human character, and, ultimately, existence, at least existence as exemplified in ideological traps such as religion and political philosophy. But *Laughable Loves* works also, and more importantly, as all of Kundera's novels do, as a higher meditation on faith in relation to language and reality. Time and again Kundera has shown how language, our primary tool in understanding and remembering, is, in and of itself, a fallible keeper of truth simply because it not only reflects reality, but through the lies of fiction creates a reality of its own that may be more believable—and more dangerous. So in *Laughable Loves* we go from "Nobody Will Laugh," a story about lying and "making it" through "Edward and God," a story about faith and "making it," both of which show the lie somehow betraying the liar with a new reality. Between those two stories Kundera portrays men and women using and abusing each other for their own purposes at all ages, from youth in the beginning to age at the conclusion, the two functioning as bookends for the various stages of adult human experience. In all stories love and sex at their least serious become the field on which highly metaphysical questions and fictions of self, existence, love, and God are debated. In "Nobody Will Laugh" the narrator Klima states the human problem succinctly, lamenting our inability to control the stories of our own lives: "They aren't *our* stories at all," he says; "they are foisted on us from somewhere *outside.*"[4] If the idea sounds suspiciously similar to the one that Jacques repeats from his former captain, we can point to it as an example of Kundera's consistency and underline Klima's words as another variation on the theme of our helplessness before external events and the inadequacy of language as a tool in controlling or understanding them.

## "Nobody Will Laugh"

Klima, an instructor of art history, sits at home with his lover, Klara, a young woman of "excellent" family, and celebrates his recent success, the publication of a study in an important visual arts magazine, while reading a letter from another scholar. The letter, from a man named Zaturetsky, asks him to review an article for publication in the same magazine that has accepted Klima's for publication. Next morning Klima reads Zaturetsky's article and finds it laughably earnest, full of platitudes, and as scholarship essentially worthless. Then the editor of the arts journal calls, encouraging Klima to say something short and negative because, he says, Zaturetsky keeps badgering them, insisting that they do not understand him and that only an expert such as Klima could appreciate his research. Flattered by Zaturetsky's good opinion, and angered because he had difficulty getting his own work published in the journal, Klima can not bring himself to write the negative evaluation. Instead, he gives a vague promise to the editor and writes to Zaturetsky himself, flattering the man at the same time he says that other specialists suspect his own opinions and that therefore his recommendation would, in the end, work against the article. Mailing the letter, Klima thinks he can forget about the article and the man, but, as he ruefully says, Zaturetsky did not forget him. There follows one of those long, complicated plot mazes Kundera runs his characters through in order to make us laugh, see the irony of frivolous behavior turned into life-changing fate (as he did with Ludvik in *The Joke*) and good intentions working against the good of those intending.

Zaturetsky confronts Klima at one of his lectures, asking for his review, and Klima, seeing stubbornness and asceticism written in the lines of the man's face, promises "something vague" (12). Instead of writing the review, however, he avoids Zaturetsky, changing the days of his lectures, asking the department secretary to lie about his whereabouts, until Zaturetsky, stubbornly seeking him out, complains to the dean and finally receives the address of Klima's apartment in Prague. In a scene baring one of Kundera's favorite themes, and one filled with potential comedy as well, Zaturetsky invades Klima's privacy: banging insistently on the apartment door while Klara sits alone, he forces her to respond at last and leaves a note to remind Klima about the review. From this point, the meeting of inept scholar and beautiful young protégée, the curve of Klima's fate turns irrevocably downward.

Zaturetsky arrives at the university again a few days later, asks Klima for the review, and Klima, seeing the man's mundane, ascetic nature as material for a joke, accuses him of making sexual advances to Klara at the apartment. Enraged, Zaturetsky denies the accusation, saying he has a wife and family, and threatens to get even as Klima, believing his own lie for a moment, dismisses the man triumphantly, believing the matter finished. But a few days later Klara receives a note from Mrs. Zaturetsky demanding that she come to her apartment to explain the accusations against her husband. Of course, Klara does not go, but in short order Mrs. Zaturetsky attempts to find Klima at the university and then she and her husband seek Klara at her job. Both attempts fail, but when Klima's department chairman calls him into the office to discuss the renewal of his contract, the Zaturetskys' presence hangs ominously over the meeting. The chairman tells Klima that his article has offended the dean and that the dean, because of Zaturetsky's complaints, now thinks Klima has missed his lectures for months. Klima tries to dismiss the complaints as frivolous or untrue but, at home that night, he finds a letter from the local Party committee asking to see him.

At the meeting Klima learns of complaints about Klara's presence from other tenants, hears about his "missed" lectures, and listens to the accusations of the Zaturetskys. Most ominous, perhaps, in light of what we know about Ludvik Jahn from *The Joke*, one of the committee members refers to Klima as an intellectual and sees him as refusing to help his fellow worker, Zaturetsky. With his job clearly threatened, and the slope of his fate seeming to slide downward, Klima searches for basic values and discovers the importance of his love for Klara. But with complaints from the other tenants and their privacy invaded by Zaturetsky, she can no longer live with him, and so they meet at a borrowed apartment. In a scene reminiscent of the ones between Lucie and Ludvik in *The Joke*, Klima learns that Klara feels uncomfortable meeting him in the apartment and they argue over the review he has to write. Pragmatic, she tells him to solve his problems by praising Zaturetsky's article, but in a second statement about his basic values, Klima insists that he cannot lie or joke about his work. In order to save himself and Klara, however, he asks Mrs. Zaturetsky to his apartment. Finally telling the truth, he says that her husband's article is scientifically worthless and reads passages from it along with passages from other writers to show its lack of originality. She leaves, stunned, but although the matter of the Zaturetskys seems at rest, Klima learns from Klara that the descent of his life has really just begun. Having spoken to the editor of the visual arts journal herself, she has learned that Klima will not continue at his teaching post, and she implies that the editor will now get her the job Klima himself had promised her. Shaking his hand "clearly for the last time" (38), Klara leaves. Alone, now facing the loss of the two things he has considered most important to him, Klima looks at recent events and, resilient, still finds amusement. Having told Klara earlier that life's purpose is to entertain, he can now find comfort in the thought that his story is comic rather than tragic.

## "The Golden Apple of Desire"

If "Nobody Will Laugh" contains in miniature many of the elements of Kundera's first novel, *The Joke*, "The Golden Apple of Desire" contains elements of his two most recent novels: in its title a major image from *Immortality* and in character and event the married Don Juan theme so powerfully developed in *The Unbearable Lightness of Being*. In addition, this second *Laughable Loves* story handles a pair of picaros, as does *Jacques and His Master*, and endows them with contrasting attitudes in the manner of Professor Avenarius and the caricature Kundera draws of himself in *Immortality*.

The narrator, apparently an art historian, sits in a Prague café leafing through a rare book on Etruscan culture and waits for his friend Martin, who can do what the studious narrator finds impossible: he can stop any woman on the street and engage her in flirtatious conversation, although he often stops at talk and passes her on to his friends. With the theme of language underlined by the narrator's comments, Martin arrives and Kundera moves on to the second part of the story, appropriately called "The Adventure Begins." Seeing a beautiful young woman at a nearby table, Martin follows her to the cloakroom and, looking for a prop, takes the narrator's rare art book, says it is too heavy to carry, and drops it into the woman's bag. They talk, Martin learns that she works as a nurse in a country hospital, and, after the three walk together to her bus to the country, he promises that he and the narrator will drive to the hospital on the following Saturday to retrieve the book. As the section ends we learn that Martin, who has recently turned forty, has a young wife at home. He loves her and fears her, the narrator tells us, and immediately Martin tries to invent a story he can tell her to get out of the house. In this way both characters reveal themselves as trapped—one by life, the other by art—and both look to language and the imagination as a means of escape.

The narrator borrows a car and the two drive to the nurse's country town. Along the way to meeting her they stop several women, and the narrator explains Martin's stages in the game of seduction: "registration," "making contact," and what the narrator refers to as the "last level," presumably sex, the exclusive interest in which he passes off as a trait of "primitive" men (46). But the more refined, stylized pursuit that Martin and the narrator practice has its ridiculous side as well, for clearly, as the "adventure" of the day continues, we see the two men as ineffectual: romantics chasing beautiful maidens in a dreamlike game of words whose world is the only reality they can control.

They meet the nurse, retrieve the narrator's book, and arrange to meet her and her girlfriend after work, at seven o'clock. Martin convinces the nurse to arrange for the four of them to go to a lakeside cabin, but as he and the narrator walk about the town to occupy the time, Martin says they have to leave for Prague by eight so he can play his customary Saturday night game of cards with his wife. Nevertheless, despite only an hour alone with the young nurses, Martin feels they have time to seduce them. Meanwhile, they "register" and "make contact" with two other women, both of whom promise to meet them in a few minutes but do not return. As the afternoon passes, we come to see how much these two Don Juans are really Don Quixotes in disguise and how, despite the lure of desire that Martin lives for and that the narrator only imitates, they have no real, physical amorous goals. They lie, to themselves and others, anticipating future adventures, eagerly planning for them, but never attaining the last level of fulfillment in them. After yet another of the women they talked to does not meet them as agreed, the narrator speculates that she did not return because she believed the fiction they concocted about shooting a film on the subject of Etruscans in Bohemia. He says that it might have gone better for them if she had not believed their story. He then discusses the danger of too much faith, saying that when people believe in something completely, their faith will "turn it into something absurd" (57), a fair comment, it seems, on the adventure the two men constantly pursue.

They return to meet the nurses at seven o'clock, park near the hospital gate, and the narrator watches for them in the rear view mirror. He sees the two nurses, obviously dressed and eager to meet them, emerge from the hospital gate. Caught up in his thoughts about the danger of too much faith, the narrator sees his friend as a forty-year-old married man playing the game of youth without knowing it. Looking at his own behavior, he considers himself more ridiculous than Martin because he knows they are merely playing: "Why at this time should I behave as if an amorous adventure lay before me, when I know that at most a single aimless hour with unknown and indifferent girls awaits me?'' (60). Without informing his friend that the nurses are there, the narrator drives away, assuring Martin that they will not arrive.

In the final scene the narrator, feeling guilty, wonders whether he can ever give up the ''gestures which signify youth'' for him (61). As they discuss a female medical student ''invented'' by the narrator for possible future adventure, he and Martin discuss passing her between themselves and decide to impress her by saying that Martin is an athlete. Martin sees it as ''in the realm of possibility,'' although he is unathletic and forty years old. The story ends pathetically, with the friends' mutual, implausible lie imposing itself upon the narrator's story, or fiction; he describes the joining as a ''beautiful, ripe, shining apple'' dangling before them (62). As they follow it down the road toward the sunset, the narrator calls it ''The Golden Apple of Eternal Desire,'' an image that some twenty years later, at the end of *Immortality,* Kundera, with ironic purpose, would resurrect as a brightly colored ball floating above a mirrored swimming pool in Montparnasse: Narcissus meeting Helen, a sign of Goethe's ''eternal feminine'' drawing us on.

### ''The Hitchhiking Game''

If ''The Golden Apple of Eternal Desire'' leaves its two main characters permanently on the road in the midst of the perpetual and futile game of the chase after women, Kundera uses the next story to carry on that theme, this time as a variation, making a woman part of the journey. A young couple traveling in a sports car sees the gas gauge turn toward empty and, after some flirtatious conversation about hitchhikers, stop for fuel at a station. As they wait for service, the young woman goes into the woods behind the station to relieve herself, and the young man reflects on her purity, as he calls it, because she speaks so shyly of her body functions. Charmed, he realizes that at her young age the shyness soon must pass.

The next section of the story elaborates on the young woman's reflections as she walks into the woods and steps behind a bush to, as Kundera says, give ''herself up to her good mood'' (68). Angry about her shyness, she longs to feel more free about her body, reminding herself that the body we receive at birth is just one out of millions of possibilities, making it random, impersonal, and strictly on loan. For the moment at one with her body, she loves her traveling companion because he accepts her wholly, in no way encouraging the usual dualism of body and spirit from which she suffers. But, like Tereza in *The Unbearable Lightness of Being,* the young woman is jealous also, worrying about keeping her lover, fearing that he will leave her one day for a more physical woman, one more comfortable (and in harmony) with her body. After she leaves the woods, instead of returning to the car, she walks along the highway in the direction they are traveling. The young man catches up, and she waves; he rolls down his window to ask if she needs a ride. Smiling flirtatiously, the woman says she does and enters the car. In that way, lightly, innocuously, the hitchhiking game begins for these two travelers, a game, or fiction, that goes to the heart of self and what Kundera might call its various possibilities.

Driving, they continue to flirt, as if they really are strangers, and although the young man, through tenderness, attempts to reestablish their normal conversational tone, the woman insists on the new one. She imagines herself as seeing her lover now as a different person, the man he is with other, more free-living, women. Jealous, she continues to flirt with him and ultimately, caught up in her act, suffers because, as with the narrator of "Nobody Will Laugh," the fiction comes to dominate their reality. Playing a "role out of trashy literature" (72), she provokes her young man to respond in kind, and the two find themselves, almost against their will, playing out the game. The young man turns off the road, taking another direction from the one they are traveling, and suddenly, but separately, both experience a refreshing rush of freedom from the ordered, frustrating existence they have lived till then. Seeking lightheartedness and irresponsibility, they drive into an unknown country town and take a room for the night. The game continues, increasing its hold on them moment by moment, and the young man wonders whether he now sees his lover's real self, freed from inhibition by the roles they are playing. She feels different herself, shameless, without history or obligations and, at last, the woman she wants to be, and that she imagines her lover wants her to be: a pickup for whom *"everything"* is *"permitted"* (79).

In their room after dinner, they play out the conclusion to the game. The young man, angry that his girlfriend performs the role of whore so well, speaks to her coarsely, refusing to kiss her and giving her money to force her to humiliate herself through obscene gestures and motions. She tries to reassert her normal behavior, but he continues to treat her like a bought woman, and in a scene with the emotional brutality of Ludvik Jahn's sexual punishment of Helena in *The Joke,* aggressively pulls her into bed, where their sex, a complex mixture of anger and impersonal desire, yields a moment that Kundera describes as one with "two bodies in perfect harmony, two sensual bodies, alien to each other" (86). The young woman, having experienced what she has always most dreaded, sex without love or emotion, admits to herself that despite her horror she has experienced sexual pleasure like no other in her life. Frightened by what she has learned about herself, she lies in the dark beside her young man, both their masks off now, and cries out "I am me, I am me" (87), while her lover, searching for compassion ("from afar," Kundera tells us), tries to comfort her. For both of them, however, the game that began so innocently, spontaneously, has irrevocably changed their lives as well as their love.

## "Symposium"

Appropriately, after two explorations of the nature of physical desire, Kundera turns to present a parody of the most famous Western work on ideal, or spiritual, love, Plato's *Symposium*, a philosophic dialogue that treats love from the perspectives of myth, poetry, reason (really false, sophistic reason), and comedy before giving itself over to Socrates's discussion defining love as intellectual rather than physical, a desire for beauty in its ideal form.

Our concept of Platonic love originates in this dialogue, and Kundera performs a parodic variation on it by staging a discussion of love in a hospital, place of bodily breakdown and repair, that decidedly emphasizes the physical even as it comically belies the validity of that very solid source of erotic power. Immediately breaking down any possible realistic reading of the story, Kundera separates it into acts instead of chapters and sets the scene of the staff room at "any hospital in any town that you like" (91). What's more, he makes obvious authorial intrusions with ironic titles to the sections of each act, and in introducing his characters says that they have gathered there under "less than important" pretexts (91), presumably to drink and chat, but also, we must remember, because the author has put them there arbitrarily. With the stage set, characters introduced, and, by means of parabasis, the author's presence very firmly announced, the drama begins.

Dr. Havel and Nurse Alzhbeta sit in a hospital staff room drinking, although they are on night duty, with three other physicians on the staff: the chief physician, elderly and bald; a thirty-year-old woman doctor from another ward; and Flaishman, the youngest of them, a ward intern whose naïve self-centeredness makes him one of those angelic innocents Kundera has treated so frequently and ironically in his fiction. The others have various degrees of experience, fitting for their years, and although the evening passes with what Kundera calls "appreciative chatter" (91), we learn of some tensions. Alzhbeta has drunk too much and begins to flirt with Dr. Havel, whose response sets off whatever drama the evening will have. Complaining that as a nurse Alzhbeta should understand the limits of the flesh, Havel criticizes her desire, a vitality that he calls "incorrigible," and declares that her body movements make his head spin. "Those boobs of yours are ubiquitous—like

God!'' he says (92), ordering her to leave him alone and go about her business of injecting patients. When she leaves to do just that, the chief physician wonders aloud why Havel refuses the nurse's advances when normally, like death, he will, as the chief says, ''take everything'' (93).

The two phrases, about Alzhbeta's breasts and Havel's desire, combine to state the basic metaphysical themes that Kundera handles in this story, ironically joining (and inverting) the spiritual with the physical and the erotic with the eternal. During a discussion that reinforces this yoking of opposites, the chief physician speaks of his greatest amorous success as one with a sexually experienced woman who refused to go to bed with him. He describes her refusal as a sign of lifelong commitment since he was her ''first and last'' refused man (94). The banter continues, with Havel admitting he does not know why he rejects Alzhbeta, since he has slept with uglier, more aggressive women, and he finally blames it on caprice, raising that capriciousness to a philosophic level by calling it a ''scrap of freedom'' in a ''world of iron laws'' (96). The three drink to freedom, and at that moment, young Flaishman enters the room, having gone off to buy a bottle of champagne.

Immediately, Havel and the chief physician take advantage of the intern's youthful egotism, claiming that for months Alzhbeta has wanted him while he has ungallantly looked the other way. Flaishman, described as slow, not because of clumsiness but because of preoccupation with his inner self, replies that he is not interested in the nurse and absolves himself from guilt, saying he is not responsible for pain he causes involuntarily. At this point Alzhbeta returns to the room, drinks champagne, and the chief physician voices one of Kundera's most prominent themes: Ignorance absolves no one, not even innocents, since ''Ignorance is a fault'' (97), and man bears responsibility for it. It is a theme Kundera would turn to again in other books,[5] and the reader may recognize in Flaishman the same self-conscious innocence (and the same attachment to his mother) that motivates Jaromil in *Life Is Elsewhere*. The woman doctor defends Flaishman, and he takes it as a sign that she is interested in him. She has apparently intrigued him since they met, and when she goes to the window and declares how lovely it looks outside under the full moon, he takes her comment as a hint that she wants to be with him in the open air. He leaves the room, his chest swelling with absolute certainty that she will follow him, and enters the garden to await her. Knowing that a great love experience is imminent, he leans against a tree and smokes, romantically seeing himself in the garden at the same time; but when he turns toward the sound of footsteps behind him he finds, rather than the woman doctor, the chief physician out to relieve his bladder. As ''Act One'' ends, this sudden change from romance to biological necessity comically underlines the dualism in Flaishman's (and we might say European) self-consciousness.

In "Act Two" Kundera accentuates the duality. Flaishman and the chief physician return to the staff room to find Alzhbeta, drunk, in the midst of a mock striptease that creates one of the most memorable parodic scenes in Kundera's fiction. With her body everywhere in the room, "like God," she circles the other characters, revolving especially about Havel, who sits with his head down as if attending a funeral. Alzhbeta encourages him to look at her, saying that she is vital, alive, at least temporarily, and, at that comment, the narrator describes her backside as "splendidly formed grief" (105) dancing close to Havel, who, despite her encouragement, keeps his eyes turned to the floor. In pantomime she removes all her clothes, and, on tiptoe at the end of her dance, in the "glory of her fictional nakedness" (107), stares down at her body, self-involved in the same way Flaishman is when he studies himself internally or stands in the garden waiting for romance to begin.

Exhausted finally, Alzhbeta collapses at Havel's feet and asks for pep pills to provide more energy. He gives her a sleeping pill instead, and when she, more tired and drunk, tries to sit on his lap, he moves his legs so she falls to the floor. Embarrassed, Alzhbeta decides to go to bed, calling the others beasts and idiots for having laughed at her. After she leaves, the doctors continue their banter. When the woman doctor refers to Havel as a Don Juan, the chief physician disagrees, again likening his colleague to death. Havel agrees with the chief physician's assessment. In a long analytic speech that lifts the consideration of love to a mythic level, he says that Don Juan is no longer a valid figure because in his time he conquered convention and innocence, defying death and God for sexual pleasure, while today's more liberal conventions would make him a collector with no tragic import. Claiming to be a mere comic figure himself, Havel says that whatever small grandeur he possesses exists only against the "background" of Don Juan's "tragic gaiety" (112). The woman doctor compliments Havel on his fine speech, noting that it contradicts his claim to a humble masculine role. Calling him an "old fraud," she remarks on the beauty of the night, and Flaishman, once more misreading her comment as a signal, excuses himself to go into the garden. But as "Act Two" ends, Flaishman again finds something unexpected. Sure that romance is imminent, he smells gas as he leaves the building, tracks it to the nurses' quarters, and finds Alzhbeta lying on her couch, unconscious and naked, with the unlit jet to the gas stove on. He opens the window and calls the others to help save her (as they do), but not before seeing, in yet another inversion (death made to look sexual and beautiful), just how lovely her body really is.

In "Act Three" Kundera begins to unwind the story, even as he continues the philosophic explorations. With Alzhbeta's life saved, the three doctors and Flaishman debate what happened in the nurses' room, disagreeing as much about the experience of death as they did earlier about erotic ones. As they debate, Kundera turns Alzhbeta's body (and her handling of it) into a sign for which each speaker seeks to find some meaning. Flaishman, self-absorbed romantic that he is, believes that Alzhbeta tried to kill herself out of love for him, condemns his egocentricity for not responding to her, and, reversing his earlier thinking, accepts responsibility for the unintended pain he caused. The chief physician, still superficially clever, believes Alzhbeta set up the suicide without intending to achieve it; she undressed, he says, turned on the gas, and, to tempt Havel, left the door to her room open so that he would discover her and see her beautiful body. Havel shrugs in resignation, saying he believes Alzhbeta intended to kill herself but not for him alone; everyone, not just Havel, refused her, he says, and she intended to be found naked, glorious, slipping into "intercourse with death" (121), so that those she left behind would be envious and long at last for her underestimated body. Practical, the woman doctor refutes the other opinions, saying Alzhbeta gassed herself by mistake. She had returned to her room, finished the strip-tease, this time removing her clothes for real, then put on coffee to await Havel, who she thought would arrive when the other doctors left for the night; tired, she fell asleep and the water for the coffee boiled over to put out the gas flame. Havel objects to this theory and asks for an explanation of Alzhbeta's comment about being alive, if only temporarily. The woman doctor, having previously called Havel a fraud for his fine talk about Don Juan, tells him that ninety-nine percent of all statements have no meaning; that is, they are fictional. Whether Kundera intends her comment as his central theme or not, he ends "Act Three" ironically with a view of patent self-delusion: Flaishman again, seated in his parents' garden, feeling words like "beloved" and "death" filling his chest and lifting him as if he wore wings (the angel motif again), and believing that in Alzhbeta he has at long last found absolute love.

To corroborate that theme, "Act Four" presents a scene of completely idle chatter. Late at night the woman doctor returns to the staff room, claiming she cannot sleep. She and Havel talk, each claiming a lack of sexual interest in the other, primarily because of their shared affection for the chief physician. Echoing Plato, Havel says friendship between men is much more important than erotic love of women, and he goes on to say that he sees his own future in the chief physician's pretentious behavior. With the decay of the body that comes with age, he says, a man must pretend, creating "everything that he no longer is" (128). The woman doctor understands and agrees that she too could do nothing to harm the chief physician. But their shared affection for the chief becomes the primary motive for their betrayal of him. Havel would do nothing to harm him, the woman doctor says, so "I can depend on you. I can make love with you" (129). She sits on Havel's knee and unbuttons his shirt. In a parabatic aside that makes up a section heading, the narrator asks a question whose answer is obvious, "What Did Dr. Havel Do?" In a teasing response the narrator also says, "Ah, that's some question" (129).

Since the answer to that question is not in words but in imagination and (as we imagine it) action, it is fitting that Kundera makes the final act of his philosophic drama revolve around a set of inventions and imaginations that in all likelihood will not be realized. He begins with Flaishman offering flowers to Alzhbeta and just avoiding the impulse to ask her to marry him. Overcome with the grandeur of his feeling, he thanks her for existing, squeezes her shoulder, and leaves to go back on duty. In the staff room he finds Havel, the chief physician, and the woman doctor still debating the suicide. Alzhbeta has confirmed the woman doctor's theory about the water boiling over, but the chief physician reminds them she could be lying since people who attempt suicide are regularly sent to asylums in their country. With the truth thus undermined, even from its source, the three continue to disagree, with each reversing a previously stated opinion. The chief physician now thinks Alzhbeta might have intended to kill herself; the woman doctor, in order "to make the world more beautiful" (132), says they should agree; and Havel, feeling guilty about the previous night, claims that only love, not friendship, is important enough to be worth a suicide. The story ends with Flaishman, ever living in his illusions, hearing the woman doctor exclaim, as she looks through the window to a beautiful day, that she is happy to be alive. Once again, he interprets her words as a romantic signal, feels grateful for having settled his feeling for Alzhbeta with flowers "and some nice words" (133), and (but we are left to imagine this, nothing more) excuses himself to go into the garden. The story begins again, Kundera tells us, but with Flaishman feeling stronger, older, having received a most romantic (and questionable) gift, a "splendid . . . invigorating death" (133) that, along with love, has been investigated and debated from positions similar to those in Plato's *Sym-*

*posium:* myth, poetry (Flaishman's emotions), specious reasoning (all that empty talk, especially about Alzhbeta's "suicide"), and, a Kunderan specialty from beginning to end, ironic comedy.

### "Let the Old Dead Make Room for the Young Dead"

"Symposium" is perhaps the high point of *Laughable Loves* so far, its joining of farce with philosophic seriousness a key to Kundera's stated ambitions for fiction,[6] while the three stories that follow serve as a coda of sorts, further exploring meaning through the experience of love, the memory of love, and the language that attempts, but finally fails, to encapsulate them.

From a discussion of the search for truth and reality in love and death, Kundera moves to a discussion of reality itself, especially in relation to human character. In "Let the Old Dead Make Room for the Young Dead," an autumnal story, he presents a pair of former lovers, meeting again in a small Czech town after fifteen years, who make the futile attempt to bring together their younger with their present selves. Complicating the situation, both have reached crisis points in their lives, moments when they are made painfully aware of the passage of time and the increased imminence of their deaths.

The woman (we never know her name) has come to this small town where her husband lies buried only to find out that the lease on the land that holds his grave has run out and the authorities have removed the body and headstone and replaced them with the remains of another. When she complains that the authorities should have let her know that the lease had run out so she could renew it, an official mutters the words that become the title and motif of this story: *"The old dead ought to make room for the young dead"* (139). The woman wanders about the town, filled with remorse for her loss and her carelessness, and upset because she knows her son, who still loves his father, will accuse her of forgetting him. Looking to pass the time until her bus leaves for Prague, she meets a younger man with whom she spent a night some fifteen years before. He, twenty years younger than she but preoccupied with his own advancing age (thirty-five) and the signs of an inevitable bald spot on his head, almost passes her by until he recognizes her smile. As he talks to her, he feels the whole experience of the single night they spent together return. With all the cafes filled and dirty, he invites her to his apartment for coffee, and there the drama of four selves in two characters plays itself out in a single room that calls to the characters' minds another, smaller one they had made love in fifteen years before.

In an elegiac tone much like the one he uses in "The Middle-Aged Man" section of *Life Is Elsewhere* and "The Dial" in *Immortality* (both are "guesthouse" chapters, separate structures that are yet still part of the formal estate that makes up the world of the novel they inhabit[7]), Kundera tells us something about the man's memory of the woman. She had been beautiful, not only older but married to an older man, more experienced, and therefore mysterious to him. After several meetings in small cafés, she had agreed to meet him in his room. Overwhelmed to be with her alone, he could not act naturally or confidently, and because of his inexperience she had to lead them into the act of love. Shamed, he had turned off the lights before they undressed and, although they were sexually intimate, he could not see her face. Now, like Rubens in *Immortality*, in the midst of evaluating his life and seeing it as pitifully uneventful, he realizes he made love to an important woman without knowing her, and seeks to redress that essential emptiness in their second meeting.

Looking at her, hearing her talk about annual visits to her husband's grave on All Soul's Day, the man analyzes her appearance and sees that with wrinkles of age, gray hair, and sagging skin, the woman eludes him still because she is not what she was. But in a narrative moment that looks forward to the genesis of *Immortality*, Kundera has the man offer the woman some cognac, and the charm of her gesture as she refuses transports him, allows him to glimpse her younger self again, in the way he recognized her through her smile when they met on the street. Moved to pity as well as recognition, he talks of the terrible trail of a life passed too swiftly, as well as the end that beckons to everyone. But she responds to his gravity without a touch of sympathy, calling his remarks "superficial" (145). To the woman, the narrator tells us, life has meaning in the work humans do, not in their bodies that so quickly decay. She speaks of her own work as an organizer of cultural programs and as a mother giving "everything that a mother can" (146) to her son while she, in age, quietly slips into the background of his life. From that statement Kundera continues to provide details of her life with her son: he has subjugated her (while other men have failed), forcing her into the confines of a proper widow's role by detesting everything youthful and sexual about her until she gave in finally, telling herself that although he nudged her toward the grave, she could live beautifully through him.

The man accepts her argument, seeing it as consistent with his impression of her as a woman intensely interested in beauty and opposed to ugliness and bad taste. He recalls their one night together, her grace and frankness a contrast to his own awkwardness and shame, and thinks of her as beyond his imagination even though they had made love. Her whispered words and the features of her face eluded him in the dark, and after their shared emotions he could only think of her as mysterious and "unreal" (150). He tells her about his experience, and she interprets his account as proof that the worth of a human life is best measured in its extension beyond the self into the memories and experiences of others. Enjoying this perception, she wonders as he strokes her hand whether he touches the skin of the woman he talks to or the woman about whom he talks. At the same time she perceives his own multiple self, acknowledging that she likes this man better than the inexperienced youth she went to bed with fifteen years before.

He embraces her and she, aware of her body's age and mortality against his memory of her youth, resists, begging him not to destroy the "memorial" (155) of her erected in his mind. He lies, telling her he still finds her beautiful, even though he admits to himself that making love will end for him in disgust. His desire for what she was, for his memory of the woman who eluded him in youth and who has remained a mystery for him through the years, becomes a symbol for everything his life has lacked; finally, it overwhelms his physical revulsion. He tells her not to fight him, aware only that should they make love today he will finally see her face and, perhaps, read the expression he lost in the dark fifteen years before. At the same time he wants "to debase this reading immediately" (158), and he realizes that he desires her now because the disgust that follows will allow him to put the lie to all she has represented through the years: the opportunities lost, the experiences missed, the pleasures never enjoyed; his disgust would render them all as "dust," mere images of memory or desire, "doomed to destruction" (158).

The woman still resists but, regretting the loss of her husband's grave site and seeing her son in the man's face, feels enraged at the trap her age, the widow's role, and her son's expectations have erected around her. She declares to herself the end of all memorials. The "old dead must make room for the young dead," she thinks, repeating the cemetery official's remark, "and yes, my boy, all memorials [are] for nothing" (159). In a complete loss of the faith that has sustained her through the years, she decides to favor physical life over memorials. She will make love to the man, the last "who would appeal to her and whom, at the same time, she could have" (159) because things outside herself, other people's thoughts and memory have no real importance now. She gives in and, in a moving narrative moment filled with the intimacy of shame and self-knowledge, begins to undress. Kundera concludes the story ironically, a grimace of despair slightly leavened with bitter laughter over what the two characters will not only feel but see: "This time the room was full of light" (160).

## "Dr. Havel after Twenty Years"

Another autumnal story about the body's mortality and the way the spirit combats decay through language, "Dr. Havel after Twenty Years"[8] does a variation on the previous story's motif of love in age. In this version, however, Kundera has age make love with youth and shows how, because of language's abilities to alter and create reality, youth, rather than age, feels privileged.

Twenty years after the events of "Symposium," Dr. Havel, now married to a beautiful, well-known actress with a film just appearing in the theaters, finds himself with gallbladder problems and taking the cure at a small spa in the country. His wife, despite her beauty, feels jealous because of Havel's well-known, and well-deserved, reputation as a lover, but to his disappointment he finds himself overlooked by the women at the spa. When, at the suggestion of Dr. Frantishka (Havel's female physician), the young male editor of the spa's newspaper comes to arrange an interview, not with Havel but his wife during one of her visits, Havel reads it as a sign of how low his reputation has sunk.

However, the editor, who has heard about Havel's conquests and is insecure about his own erotic abilities, asks the older man to meet his girlfriend and evaluate her from his expert point of view. Dr. Havel agrees, and finds himself repelled by what he calls the young woman's small-town looks—she is thin, with freckles around her nose—and especially her talkativeness. Embarrassed, the editor defends his girlfriend as being "nice," but Havel replies that dogs, canaries, and ducklings can also be nice. He urges the editor to cultivate his taste by throwing "small fish back into the water" (183) and learn to find true erotic beauty by seeking the unusual. Genuinely loving the young woman, the editor nevertheless accepts Havel's judgment and, when he meets the beautiful Mrs. Havel, becomes convinced he has taken a lesson from a master.

In the meantime, Havel, seeing new respect from others as he walks through the spa with his wife on his arm, feels more confident about himself and, in a playful mood, recommends Dr. Frantishka to the editor. She does not conform to the "ready-made prettiness" (186) of small-town tastes, he says, and possesses very "expressive" legs (187). Urging the editor to listen to what those legs are "saying," Havel plants the seed of desire in the editor's imagination, just as his wife's presence creates attention from two of the women who previously spurned him. The love scene between the editor and Dr. Frantishka takes on a central role, ranking as one of the funniest that

Kundera has written. In a sweet yet farcical variation of the son and lover motif he treated in "Let the Old Dead Make Room for the Young Dead," Kundera describes the editor fighting to maintain his sexual ardor as Dr. Frantishka, more talkative than his girlfriend, babbles about her children: "Beautiful, beautiful!" she calls them (196); and when the editor, striving to maintain physical passion, says how much he wanted to make love to her when they first met, she replies by comparing him to her son: "That kid wants everything too" (196). Finally, their sex at last completed, she gives his hair a matronly stroke, saying he has a "cute little mop" just like her son's, although Kundera, humanely and in good humor, describes her as feeling younger and, with gratitude, "foolishly good" (197).

The story ends with Havel and the editor meeting next day. Havel's wife has returned to Prague and the doctor himself awaits another woman. The editor, slightly ashamed of his experience with Frantishka, hides it at first, but eventually provides details when Havel questions him. Enthusiastic about his own prospects now, Havel responds positively to the tale of Frantishka's conversation. He tells the editor that bodily pleasure felt in silence only grows "tiresomely similar" (199), making one woman become like all the others. Yet we seek sexual adventures, he says, "to remember them" (199) and, anticipating a theme from *The Book of Laughter and Forgetting,* Havel adds that it takes language, words spoken "at this most banal of moments" (199), to make the sexual experience unforgettable. Although he is known as a collector of women, Havel tells the editor he has a different assessment of himself. Baldly stating one of Kundera's most prominent ideas while underlining the thematic role of language in *Laughable Loves,* he says, "In reality, I'm far more a collector of words" (199)—that is, words spoken during coitus—than of women. Ironically, he follows that self-assessment by walking away hand in hand with a young woman he has met at the spa. Described as resembling a "riding horse" (199), she heads with him toward the spa promenade where, presumably, instead of listening to her words, he will treat her like a prize possession and show her off.

## "Edward and God"

In *Immortality* Professor Avenarius says that most men, given the choice, would rather be seen with a beautiful woman than sleep with her, and Havel, the self-proclaimed "collector of words," serves to confirm that assessment at the end of the previous story, making him a collector of images (and self-images) as well. As Kundera probes the reality behind the lies of language in *Laughable Loves,* he moves through various shadowy areas of philosophic truth, and in this last story of the collection he takes as his final topic the essence of the self as it relates to religious and ideological faith. A companion piece to "The Hitchhiking Game," it is perhaps the most ambitious of the stories in this book, one that embodies most of the narrative techniques and themes that we associate with Kundera in his novels: parabasis and authorial intrusion, variation, social and physical necessity as a method of character motivation, use of theatrical tableaux, gravity of subject handled with light technique, parody of ideological innocence, irony, and finally laughter at the way fate turns against the best human intentions. In its concern with Communist Party guilt and restitution it parallels *The Joke* and *Life Is Elsewhere*; in its exploration of the trap that life has become it looks forward to *The Farewell Party* and *The Book of Laughter and Forgetting*; and in the farce it makes of the mysteries (and lies) inflating and deflating reputations as well as love affairs it joins *The Unbearable Lightness of Being* and *Immortality*.

Edward, a schoolteacher, not by choice, visits his brother in the country to discuss problems he will have in obtaining a teaching position from a school supervisor, Miss Chehachkova, a party zealot who many years ago caused Edward's brother to lose his status as a university student for behaving with unbecoming levity after Stalin's death. Edward's brother was forced to leave Prague and work in the country as a result of Miss Chehachkova's denunciation, but he has adjusted well to his fate, acquiring a house, a family, a dog, and a cottage. Edward's brother tells him not to worry about the supervisor, saying that she has always gone after young men and so she will probably look favorably on him. She may even wish to redress the old wrong she did to him, he says, believing that even party zealots possess consciences.

Edward has just graduated from a teacher's college, and to his relief he finds that his brother is right about Miss Chehachkova. Tall, ugly, with black eyes and just a hint of a black moustache, she responds well to Edward and succeeds in finding a teaching position for him. The position, Kundera says, makes Edward "neither happy nor sad" (204), since he puts a teaching career in the category of the "*unserious*" things in life, principally because it did not fit what he considered to be his true nature and he did not freely choose it. Rather, external conditions, such as the accident of academic and party affiliations (and successful performance during examinations), had chosen him for the career. Thus, he sees chance as the primary cause of his occupation, and because of that he regards it as "laughable," a key word in terms of the title of the book and the theme of this particular story. Kundera explains further: "What is *obligatory* was unserious (laughable) . . . what is *non-obligatory* was serious" (205), and so chance, operating as necessity through Edward's grades, party membership, and scores, leads Edward into his career, allowing him no freedom of choice. But Kundera reveals the non-obligatory and serious side of Edward's experience through his love life, in this case a beautiful young women whom he meets at school.

However, the young woman, Alice, believes in God, presenting a difficulty for Edward. Saying she could not live without meaning, Alice asks Edward whether he has religious faith, and as he, not wanting to lose her, struggles for a fitting reply, encourages him to speak honestly. Without such honesty, "there wouldn't be any sense" in their being together (206), she says. Edward confesses to religious doubts but goes to church with Alice on Sunday and finds himself moved by the ceremony. Emotionally compelled to kneel on the floor, he feels "magnificently free" (207) at the same time, perhaps because in religious faith he senses the operation of choice rather than necessity. He lies, telling Alice he no longer harbors doubts about God, but unfortunately, as they leave the church together, with his soul "full of laughter" (207), Miss Chehachkova passes and sees them on the steps.

When he meets the supervisor at school during the week, he explains his presence at church by citing an interest in baroque architecture. Clearly, Miss Chehachkova does not believe him, and therefore he excuses himself from church with Alice the following Sunday. Annoyed, she criticizes his wavering belief, and Kundera, in a parabatic aside that prefigures the technique of the novels that come afterward, describes how Edward burns with desire for Alice's body while the Seventh Commandment, forbidding adultery, remains Alice's primary means of testing her faith. The other nine commandments, Kundera says, about honoring parents, not killing, and not coveting neighbors' goods or wives, seem self-evident to her, while the seventh is inconvenient and therefore requires commitment. Using faith to fight her, Edward raises the issue of a less forbidding New Testament God allowing and encouraging love, even including sex. He quotes St. Paul, "Everything is pure to the man who is pure at heart" (211) and refers to Augustine's "Love God and do what you will." When Alice continues to refuse him, romantically and sexually, he begins to exaggerate his religious zeal, accusing Alice of being too complacent to be truly religious. Finally, performing what amounts to a parody of faith, he ostentatiously crosses himself before a crucifix in the street. A woman janitor from his school sees him, reports him to the Party Committee, and, as Kundera says, making use of a pun on ideological as well as religious faith, "Edward realized that he was lost" (213).

Called before the committee, presided over by Miss Chehachkova, Edward feels overwhelmed by the situation. He cannot, like Ludvik Jahn, bring himself to call his actions a joke because he is sensitive to the gravity with which the committee members regard the situation. Instead, he asks permission to be frank, and the supervisor, echoing Alice when she and Edward discussed religion, tells him he must be frank or else there is no point in their meeting. Gratified, he confesses that he does in fact believe in God even though he does not want to, since religious faith has no place in modern life. Acknowledging the contradiction between what he knows and what he believes, Edward simply hangs his head and says he feels that "He exists" (217). Sympathetic, probably because Edward is a young man, Miss Chehachkova urges the committee to give reason a chance to defeat faith and promises to take charge of his reeducation.

At this point some readers may begin to see Edward as a manipulator of women, playing on their political and religious beliefs for his own gain. Perhaps. And, consistent with that viewpoint, Kundera tells us that Edward felt relieved to be in the supervisor's hands, resolving immediately to gain her favor "as a man" (218). But let us not forget that the social, political world manipulates him, and he must defend himself against it any way he can.[9] From that viewpoint the women also manipulate Edward, and we should remember that with this story's title Kundera has set out to examine, through irony, the larger philosophic issue of belief; erotic romance happens to be the field upon which he studies it.

Alice and Miss Chehachkova represent two possible directions for personal belief to take in life, as well as two possible sources of manipulation. Edward is caught between them. Discussing the Communist Party and the pain that she admits it has caused, Miss Chehachkova gives a clear variation on Alice's statement about God: Without something other than herself to believe in, she says, "I couldn't perhaps live at all." Edward asks about her personal life, whether it could not be satisfying in and of itself, and her bitter smile makes him see her evident loneliness and passion, with political commitment being an inadequate substitute for love. They go on to discuss the nature of belief and recognize the impossibility of joining religion and Communism. Miss Chehachkova, responding to the intimacy of her pupil's sympathetic attention, tells Edward that she likes his youth and especially likes him. At this moment, as Kundera points out, something important happens: the trap Edward has been working so hard to construct for his supervisor suddenly springs, but not on her. Instead, it closes on him.

Edward replies to Miss Chehachkova's statement by saying, "not too expressively" (222), that he likes her also. She reacts with surprise, saying she is an old woman, and Edward feels obligated to deny it, calling her sense of age "nonsense" (222). She tells him not to lie. He says, seemingly sincere, that he finds her pretty, that he likes women with black hair. The scene, humorous and wrenching at the same time, reads very much like a passage from Witold Gombrowicz,[10] 'with Edward feeling himself pushed deeper and deeper into a performance made necessary by the situation, even as he plays (to himself) the character of the freewheeling Don Juan. When the directress asks why he has never spoken to her about his feelings before, he delivers a plausible response, but one that only makes things worse for him. People would have thought "I was sucking up to you," he tells her, and she replies that he should not be ashamed: "It has *been decided* that you must meet with me from time to time" (223). That their meetings are obligatory places them under Edward's category of the "unserious" or laughable; more important, as the story develops, the scene itself signals a drastic turn in Edward's fate, placing him solidly in the Kafkan realm of what Kundera calls the "horror of the comic,"[11] where the jaws of necessity have sprung closed on his freedom. But Edward does not know that yet, and as he leaves, Miss Chehachkova strokes his hand, sending him home like a successful Don Juan, "with the sprightly feelings of a winner" (223).

For a time Edward's sense of his situation seems correct. He has become the stuff of legend among his friends, and the virtuous Alice, now perceiving him as a martyr for his religious beliefs, agrees to spend a weekend in the country with him. But before that occurs he meets again with the supervisor in her apartment, and he learns that, for her too, principles fall easily before passion. In a parabatic passage that lays out the theatrical as well as philosophic content of the following scene, Kundera reminds the reader how fallible is man's sense of his future before the workings of external forces: "A man imagines that he is playing his role in a particular play, and does not suspect that in the meantime they have changed the scenery without his noticing" (227). Finding himself in the "middle of a rather different performance," he must, in all innocence, improvise his actions and his words, with the plot now inevitably working against him. Such is Edward's experience with his supervisor.

Feeling confident when he arrives at her apartment, Edward finds himself trapped by what Kundera calls "*the change of program*" (228) and realizes that the bottle of cognac, the intense look in Miss Chehachkova's eyes, and their increasingly personal rather than ideological conversation will lead them directly into each other's arms. Repelled by her ugliness, Edward feels his livelihood threatened, and as he leads her around the room in a romantic dance, drinks glass after glass of cognac to numb himself against his feelings.

The comic and philosophic point to the scene, of course, is that Edward *must* make love to Miss Chehachkova in order to keep his job, "unserious" though he thinks it may be. Touching her breast, he gives himself up to "irreversible necessity" (230), placing the scene (and himself) in the realm of the laughable, despite the genuine terror he must feel when his body rebels against the moment's needs. With the supervisor standing naked before him, he finds he must improvise, and he calls upon religion to cover this physical lack of desire. Declaring their actions sinful, he demands that she kneel, clasp her hands, and pray, and the "threefold image of degradation" (233), as Kundera calls it, excites him at last. As she finishes her prayer, he lifts her off the floor and carries her to the couch.

Kundera follows Edward's near physical failure with a scene about a spiritual one. The next weekend Edward travels to the country with Alice and finds, now to his dismay, that she no longer feels reluctant to go to bed with him. The change bothers rather than enchants him because it occurs independent of his efforts and without any acceptable logic. In fact, as Edward analyzes it, Alice will sleep with him now because of a mistaken belief that he has been martyred for his religious beliefs. Yet if he did not betray God before the Party Committee, Edward wonders, why should she betray her religious principles (as the supervisor did her political ones) before Edward? With such doubts in mind, he speaks to his brother, who turns the table of ethics on him and his own actions. When Edward tells about his seduction of Miss Chehachkova, Edward's brother disapproves, saying that whatever else he has done, he has never lied. In reply Edward talks of the madness of speaking truthfully to a madman. Seeing the world as insane, he says, "If I obstinately told the truth to its face, it would mean that I was taking it seriously" (237). And taking the world, or a madman, seriously, Edward tells his brother, would make him unserious (or laughable) and mad himself.

The conversation reaches the heart of Edward's feelings and, we might say, relates the primary question in Kundera's fiction: What is the real value of truth, beauty, and human goodness in an insane, chaotic world made comprehensible only through fictions? Having realized his physical desires at last, Edward becomes obsessed with Alice's lack of faith as they journey homeward. His conscience revolts against her and, with the plot of his life changing despite his passionate desire for her body, Edward comes to see Alice, and everyone else he knows, as "beings without firm substance," people "with interchangeable attitudes" (238), and admits himself to be a mere shadow, or imitation, of them. Remorseful despite his physical attraction to her, he tells Alice that she disgusts him, and when they arrive in Prague the good-byes they say are clearly final.

Kundera ends the story and the book with images of spiritual ambivalence: Edward, done with both his desire and regret for Alice, sees Miss Chehachkova weekly, with the intent of doing so until his position at the school is secure. Meanwhile, he has begun to seek other woman, and his success with them more than satisfies his physical needs. A pensive, perhaps even monkish, Don Juan, he appreciates quiet moments alone, and his nostalgic longing for deity dramatizes the spiritual dissatisfaction in his life. Too bright to see God as real, Kundera says, Edward is yet too weak to ignore his wish for Him. In a scene of spiritual emptiness reminiscent in tone of the one that closes *The Book of Laughter and Forgetting,* he presents a theatrical tableau: Edward, in church, thoughtfully looking up at the cupola and, in his melancholy, suddenly seeing the face of God. Not mythically sexual, like the golden apple of eternal desire or a brightly colored ball tossed from a woman's outstretched hand, the image clearly, and sadly, draws everyone, including Edward, on.

So a book that begins with laughter, ends with poetry. Unlike Klima, in "Nobody Will Laugh," Edward lacks an ironic sense of himself. Still, he smiles and, Kundera says, feels happy. He asks us to keep that sad fictional image of Edward (keeping that charged fictional image of spiritual longing) in our memories. It is a paradox of longing, Kundera says,[12] and a poetry of need. In the world that neither Edward nor any of the other characters made, it is a truth whose only expression comes in the fictional world of dreams.

## NOTES

1. From the author's note, Czech edition of *The Joke;* my translation, from French, of Kundera's own translation from the Czech.

2. *The Art of the Novel* (New York: Grove, 1988) 85.

3. Personal letter to the author, May 13, 1990: "It is a collection of short stories, but it has almost the same thematic unity as *The Book of Laughter and Forgetting.* In Germany and in Spain *Laughable Loves* appeared under the title *The Book of Laughable Loves.* (It was my idea, that title.)"

4. *Laughable Loves* (New York: Penguin, 1987) 34. Further references will be noted parenthetically.

5. *The Book of Laughter and Forgetting* (especially in the passages about the French poet, Éluard) and *The Unbearable Lightness of Being* (when Kundera discusses Oedipus and his acceptance of guilt).

6. "To bring together the extreme gravity of the question and the extreme lightness of the form—that has always been my ambition" *Art of the Novel* 95.

7. See *Life Is Elsewhere* (New York: Penguin, 1986) 269–73.

8. Originally "Dr. Havel after Ten Years"; Kundera changed the title when he published the definitive French and English versions of *Laughable Loves*. The change allows for a greater emphasis on bodily change and decay, even as the spirit retains desire.

9. Kundera sees Edward as powerless, not as a manipulator: "He lies not to manipulate women, but to be able to live in the world, such as it is" (personal letter to the author, November 1991).

10. See ch. 1 of this study for further comment, particularly on Gombrowicz's *Ferdydurke*.

11. *The Art of the Novel* 104.

12. "The final passage isn't ironic. It is paradoxical, not ironic" (personal letter to the author, November 1991).

# CHAPTER TEN

# Conclusion: *The Art of the Novel*

*Man thinks, God laughs.* —Jewish proverb quoted in *The Art of the Novel*

"The object of structuralism," said the French essayist Roland Barthes, "is not man endowed with meanings, but man fabricating meanings."[1] While it is not the aim of this study to place Kundera in the category of structuralist or poststructuralist critics, we can see Barthes's comment as a model for one of the key scenes that Kundera repeats, with certain variations, in many of his novels: A character sits, framed by a window, room, or mirror, and contemplates his life, his fate, his existence, trying to give it meaning even as it is made clear by the narrator's tone, sometimes ironic, sometimes sympathetic, that there is little if any meaning to be found. Such an image concludes *Laughable Loves.* Edward sits in church and looks for God while we, and the author, look at him and possibly laugh, exemplifying the serious yet playful spirit of all Kundera's fiction. "The novel is a meditation on existence as seen through the medium of imaginary characters," Kundera says in his theoretical work *The Art of the Novel* (83), and we can see that idea as the primary source of seriousness, gravity, or "weight" in his art as well as its ironic humor.

Kundera repeats the key scene frequently: when he himself stares at the wall and conceives his character Tomas, in *The Unbearable Lightness of Being;* when Tomas stares out at the wall and contemplates his fate in the same novel; when Kundera writes of his highrise apartment in France whose window faces his former home in Prague (*The Book of Laughter and Forgetting*); when he describes how in 1971 he and a friend stared out his window at the spires of Prague Castle and discussed the dismissal of one hundred and forty-five Czech historians; when Klima, the instructor of art history abandoned by love and profession, laughs at his own fate at the end of the ironically titled "Nobody Will Laugh"; and finally when Jaromil, caught in the frame of a cinematographer's image in *Life Is Elsewhere,* silently mouths his words to the camera while standing before the probable site of his own conception.

Kundera places other, less obvious tableaux throughout his work: Ludvik, in *The Joke,* staring in the mirror while Lucie shaves him, feeling his whole experience with her flood his consciousness; Rubens, in *Immortality,* studying pictures of Agnes and interpreting the mysteries of his own futile life; Jakub, in *The Farewell Party,* watching himself commit senseless murder to understand how far his moral nature will let external circumstances control him; and finally Tereza, in *The Unbearable Lightness of Being,* staring at her naked body in the mirror and wondering: If I had a different nose (or face or arm), would I still be Tereza?

Along with the motif of the framed moment of contemplation, Kundera creates corollary scenes of characters separated from life by height or distance and gazing over it: Kundera and Avenarius beside the swimming pool at the top of a tower in Montparnasse; Tamina behind the counter in her café, wondering about her journals across the border; the middle-aged man in his apartment reading the works of ancient literature in *Life Is Elsewhere*; and Jaromil, in the same novel, out on the balcony, considering suicide while separated from the erotic life of the party behind the glass door in back of him as well as the active, social life of the city lying at his feet.

From parabasis to the exemplary framed scene, Kundera has created a thematic and stylistic continuum that works as a model for his special kind of narrative structure. Mixing fictional materials with other modes of prose such as essays, philosophic speculation, fantasy, and autobiography, he has created a narrative persona who increasingly steps from behind his mask to address the audience and discuss the characters, setting, or idea behind the story he tells, as well as any other bit of information or thinking that occupies his mind. In light of such a technique, we can say that for Kundera a novelist operates with a method similar to the one Barthes describes for structuralists: From an observatory, arbitrarily placed, as Kundera says in *Life Is Elsewhere* (269), the novelist studies men and women (including himself, from time to time) who, in thought and language, try to make meaning of the mystery of self while physically living the greater mystery of an existence that increasingly overwhelms them. Thus, while characters think, speak, and act in order to make meaning, the novelist, like history or, in a larger context, God, lifts the veil of illusion, exposing whatever once lay there, unseen, beneath our eyes.

It is a serious method, filled with potential pessimism, of course, but the form of the European novel as Kundera conceives of it also provides for exhilaration: a playful, ironic attitude that dramatically lightens the theme with form and, as critics say in discussions of literary theory, deconstructs it at the same time. With irony, which Kundera sees as the primary tone of the European narrative, the novelist portrays things both as they seem and as they might be, causing the reader to laugh, either at seeming fact or acknowledged fiction. At the same time, since ironic effect depends upon heightened audience awareness, the author must work to keep the reader alert to multiple, even contradictory, interpretations. So for Kundera, the use of parabasis is critical to the ironic tone, allowing him to enrich his narratives with information, ideas, and "human possibilities" that go beyond the limits of an ordinary story and may, in a sense, jar the reader into thought, negating a first reading (or second, or third) by posing other points of view, other angles from which to regard the story.

In effect, therefore, we can say about Kundera's narratives what the French theoretician Jacques Derrida says about all language, that it "bears within itself the necessity of its own critique"[2] and that Kundera, whether through study or observation, has learned to work both the subjective and objective points of view into his narratives, allowing rhetorical and grammatical meanings to stand side by side[3] because each is valid and yet canceled out by the other. In such a situation, filled with complex, ambiguous meaning, the narrator's personality and skill, his ability to balance and control opposites, may determine a reader's attitude toward the text. For Kundera parabasis furnishes a practical novelistic method of having things two ways (serious yet playful, tragic yet comic, meaningful yet meaningless, and, to use one of his own contradictory couplings, heavy yet light), with narrative tone and theme working as the glues that hold opposites together.

## "The Depreciated Legacy of Cervantes"

If Kundera reaches similar conclusions about human life as Derrida, he does so through an analysis of a different field: culture, not language. He begins the first essay in *The Art of the Novel* with a reference to the German philosopher Edmund Husserl,[4] who, according to Kundera, conceived of the European spirit as extending beyond the Continent and described it as having an inquiring habit of mind that "apprehended the world . . . as a question to be answered."[5] That empirical attitude allowed for great cultural and technological advances throughout the nineteenth and early twentieth centuries, but for Kundera the triumphs are not pure. The European spirit also includes people who, in the process of making technological advances, lost all sense of themselves as living beings. In light of their experience, Kundera sees human life as increasingly diminished, "a mere thing" before huge cultural forces, historical, technological, and political, that now "bypass," "surpass," and even "possess" their very makers (4), putting into doubt all urgent (and timeless) human questions: of self, of individuality, and destiny.

Rather than find this situation negative, however, Kundera takes a more complex point of view, describing the past three hundred years of the Modern Era in Europe as a time of decline mixed with progress, a period that "like all that is human, carries the seed of its end in its beginning" (4). That complexity does not diminish the era's value, because it is precisely that complexity, and a consequent sense of increased irrationality and doubt, that makes the European novel the perfect expression of the times. While philosophy and science have so far failed to grapple with ambiguity in a satisfying way, the novel has done so systematically and with great success since its beginning. European novelists "discovered the various dimensions of existence one by one": with *Don Quixote* Cervantes examined adventure in the physical world; in *Pamela* and *Clarissa* Richardson studied internal events "to unmask the secret life of the feelings" (5); Balzac, in the many volumes of *The Human Comedy,* plumbed man's place in history; Flaubert, especially in *Madame Bovary* and *Three Tales,* examined the banal facts of everyday life; Tolstoy studied the irrational and its effects on human behavior in *Anna Karenina;* with *Ulysses* and *Remembrance of Things Past* Joyce and Proust meditated on time, present and past respectively; and Thomas Mann, in *Death in Venice* and *Doctor Faustus,* showed how ancient myths control present human actions.

Within the spirit of discovery that such a list implies, at its very center in fact, Kundera perceives knowledge as the European novel's only reason for being, especially since, in the thinking of the Modern Era, God has played less and less of a role in daily life. With the resultant ambiguity of that absence, small truths have replaced one divine truth in Western thinking, and the novel, beginning with Cervantes and Rabelais, came into its own. Taking what Husserl called the "world of life" as its laboratory, the European novel abandoned old truths and values, embraced ambiguity, and made knowledge its only morality (6). Discussing the various interpretations of Cervantes's intent in *Don Quixote,* Kundera cautions the reader that the European novel's province is "inquiry," not simple moral positions, and he says that the search for clear moral interpretations, whether religious, political, psychological, or historical, reflects an intolerance of the "essential relativity" of human life and an inability to accept, in the absence of a Supreme Being, the "wisdom of uncertainty" that is the novel's special province (7). Kundera's view is distinctly contemporary, rational and scientific as he describes it, and reflects for the novel, which takes its text from life, the same concerns that Derrida enumerates for literary criticism.

Continuing from that point in his essay, Kundera briefly discusses the work of Kafka, Hasek, Musil, and Broch, calling them the "pleiad of great Central European novelists" (11–12), and saying that the cataclysmic political and cultural changes in Europe brought about by World War I enabled the novel to move outside the boundaries of the soul and again regard the outside world, as Cervantes did. If Joyce and Proust memorialized the battle for control of the monster within the human soul, Kafka, Hasek, Musil, and Broch described a monster that "comes from outside and is called History." Kundera describes this monster as "impersonal, uncontrollable, incalculable" and, most important for individual destiny, "inescapable" (11). The novels of these great Central Europeans reveal what "only the novel can" (12), that all the previously discovered dimensions of existence (now called "existential categories") as described by Cervantes, Richardson, and the others have changed in the course of the twentieth century. We now have a different set of questions: What is adventure without freedom of action (Kafka, *The Trial*), history if intellectuals have no idea their lives will change irrevocably in twenty-four hours (Musil, *The Man without Qualities*), crime if a murderer can actually forget his act (Broch, *The Sleepwalkers*), the comic if war is the novelist's primary source for humor (Hasek, *The Good Soldier Svejk*), and solitude if there is no longer a division between public and private lives (Kafka, *The Castle*)? Complicated, the questions provide a rich area of human experience to contemplate, and because of that, according to Kundera, the potential for the "post-Proustian novel" remains far from fulfilled, therefore far from over. Citing four appeals of the form that still need to be explored—play, dream, thought, and time—he says that if the novel disappears, it will not be attributable to exhausted powers. Instead, it will be because the novel as he sees it "exists in a world grown alien to it" (16), a world limited and controlled by the demands of the mass media that "amplify and channel the reduction process" in human thought. The media serve to unify earth's history (that is, its memory of experience), promoting oversimplification instead of complexity, so that "sound bites" replace fully developed political thinking,[6] and the world no longer proves hospitable to the novel's special gifts.

And, after all those changes, what is left? Despite everything, Kundera answers, stepping forth at the end of the essay as an anachronistic Don Quixote figure himself, he remains dedicated to his chosen literary form: the European novel, "the depreciated legacy of Cervantes" (20).

## Notes and Dialogues

His discussion of the novel extends, with variations of subject and theme, through the rest of the book. Parts Two through Six, "Dialogue on the Art of the Novel" (a composed interview, edited in collaboration with Christian Salmon), "Notes Inspired by *The Sleepwalkers*" (an essay on Hermann Broch's trilogy of novels), "Dialogue on the Art of Composition" (another edited interview, also in collaboration with Christian Salmon), "Somewhere Behind" (the essay on Kafka discussed in some detail in chapter two of this study), and "Sixty-three Words" (a meditation on words, "key words," "problem words," "words you love"), continues Kundera's investigation of the special problems and capabilities of the novel form, with emphasis in the two dialogues on his own particular practices as a novelist. In the first dialogue he brings special emphasis to the novel's exploration of what he calls the "enigma of self" (23) and says that for him, making a character come to life means "getting to the bottom of his existential problem," that is, unveiling situations, motifs, and even words that "shape him" (35). Emphasizing what he sees as the novel's particular interest in history, he argues that a novelist's task is not to illustrate historical situations as, say, a television docudrama might, but to examine the *"historical dimension of human existence"* (35), seeing that existence as the realm of human possibilities, everything that man has become and "can become" (42) in life.

In the second dialogue Kundera emphasizes novelistic form, discussing in particular the use of ellipsis, a technique he says he learned from the work of the Czech composer Leos Janacek; novelistic counterpoint, which he also calls polyphony because it blends narrative, philosophic essays, and dreams into "one music" (71); and the novelistic essay, which Kundera claims has no clear message but instead "remains hypothetical, playful, or ironic" (71). In this section Kundera most fully and clearly delineates his ideas concerning thematic, as opposed to narrative, unity and discusses the importance of tempo as a means of developing pace and variation in his novels. Rejecting the value of verisimilitude, he says that the first novelists, such as Cervantes and Rabelais, did not seek to convey an impression of reality; rather they sought to "amuse, amaze, astonish, enchant" (94), goals that he shares with them as he attempts to expose human dramas "in all their terrible insignificance" (96).

In "Notes Inspired by *The Sleepwalkers*," Kundera discusses the philosopher-novelist Hermann Broch's special interest in character as "ontological hypothesis," another way of saying that for Broch characterization is an investigation into human possibilities. Kundera sees the three principal characters of *The Sleepwalkers* trilogy, Pasenow, Esch, and Huguenau, as a bridge "erected above time" (55) by Broch so that he can investigate the ideological and philosophic shift that occurred between the nineteenth century's "reign of irrational faith" and the twentieth century's "reign of the irrational in a world without faith" (54). Describing human history as "the story of a few characters" (56) such as Faust or Don Quixote, Kundera sees Broch's characters as types who express the increasing secularization and loss of responsibility in the modern era. He discusses Broch's concept of action as a means of defining character, revealing what Kundera calls a "subterranean" order to the seemingly irrational choices *The Sleepwalkers* characters make (63). Attacking "establishment modernism" for what he perceives as its hostility to the form of the novel, Kundera praises Broch for the following achievements: (1) He keeps his own character out of sight during the narration; (2) he shows the novel as being one of the last means of artistic expression that connects with "life in its entirety"; (3) he continues the novelistic quest of the great classical novelists; and (4) he possesses a "melancholy awareness" of history drawing to a close, leaving in its wake an environment hostile to the "evolution of art and of the novel in particular" (67).

After "Somewhere Behind," the essay in which Kundera describes the world of Kafka's novels and which is discussed in some detail in chapter two above, he moves on to one of the most extraordinary essays in *The Art of the Novel*, "Sixty-three Words," a collection of comments on subjects ranging from "Aphorism" ("poetic form of definition") through "Novelist" ("an explorer feeling his way in an effort to reveal some unknown aspect of existence"), to "Youth" ("that stupid *lyrical* age"). Working through this list of words, Kundera comments on topics such as Europe, Central Europe, and the intellectual traditions they have spawned, emphasizing changes in the three-centuries-old Modern Era that have yielded, after humanism, a historical situation he calls "a laboratory of twilight" (125). The scientifically based pessimism inherent in that metaphor parallels Kundera's comment on Broch's sense of history drawing to a close, and on his own experience in Prague, described in the introduction to *Jacques and His Master,* of "the violent end of Western culture" (11). We have witnessed such pessimism throughout the course of discussion in this study and seen that Kundera perceives the end of the West as inevitable, a historical phenomenon existing beyond the old political problem of Soviet expansion and resting squarely on the human situation in general and, as "Sixty-three Words" demonstrates, especially in the present cultural climate.

Perceiving the European world as flourishing without God for a few brief centuries under the reign of humanism and its emphasis on reason and doubt, Kundera regrets the gradual ending of that era, evidence of which he sees all around him (See his comments on "Misomusist," "Modern," "Non-thought," and "Rhythm"). Contemporary life, with its questions about the adequacy of language, its faith in technological development, and its belief in media expansion, no longer values the individual as the measure of things. And, with an end to "personal originality," as represented by the European novel, heralding an "era of unparalleled uniformity" ("Temps Modernes," 149–150), the culture of Europe may no longer provide a lamp to shine into the meaningless void. It is a terrifying, even beautiful, vision, and Kundera adheres to it throughout his work, letting his sense of irony and play contradict each other in a highly charged philosophic atmosphere that at one moment promotes questions and at the next undermines definitive answers.

## Jerusalem Address: "The Novel and Europe"

In the final chapter of this book, a speech he delivered in 1985 upon receiving the Jerusalem Prize for literature, Kundera restates his themes and, in the optimism of the moment, provides hope, however little it may be, through his discussion of the novel's art. He begins the address by invoking the Jewish tradition of exile and relating it to the fact that Israel's most important literary prize is an international one. Saying that because of their experience of exile great Jewish leaders have been especially sensitive to the idea of a "supranational" European culture, Kundera accepts the prize not as a writer, but as a novelist with an appreciation of the "great cosmopolitan Jewish spirit" (157). He goes on to say that, along with Flaubert, every "true" novelist attempts to disappear behind his work, renounce a public persona, and refuse the role of public figure. Lamenting the mass media–bred taste for public actions and declarations, he says that the novelist is never a spokesman for ideas, his own or any others, and refers to a "suprapersonal wisdom" that every novelist listens for while writing and declares that wisdom an explanation of "why great novels are always a little more intelligent than their authors" (158).

Discussing that "suprapersonal wisdom" as well as the novel form, Kundera turns to a piece of folk wisdom, a Jewish proverb: "Man thinks, God laughs." He uses the saying to discuss humility as a necessary means for attaining the novel's wisdom. While doing so, he underlines the limits of man's knowledge of himself, his world, and, of course, his ultimate reality: "man thinks . . . the truth escapes him"; "the more men think" the more their thoughts diverge; and "man is never what he thinks he is" (158). But a corollary to the humility that Kundera advocates is the necessity for laughter, presumably God's laughter, because it is just such laughter that provides a larger, ironic perspective on human life. "The novel is born not of the theoretical spirit but of the spirit of humor," Kundera says (160), calling it one of Europe's major failures that it never understood the form or the humor intrinsic to it. Calling human existence and the poetry inherent in it the novel's field of knowledge, he describes the poetry of existence discovered by three major European novelists: Sterne perceived it in digression; Flaubert saw it in the banality of daily life; and Broch studied it in kitsch, "the attitude of those who want to please the greatest number, at any cost" (163). Seeing kitsch as more present today than fifty years ago, when Broch wrote about it in his trilogy, Kundera calls kitsch the "aesthetic of the mass media" (163) and predicts that as mass media reaches more and more deeply into daily life, kitsch will inevitably become our "everyday aesthetic and moral code" (164). Modernism, which once implied nonconformity of taste and behavior but, now infused with the "enormous vitality" of the mass media, exerts a pressure to conform, to be "up to date," and as a result has "put on kitsch's clothing" (164). Kitsch, people who do not laugh (*agelastes*, he calls them, a word invented by Rabelais), and the automatic acceptance of received ideas, are the "three-headed" enemy of the novel, the art "where no one owns the truth and everyone has the right to be understood" (164).

Finally Kundera discusses the tradition of tolerance in Europe. Acknowledging that tradition as "our dream of Europe" and not always Europe's reality, Kundera says that despite its many betrayals the dream is strong enough to unite people beyond Europe's borders. Recognizing that tolerance as under threat, particularly in the Mideast, a region marked by violent intolerance for five thousand years, Kundera excuses himself for speaking only of the novel, especially in Israel and in a city as tense and unstable as Jerusalem. But he reminds his audience that for him the spirit of Europe, its respect for the individual, original thought, and the right to privacy, is still contained, "as in a treasure chest," in the history and special "wisdom" of the novel. He closes the speech by reminding the audience of the previously cited Jewish proverb. Lightly poking fun at himself, he undercuts his own ideas with irony: "I was forgetting that God laughs when he sees me thinking" (165). Donning his novelist's mask once more, he retreats from public view. Like the middle-aged man in *Life Is Elsewhere* (a character whom Kundera calls the closest to himself [129]), he leaves a light in the window of European culture at the end, "a lamp of kindness,"[7] shining, however briefly and faintly, in the dark.

## NOTES

1. Roland Barthes, "The Structuralist Activity," *Critical Essays* (Evanston: Northwestern University Press, 1972) 218.
2. Jacques Derrida, "Structure, Sign, and Play in the Discourse of the Human Sciences," *The Structuralist Controversy* (Baltimore: Johns Hopkins University Press, 1972) 254.
3. See Paul de Man, "Semiology and Rhetoric," in *Allegories of Reading* (New Haven: Yale University Press, 1979), 3–20, which argues for conflicting readings of a text based on the certainty of grammatical code countered by the uncertainty of rhetorical tone or reading.
4. German philosopher (1859–1938), one of the founders of phenomenology, the school of thought that conceives of human consciousness as being deeply connected to, rather than separate from, the physical world.
5. *The Art of the Novel* (New York: Grove, 1988) 3. Further references will be noted parenthetically.
6. And imagologues replace ideologues. See ch. 8 of this study for further discussion.
7. *Life Is Elsewhere* (New York: Penguin, 1986) 286.

# BIBLIOGRAPHY

## Books by Milan Kundera

For Kundera's ideas about the final shape of his oeuvre, see his essay at the beginning of chapter nine of this study. This bibliography lists English editions of his books in the order that they are covered in this study.

*Jacques and His Master: An Homage to Diderot in Three Acts.* Trans. Michael Henry Heim. New York: Harper, 1985. First published in French as *Jacques et son maître, hommage à Denis Diderot* (Paris: Gallimard, 1981). Play.

*The Book of Laughter and Forgetting.* Trans. Michael Henry Heim. New York: Penguin, 1981. First published in French as *Le livre du rire et de l'oubli* (Paris: Gallimard, 1979); published in Czech as *Kniha smichu a zapomneni* (Toronto: Sixty-eight Publishers, 1981). Novel.

*The Joke.* Trans. Michael Henry Heim. New York: Penguin, 1983. Published in Czech as *Zert* (Prague: Ceskoslovensky Spisovatel, 1967); published in French as *La plaisanterie* (Paris: Gallimard, 1968). Novel. (Note: A new and definitive English version of *The Joke,* fully revised by Kundera and published by Aaron Asher Books/ Harper Collins Publishers, appeared in Spring 1992, too late for use in this study.)

*Life Is Elsewhere.* Trans. Peter Kussi. New York: Penguin, 1986. First published in French as *La vie est ailleurs* (Paris: Gallimard, 1973); published in Czech as *Zivot je jinde* (Toronto: Sixty-eight Publishers, 1979). Novel.

*The Farewell Party.* Trans. Peter Kussi. New York: Penguin, 1981. First published in French as *La valse aux adieux* (Paris: Gallimard, 1976); published in Czech as *Valcik na rozloucenou* (Toronto: Sixty-eight Publishers, 1979). Novel.

*The Unbearable Lightness of Being.* Trans. Michael Henry Heim. New York: Harper, 1984. Published in French as *L'insoutenable légèreté de l'être* (Paris: Gallimard, 1984); published in Czech as *Nesnesitelna lehkost byti* (Toronto: Sixty-eight Publishers, 1985.) Novel.

*Immortality.* Trans. Peter Kussi. New York: Grove Weidenfield, 1991. First published in French as *L'immortalité* (Paris: Gallimard, 1990). Both editions are translations from Kundera's Czech manuscript ''Nesmrtelnost.'' Novel.

*Laughable Loves.* Trans. Suzanne Rappaport. New York: Penguin, 1987. Revised, edited, and rearranged translation of *Smesne lasky* (Toronto: Sixty-eight Publishers, 1981). Also published in French as *Risibles amours* (Paris: Gallimard, 1986). Novel/stories.

*The Art of the Novel.* Trans. Linda Asher. New York: Grove, 1988. First published in French as *L'art du roman* (Paris: Gallimard, 1986). Criticism.

## Other Texts by Kundera

"Appendix: Speeches made at the Fourth Congress of the Czechoslovak Writers' Union June 27–29, 1967." Trans. D. Orpington. In Dusan Hamsik, *Writers against Rulers.* New York: Random House, 1971. 167–77. A very important document containing a clear, early statement of Kundera's ambitions as a writer who wants to write for Europe and the world, not just for Czechoslovakia.

"Interview." Trans. Peter Kussi. In Antonin J. Liehm, *The Politics of Culture.* New York: Grove Press, 1973. 131–50. Important for Kundera's biography and literary theories before he became well known.

"The Czech Wager." *New York Review of Books* 22 Jan. 1981: 21–22. The fundamental importance of Czech literature to the fate of the nation and the history of Europe in an era, and under a regime, where politics were everything. The original text is in French: "Le pari de la litterature tcheque" in *Liberté* 23 (1981).

"Xenakis, 'prophète de l'insensibilité'." In *Regards sur Iannis Xenakis.* Paris: Editions Stock, 1981. 21–25. An important musicological comment on the contemporary Greco-French composer and on the history of European music.

"Le choc de l'irrationnel." French preface to "Prague 68" by Petr Kral. *Le Matin de Paris* 17 Aug. 1981: 15–17. An essay for those who see Kundera looking back at his country without commitment or passion.

"Janacek: He Saw the Coming Night." Trans. Susan Huston. *Cross Currents* 23 (1983): 371–80. Some technical musicology here, but the essay is very important for understanding Kundera's musical roots and Janacek's influence on his work. The original essay, written in French, is "La situation de Leos Janacek."

"A Kidnapped West or Culture Bows Out." Trans. Edmund White. *Granta* 11 (1984): 93–118. Kundera elaborates on Czechoslovakia, its culture and history, and his concept of Central Europe. The original text, written in French, is "Un Occident kidnappé ou la tragedie de l'Europe centrale." *Le Débat* 27 (Nov. 1983).

"Paris or Prague." *Granta* 13 (1984): 11–19. A translation of Kundera's preface to the French version of Josef Skvorecky's *Miracle en Bohème.* Kundera holds that while the Paris spring of May 1968 attacked the foundations of European culture, the Prague Spring was a vehement expression of that culture.

"Prague: A Disappearing Poem." *Granta* 17 (1985): 87–103. The heartfelt title describes the tone. In addition, this essay treats Czechoslovakia's cultural heroes: Kafka, Hasek, and Janacek. They pushed European culture to the edge of a new awareness, and the USSR had to subjugate the Czechs because it could not contain them culturally. The original essay, written in French, is called "Prague, poème qui disparaît."

"Encore sur le roman." Interview. *Lettre Internationale* 4 (Spring 1985): 3–7. With Christian Salmon. Parts of this interview are included in *The Art of the Novel*, but there is additional material here on Kafka and the European novel in general.

"L'ombre castratrice de Saint Garta." *L'infini* 32 (1990): 3–12. An essay on Kafka and the twisted impressions of his work given to us by, as Kundera calls them, "Kafkologues."

"The Umbrella, the Night World, and the Lonely Moon." Trans. David Bellos. *New York Review of Books* 19 Dec. 1991: 46–50. An essay on French-speaking Caribbean culture, with special attention to the works of Patrick Chamoiseau and René Depestre. The original version of this article, written in French, appears as "Beau comme une rencontre multiple" in *L'infini* 34 (1991): 50–62.

"Une phrase." *L'infini* 35 (1991): 42–53. In this essay Kundera analyzes the art, or lack of it, in various published translations into French of a sentence from *The Castle* by Kafka.

"Improvisation en hommage à Stravinski." *L'infini* 36 (1991): 19–42. Interesting and valuable essay on what Kundera sees as shared problems in the history of music and the novel.

"À la recherche du présent perdu." *L'infini* 37 (1992): 22–34. An intriguing and illuminating essay that compares Hemingway's "Hills like White Elephants" to the operas of Janacek. Kundera sees them all as works that, in the tradition of Flaubert, seize a fleeting image of the present moment.

## Critical Works on Kundera

Aragon, Louis. "Ce roman que je tiens pour une oeuvre majeure." Preface to *La plaisanterie (The Joke)*. Paris: Gallimard/Folio, 1968. An important comment, despite its obvious political leanings.

Banerjee, Maria Nemcova. *Terminal Paradox: The Novels of Milan Kundera*. New York: Grove Weidenfield, 1990. Essays on Kundera's novels through *The Unbearable Lightness of Being*. Thorough, valuable textual notes, and the essays are interesting, if densely written, emphasizing Kundera's ideas about life's paradoxes during the twilight of Western culture.

Brand, Glen. *Milan Kundera: An Annotated Bibliography*. New York: Garland Publishing, 1988. Commentary on articles by Kundera as well as on the criticism of his work make this book a useful research tool. However, it neglects some of Kundera's French texts.

Des Pres, Terrence. "Poetry and Politics." *TriQuarterly* 65 (Winter 1986): 17–29. An interesting, reflective essay on the relationship of authors and their audiences in a world dominated by media. Kundera, Milosz, and Orwell are the examples.

Eiland, Howard. "The Novel in the Age of Terminal Paradoxes." *Gettysburg Review* 4 (Autumn 1988): 708–22. Useful for elucidating Kundera's fiction as cultural criticism.

Faris, Wendy B. "Desire and Power, Love and Revolution: Carlos Fuentes and Milan Kundera." *Review of Contemporary Fiction* 8 (Summer 1988): 273–84. Useful, but more illuminating on Fuentes than on Kundera.

Feintuch, Burt. "The Joke, Folk Culture, and Milan Kundera's *The Joke.*" *Western Folklore* 46 (Jan. 1987): 21–35. A good article on Kundera's narrative methods, tying folk tales and jokes to classical forms.

Fuentes, Carlos. "The Other K." *TriQuarterly* 51 (Spring 1981): 256–75. The Mexican novelist reminisces: meeting Kundera in Prague in 1968, reading *Life Is Elsewhere*, relating literature to history and politics.

Hamsik, Dusan. *Writers against Rulers.* Trans. D. Orpington. New York: Random House, 1971. Invaluable for its portrait of writers in action and the inclusion of Kundera's speech to the 1967 Czech Writers' Congress.

Harkins, William E. and Paul I. Trensky, eds. *Czech Literature Since 1956: A Symposium.* Columbia Slavic Studies. New York: Bohemica, 1980. Essays on various literary movements; two particularly useful ones are "Kundera's Novel and the Search for Fatherhood," by Peter Kussi, and "Milan Kundera: Czech Writer," by Antonin J. Liehm.

Kimball, Roger. "The Ambiguities of Milan Kundera." *New Criterion* 4 (Jan. 1986): 5–13. A good introductory article on Kundera and his work with special emphasis on cultural and political themes.

"Kundera, Milan 1929– " *Contemporary Authors.* Ed. Frances Carol Locher. Vols. 85–88. Detroit: Gale Research Company, 1980. 323–25.

Kusin, Vladimir. *The Intellectual Origins of the Prague Spring: The Development of Reformist Ideas in Czechoslovakia 1956–1967.* London: Cambridge University Press, 1971. Useful history of intellectuals' role in the politics of Czechoslovakia's post-Stalinist years.

Kussi, Peter. "Essays on the Fiction of Milan Kundera." Ph.D. Diss., Columbia University, 1978. Ann Arbor: UMI, 1978. 7819373. Kussi comments in some detail on Kundera's poems and plays and provides some speculative commentary on the fiction, stylistic influences, and philosophic foundations.

——— . "Milan Kundera: Dialogues with Fiction." *World Literature Today: A Literary Quarterly of the University of Oklahoma* 57 (Spring 1983): 206–9. A judicious comment on Kundera's writing style and his aims as a novelist.

Liehm, Antonin J. *The Politics of Culture.* Trans. Peter Kussi. New York: Grove, 1973. Excellent on the historical role of intellectuals in Czech politics. Liehm's interview with Kundera has interesting biographical and theoretical information.

Lodge, David. "Milan Kundera and the Idea of the Author in Modern Criticism." *Critical Quarterly* 26 (Spring-Summer 1984): 105–21. Excellent commentary, especially useful in relation to Kundera's narrative persona.

"Milan Kundera." *World Authors, 1970–1975.* Ed. John Wakeman. New York: H. W. Wilson, 1980. 459–63.

Misurella, Fred. "Milan Kundera and the Central European Style." *Salmagundi* 73 (Winter 1987): 33–57. About Kundera, a course he teaches on the Central European novel at the École des hautes études en sciences sociales, and two novelists, Kazimierz Brandys, from Poland, and Danilo Kis, from Yugoslavia.

Porter, R. C. *Milan Kundera: A Voice from Central Europe.* Aarhus, Denmark: Arkona Publishers, 1981. Very useful ground-breaking study of Kundera's early works and career.

*Review of Contemporary Fiction* 9 (Summer 1989). Ed. Lois Oppenheim. Issue dedicated to Kundera and Zulfikar Ghose, with especially interesting articles on Kundera by Italo Calvino, Kvetoslav Chvatik, Francois Ricard, and Kundera himself.

Ricard, François. "Le point de vue de Satan." Afterword to *La vie est ailleurs* (*Life Is Elsewhere*). Paris: Gallimard/Folio, 1982. 465–74. Excellent for an appreciation of Kundera's "devilish" laughter. Appears in English in the special issue of *Salmagundi* listed below.

————. "L'Idylle et l'idylle." Afterword to *L'insoutenable légèreté de l'être* (*The Unbearable Lightness of Being*). Paris: Gallimard/Folio, 1989. 457–76. On Kundera's analysis of the idyll as a form of literature and belief. Appears in English in the special issue of *Review of Contemporary Fiction* listed above.

Robinson, Fred Miller. "The History and Significance of the Bowler Hat: Chaplin, Laurel and Hardy, Beckett, Magritte and Kundera." *TriQuarterly* 66 (Spring-Summer 1986): 173–200. Interesting. The title tells all.

*Salmagundi* 73 (Winter 1987). Ed. Robert Boyers. A special issue, "Milan Kundera: Fictive Lightness, Fictive Weight," with interesting articles and interviews, especially those by Terry Eagleton, Guy Scarpetta, and François Ricard.

Scarpetta, Guy. "Kundera: le roman: la musique et le vérité." *Art press* 108 (Nov. 1986): 42–8. Kundera calls this "the best text" on his theory of the novel.

Straus, Nina Pelikan. "Erasing History and Deconstructing the Text: Milan Kundera's *The Book of Laughter and Forgetting.*" *Critique: Studies in Modern Fiction* 28 (Winter 1987): 69–85. Useful for relating Kundera's work to structuralism and other modern critical schools.

## Other Works Cited

Barthes, Roland. "The Structuralist Activity." *Critical Essays.* Trans. Richard Howard. Evanston: Northwestern University Press, 1972. 213–20.

Derrida, Jacques. "Structure, Sign, and Play in the Discourse of the Human Sciences." Trans. Richard Macksey. *The Structuralist Controversy.* Ed. Richard Macksey and Eugenio Donato. Baltimore: Johns Hopkins University Press, 1972. 247–72.

Diderot, Denis. *Jacques le fataliste.* Ed. Paul Verniere. Paris: Flammarion, 1970.

Gombrowicz, Witold. *Ferdydurke*. Trans. Eric Mosbacher. Writers from the Other Europe. Ed. Philip Roth. New York: Penguin, 1986.

———. *Diary*. Ed. Jan Kott. Trans. Lillian Vallee. Evanston: Northwestern University Press, 1988.

Kafka, Franz. "A Hunger Artist." Trans. Willa Muir and Edwin Muir. *The Complete Stories*. New York: Schocken Books, 1976. 268–77.

Lévi-Strauss, Claude. "The Structural Study of Myth." Trans. Claire Jacobson and Brook Grundfest Schoepf. *Structural Anthropology*. New York: Basic Books, 1963. 206–31.

McKay, Kim. "Narrative Voices in the Bildungsroman." Ph.D. Diss., Lehigh University, 1990. Ann Arbor: UMI, 1991. 9109576.

Skvorecky, Josef. *The Engineer of Human Souls*. Trans. Paul Wilson. New York: Knopf, 1984.

# Index

First World War, 3

Flaishman (character in "Symposium"), 174–79; compared to Jaromil, 175

Flaubert, Gustave, 194, 198; and the banal, 199

Framed moments of contemplation: as tableaux, 147, 192

Framing: as technique for narrative perspective, 191

Franta (character in *The Farewell Party*), 90–104

Frantishka, Dr. (character in "Dr. Havel after Twenty Years"), 182–83

Franz (character in *The Unbearable Lightness of Being*), 117–33, 146, 159

Freud, Sigmund, 68, 113

Freudian, 156. *See also* Oneiric Narrative

Fucik, Julius, 59

Fugue: use of in Kundera's narration, 8, 12–13, 56, 62–64

German romanticism, 94

Germany, 47, 67

Gesture: of longing for immortality, 146–47, 160; of tossing, 139, 140, 143, 155, 160–61; as sign of character, 180

Goethe (pseudonymous character in *The Book of Laughter and Forgetting*), 34–36

Goethe, Johann Wolfgang von, 68, 83 n. 7, 135–36, 138, 140–43, 148–50, 160, 172; and his *Faust*, 89, 93, 143, 160, 197. *See also* Bettina Brentano

"Golden Apple of Desire, The," 170–72; compared to *Immortality*, 170, 172

Gombrowicz, Witold, 3, 5, 74, 134, 155, 187; *Diary*, 3; *Ferdydurke*, 3–4, 53, 95, 114, 140, 190 n. 10

*Good Soldier Svejk, The*, 15

Gottwald, Klement, 21, 29, 36, 71, 145

Grand March: of Europe, 117–18, 129–30, 146. *See also* Marching in step

"Graphomania," 32–33, 87

Greco-Roman tradition. *See* Christian and Greco-Roman traditions; Judeo-Christian, Greco-Roman tradition

Guesthouse chapter: "The Middle-Aged Man" in *Life Is Elsewhere* and *"The Dial"* in *Immortality*, 78–79, 180

Hasek, Jaroslav, 195. *See also Good Soldier Svejk*

Havel, Dr. (character in "Symposium" and "Dr. Havel after Twenty Years"), 174–79, 182–83

Havel, Vaclav, 163, 164

Hawthorne, Nathaniel, 21

*Heinrich von Ofterdingen*, 93

Helena Zemanek (character in *The Joke*), 50–65, 79; her narration, 50–52

Hemingway, Ernest: as fictional character, 142–43, 150

Highways and roads: compared as views of life, 151

"Hitchhiking Game, The," 172–74